IMAGES
of America

BROOKLYN'S CENTRAL LIBRARY

On the Cover: Taken shortly before Central Library opened to the public for the first time in 1941, this photograph shows staff working to fill the shelves of the much-anticipated library. Stocking the new facility was a major undertaking: 460,000 books were shipped in from branches around the borough, and a small army of workers, including 30 temporary staffers hired by the Works Progress Administration (WPA), toiled to prepare the building for Brooklyn's readers. (Courtesy of Brooklyn Public Library, Brooklyn Collection.)

IMAGES
of America

BROOKLYN'S CENTRAL LIBRARY

Brooklyn Public Library
Foreword by Francis Morrone

ARCADIA
PUBLISHING

ISBN 978-1-4671-2444-7

Published by Arcadia Publishing
Charleston, South Carolina

Printed in the United States of America

Library of Congress Control Number: 2016941975

For all general information, please contact Arcadia Publishing:
Telephone 843-853-2070
Fax 843-853-0044
E-mail sales@arcadiapublishing.com
For customer service and orders:
Toll-Free 1-888-313-2665

Visit us on the Internet at www.arcadiapublishing.com

To the people of Brooklyn, New York.

Contents

FOREWORD

Brooklyn's Central Library had a long and arduous gestation, beginning in 1888. New York City's construction of its magnificent central library on Fifth Avenue jolted Brooklyn into action. In 1906, the 37-year-old Raymond Francis Almirall was hired to design the library at Grand Army Plaza. The Brooklyn native had attended Brooklyn Polytechnic Institute and the fabled École des Beaux-Arts in Paris and had already distinguished himself with such buildings as Binghamton City Hall (1897–1898) and two of the most distinctive neighborhood libraries in Brooklyn, the Pacific Branch (1903) and the Prospect Branch (1906). His Beaux-Arts classical design for Central Library, and his suggestion that the plaza be ringed by classical buildings in the same grand manner, came to naught. Though construction began in 1911, financial and political difficulties, especially with regard to securing funding from a Manhattan-centric city government, forced frequent suspensions of work, such that by 1935 only a third of Almirall's building had been constructed. In that year, a new library regime commissioned Alfred Morton Githens and Francis Keally to redesign the library.

In keeping with the spirit of the times, Githens and Keally produced a monumental edifice sheathed in Indiana limestone that is one of the nation's most notable examples of 1930s modernism—Art Moderne, though others have called it Art Deco and even Modern Classical. Ornament, in the form of gilded reliefs by Carl Paul Jennewein and a sculptural metal screen by Thomas Hudson Jones, both major sculptors of the time, is concentrated around the entrance. Jennewein's reliefs embellish the two giant cylindrical piers on either side of the triple doorway. I cannot think of anything else in American architecture that is quite like these piers. This thrilling entrance is set in the middle of a vast concave facade and leads into one of the great monumental interiors in New York and probably the finest in a modernist idiom. Here, the exterior limestone yields to wood. Great wooden piers echo the limestone piers on the exterior, and a sweeping second-floor balcony echoes the concave facade.

The building is a modern masterpiece. It is one of the finest public library buildings in America. We may regret the failure of Almirall's vision for Grand Army Plaza to be realized. But how often do we fail to get what we most fondly desire, only to get something just as good?

—Francis Morrone

Acknowledgments

This book represents the efforts of many staff members and library supporters, both past and present. The work started with the support of Brooklyn Public Library president Linda Johnson and chief librarian and director Lisa Rosenblum. Alla Roylance, Jack McCleland, Norman Eriksen, and Jesse Montero formed the committee that first envisioned and shepherded the project. Ivy Gocker selected the historical photographs, researched library history, and wrote the book's captions to flesh out the story of the building, and Diana Bowers provided access to the library's archival holdings. Adam Leddy, Ally Malinenko, and Lauren Rochford provided editorial guidance. Past librarians, historians, and patrons—Margaret Freeman, Ruth Ferguson, Marcia McKee, Matthew Postal, and Signe Steen, among others—all provided indispensable groundwork with their explorations of the history of Brooklyn Public Library.

All images appear courtesy of Brooklyn Public Library, Brooklyn Collection.

Introduction

In 1888, Brooklyn was an independent city, the fourth largest in the United States. It had all the trappings of a modern metropolis—a thriving industrial waterfront, an extensive subway and streetcar system, and even a major league baseball team—with one glaring exception. City leaders authorized the Brooklyn Parks Commission to select a site for a new world-class library, a grand civic institution that would join the Brooklyn Museum, then under construction, in forming the cultural heart of the city. As it happened, by the time the library site—a triangular plot between Flatbush Avenue and Eastern Parkway, facing Grand Army Plaza—was identified in 1905, Brooklyn was no longer a city at all, having been consolidated into Greater New York as one of its five boroughs.

The construction of architect Raymond F. Almirall's elegant Beaux-Arts design began in 1911, but the project was soon beset by economic and political challenges. When work on the new library was halted a few years later, only one wing had been built; for years, what is now Central Library's Languages and Literature Division stood like a ruin on Flatbush Avenue. Mayor John Francis Hylan routinely referred to the construction site as "that hole in the ground," while others were even less generous in their assessment of Brooklyn's civic folly.

In the 1930s, with renewed public interest and under the determined leadership of Brooklyn borough president Raymond Ingersoll, architects Alfred Morton Githens and Francis Keally were commissioned to reimagine the library. Their Art Deco design was more streamlined (and more affordable) than Almirall's original vision. When it finally opened to the public on February 1, 1941, the Ingersoll Memorial Library, as it was known then, closed the chapter on a construction process that lasted nearly 30 years and a planning period that spanned more than 50.

The long wait was worth it. In comparing the new building to New York Public Library and the academic libraries of Harvard and Yale, the *New Yorker* declared, "Brooklyn's new one is tops." The public response was equally rapturous as bibliophiles flocked to the building in great numbers from the day it opened.

In the library's early years, children could only access the building through its Eastern Parkway entrance, and they were forbidden outside of the Children's Library, now known as the Youth Wing. In fact, until 1955, only the library's first floor was accessible to the public. The second floor housed a carpentry shop for furniture repair, and the third floor was dedicated to the binding and cataloging of books for the entire library system.

Times have changed. The card catalogues that once dominated the Grand Lobby were long ago supplanted by a computerized system. Today, all three floors are open, and the Ingersoll Memorial Library is now known as Central Library. The name is apt: while many of the borough's educational and civic institutions are clustered downtown, as close to Manhattan as possible, Central Library is nearer to the borough's geographic center, at the intersection of two of its most important thoroughfares. From its location at the head of Grand Army Plaza, Central Library stands at the center of several Brooklyn cultural landmarks: Prospect Park to the south, the

Soldiers and Sailors Memorial Arch to the west, and the Brooklyn Botanic Garden and Brooklyn Museum to the east.

The building is also central to Brooklyn Public Library (BPL), the nation's fifth-largest library system. At 352,000 square feet, it is by far the largest public library in the borough, accounting for more than one third of BPL's 1.1-million-square-foot physical plant. Its three floors and four underground storage decks offer more than 35 miles of shelving and house over a million items, most of which can be requested and delivered to any library in Brooklyn.

But Central Library is far more than a repository of books. Its inspiring 50-foot portico entrance welcomes patrons from throughout Brooklyn and visitors from all over the world. Readers and researchers lose and find themselves in its vast collections, while in the Shelby White and Leon Levy Information Commons, freelancers and aspiring entrepreneurs connect to the borough's largest free wireless network and gain access to sophisticated software and databases. Parents and caregivers bring their children to a wide range of free programs in the Youth Wing. In the Brooklyn Collection, genealogists trace their family trees, and students learn about the history of their neighborhoods. Jobseekers write résumés and submit employment applications in the computer lab. Immigrants and beginning readers attend classes in the Adult Learning Center. Patrons of arts and culture attend author talks and musical performances at the Dr. S. Stevan Dweck Cultural Center.

After 75 years, Central Library remains a Brooklyn landmark. In 2015, the facility received 1.3 million visits, and items from its collections circulated over 1.7 million times. Its public computers offered more than 350,000 individual sessions, and its wireless network facilitated over 300,000 connections. More than 100,000 people attended its free programs. Still more joined the millions of New Yorkers who have found the inspiration to do their best thinking and the free resources to transform their lives, all at Central Library.

New technologies have broadened Brooklyn Public Library's mission so much that our work—and often our facilities—would be unrecognizable to librarians and patrons of generations past, and the years ahead promise technological breakthroughs beyond the contemporary bounds of our imagination. New means of communication, of engaging with the world, will continue to emerge at an astonishing pace.

Yet whatever the future brings, Central Library will continue to adapt to meet the needs of its patrons and visitors—just as it has, proudly, for 75 years.

—Linda E. Johnson
President and CEO

One

Inspirations

Originating as a small network of libraries throughout the independent city of Brooklyn, the Brooklyn Public Library system was approved by an act of legislature of the State of New York on May 1, 1892, and later passed by resolution of the Brooklyn Common Council on November 30, 1896. Perhaps because Brooklyn itself was cobbled together from independent villages, the idea of a central, unifying library was not inherent in the foundation of the free branch system. The spokes came before the hub; when the public library was established, many small libraries had already been operating in neighborhoods throughout the city for years. These were consolidated under the Brooklyn Public Library banner from the late 1890s and into the early 20th century and included small branches like the Bay Ridge Free Library (established independently in 1888), as well as larger research collections like the Mercantile Library in downtown Brooklyn, which dated to 1857.

The possibility of erecting a large, central library for Brooklyn was first raised in 1888, when a subcommittee of the Brooklyn Park Commission suggested that an odd triangular plot at the top of Prospect Park could make a proper home for such an institution. Their recommendation did not gain traction right away, as the leadership of the new Brooklyn Public Library system was initially concerned with building neighborhood branches throughout the borough. Thanks to donations from steel magnate Andrew Carnegie, new libraries were being established all over the country, and many of Brooklyn Public Library's first branches were built with Carnegie funds.

With all that growth came the need for a centralized location to serve the scattered branches. In 1904, the library's president (and former Brooklyn mayor) David A. Boody declared that a "great library building" would soon be necessary to house the nearly one million volumes in the library's collection. The triangular Grand Army Plaza plot was approved the next year. But it would prove to be decades before a central library opened. In the meantime, other libraries in Brooklyn served some of the functions of a central library, especially the former Mercantile Library in downtown Brooklyn.

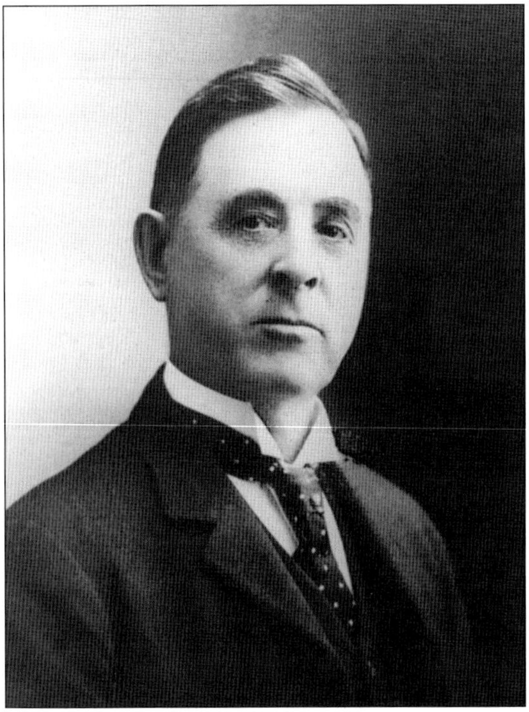

The first meeting of Brooklyn Public Library's board of trustees was held on February 11, 1897. David A. Boody, pictured here, was elected as the first president of the board, a position he held until his death in 1930. Boody would advocate for a central library in 1904, but first, the library focused its energies on building new branches and absorbing existing ones.

The Brooklyn of today was first a collection of small, independent villages. Among them was the Dutch colony of New Utrecht in Brooklyn's southwest corner. In 1894, the village created its own free library, founded by members of a literary club called the Winter Society. The library joined the Brooklyn Public Library system in 1901 and is pictured here in 1911.

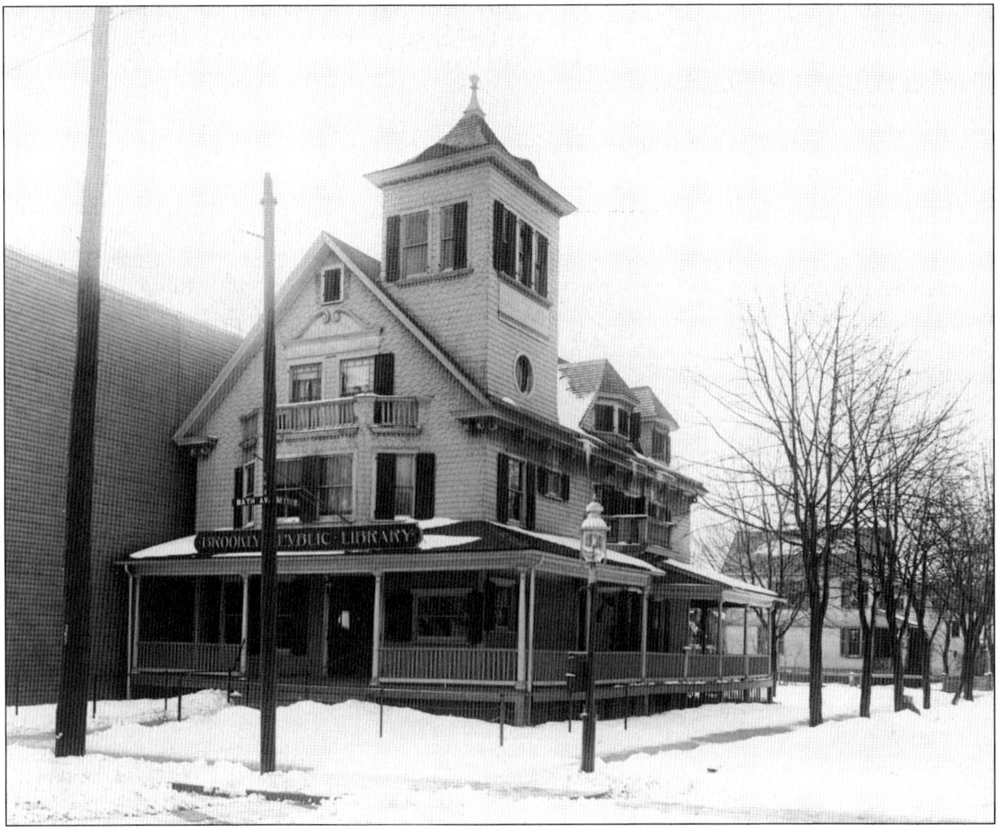

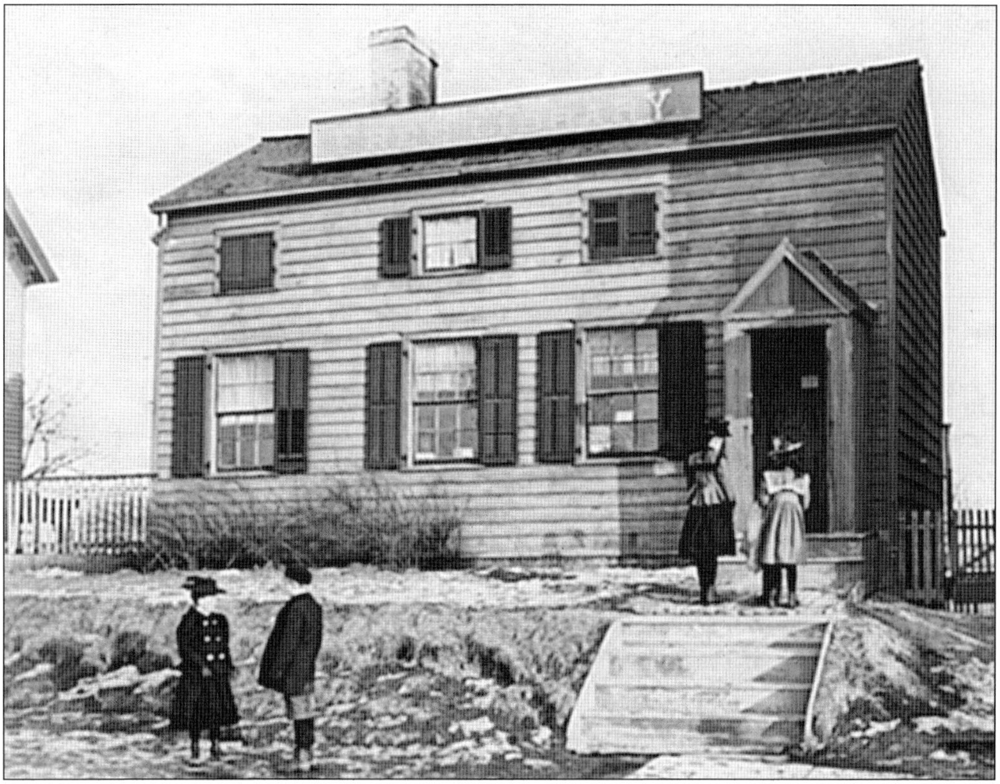

The Fort Hamilton Free Library, pictured here in the early 1900s, was founded by a Miss A.M. Gelston of Shore Road in 1889. It was also transferred to the Brooklyn Public Library system in 1901. This two-story frame building was demolished to make way for a new Carnegie-funded building, which opened in 1907.

The Bay Ridge Free Library was organized by the Bay Ridge Reading Club in 1888. In 1896, the building pictured here opened on the site of the present-day branch at 73rd Street and Ridge Boulevard. In 1901, this building and its collection of 6,000 books were incorporated into Brooklyn Public Library. A new library was built on the site in 1958.

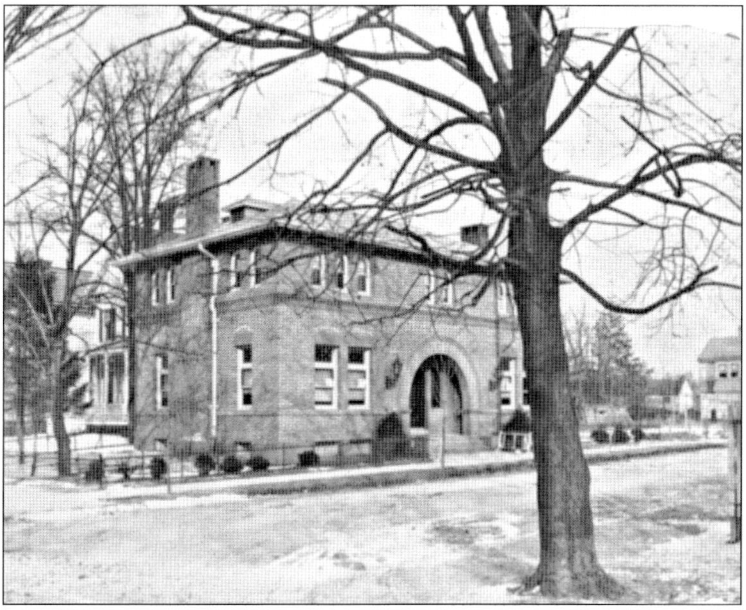

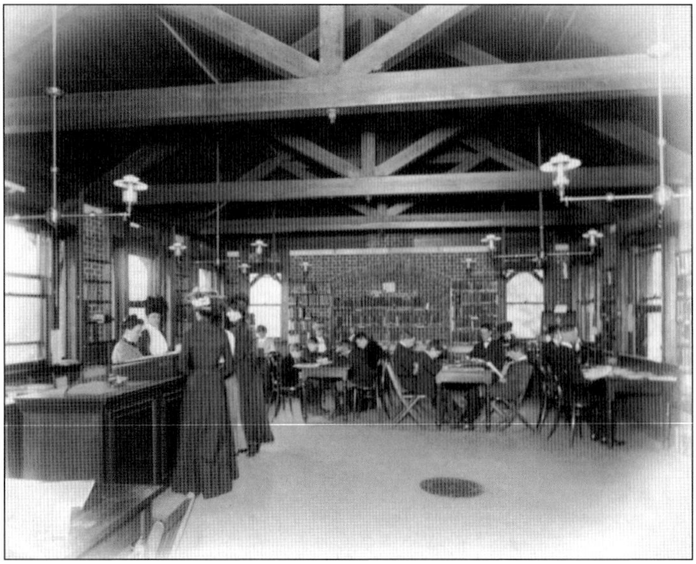

The Tompkins Park Free Library, pictured here in the early 1900s, opened in a Grecian-style shelter at the center of Tompkins Park in today's Bedford-Stuyvesant neighborhood in 1899. Brooklyn Public Library absorbed the branch into the new borough-wide system in 1901. The original building was replaced in 1969.

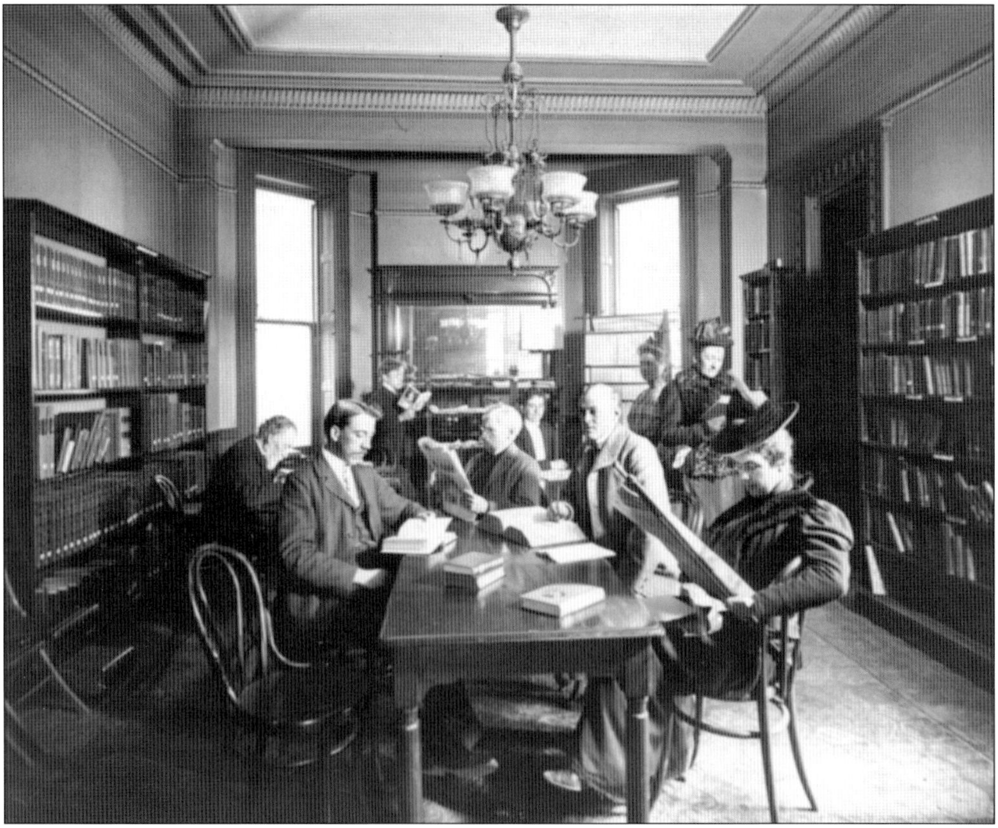

The first completely new library branch to be established by Brooklyn Public Library was the Bedford branch in today's Bedford-Stuyvesant neighborhood. When the branch opened on December 20, 1897, it was first based in the old Public School No. 3 on Bedford Avenue, pictured here in 1899. It moved several times in the succeeding years before finally settling into a new location funded by Andrew Carnegie in 1905.

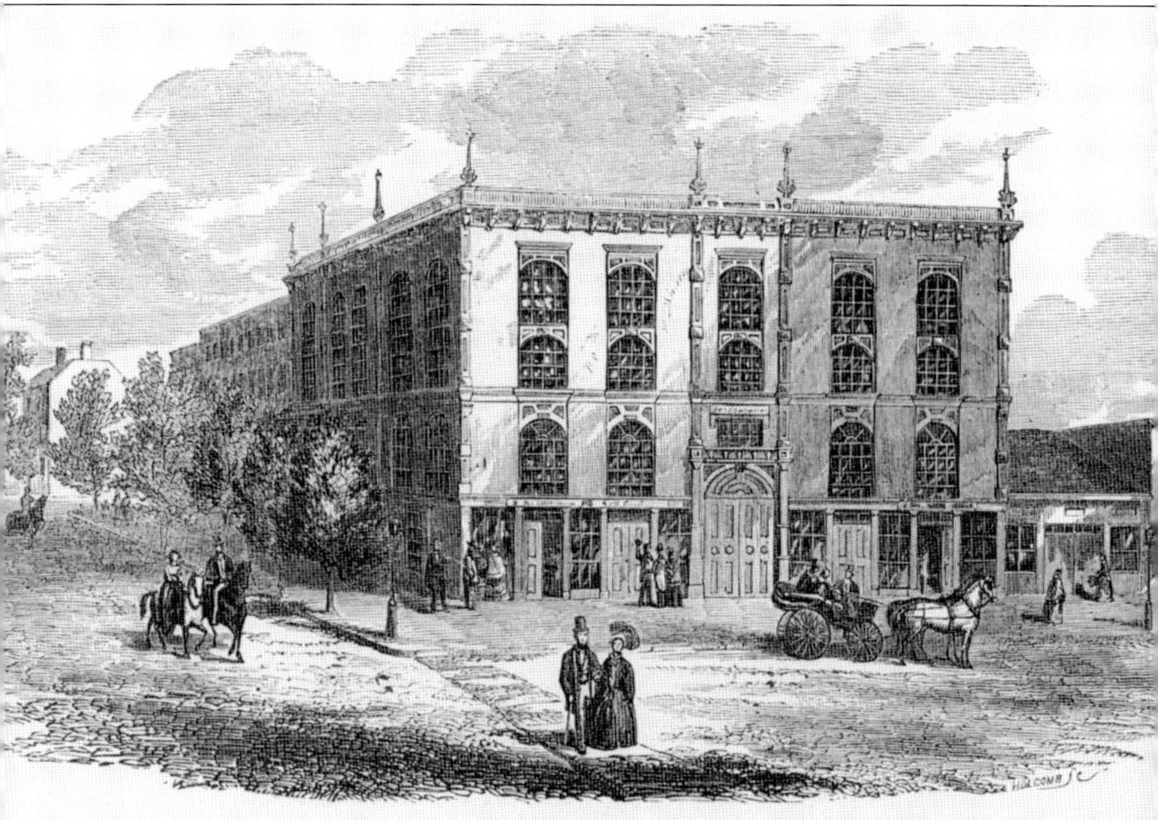

BROOKLYN ATHENÆUM.

Before free libraries dotted the suburban villages near Brooklyn, subscription organizations formed in the growing city's core. The Brooklyn Athenaeum and Reading Room was incorporated as a paid membership library on January 31, 1852. With the mission "to foster and encourage science, literature and the arts and to promote the moral and intellectual improvement of the community," the Brooklyn Athenaeum opened in this building at the corner of Atlantic Avenue and Clinton Street in 1853. A row of stores occupied the lower part of the building, making the enterprise self-sustaining, while the library, classrooms, and a lecture room seating nearly 1,500 were housed on the upper floor. The organization lent books and sponsored lectures. One detail to note was that the loan period was based on a book's size; larger books could be kept for four weeks, while smaller volumes were due back after two weeks. Overdue fines followed the same scheme.

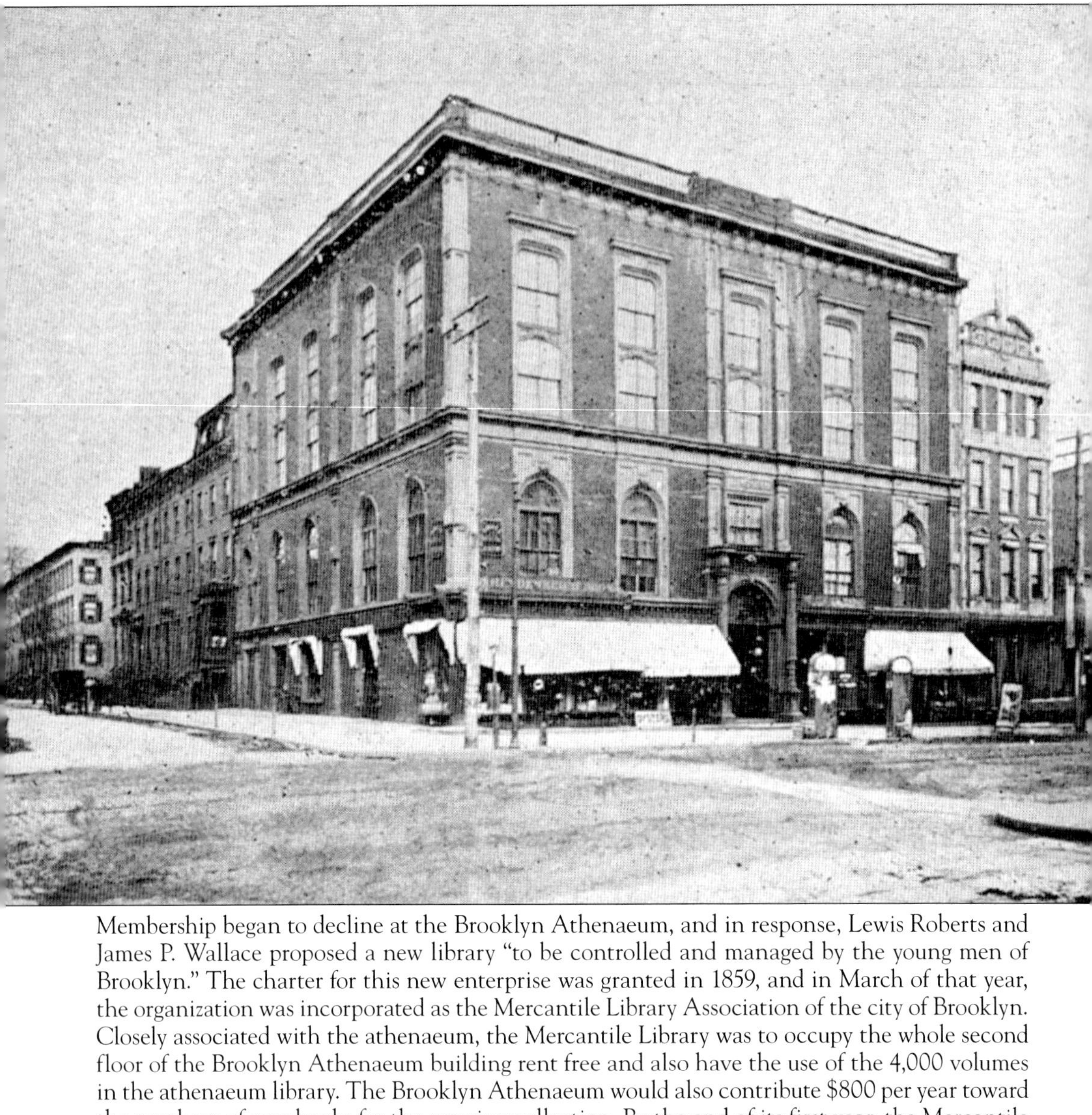

Membership began to decline at the Brooklyn Athenaeum, and in response, Lewis Roberts and James P. Wallace proposed a new library "to be controlled and managed by the young men of Brooklyn." The charter for this new enterprise was granted in 1859, and in March of that year, the organization was incorporated as the Mercantile Library Association of the city of Brooklyn. Closely associated with the athenaeum, the Mercantile Library was to occupy the whole second floor of the Brooklyn Athenaeum building rent free and also have the use of the 4,000 volumes in the athenaeum library. The Brooklyn Athenaeum would also contribute $800 per year toward the purchase of new books for the growing collection. By the end of its first year, the Mercantile Library boasted more than 1,500 members. Within 10 years, it had outgrown its original quarters, shown here on a postcard from the early 1900s.

This rendering of the Mercantile Library shows the organization's new building at 197 Montague Street as it appeared when it opened in 1869. The *Brooklyn Daily Eagle* praised architect Peter Bonnett Wright's design, calling the edifice "one of the most ornamental as well as useful institutions" in the city. The Reverend Henry Ward Beecher spoke at the library's opening ceremonies.

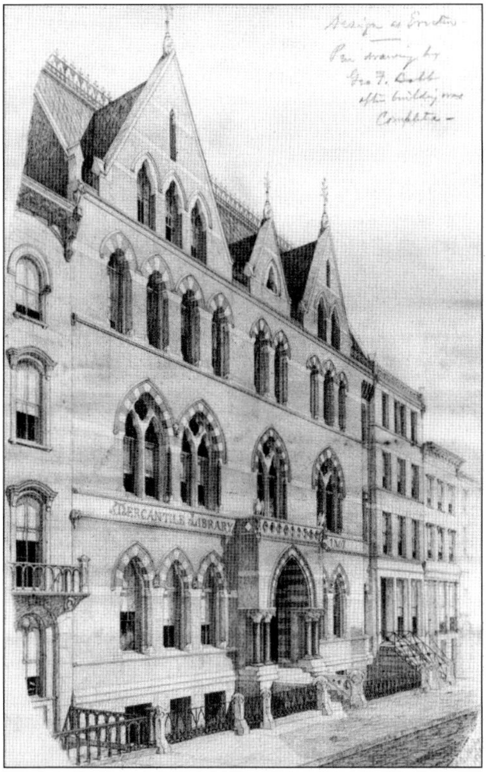

The constitution of the Mercantile Library established that "any person engaged as a clerk, student, journeyman, mechanic or apprentice could become a member . . . upon payment of one dollar initiation fee and fifty cents for each three months thereafter." These privileges were extended to women as well as men.

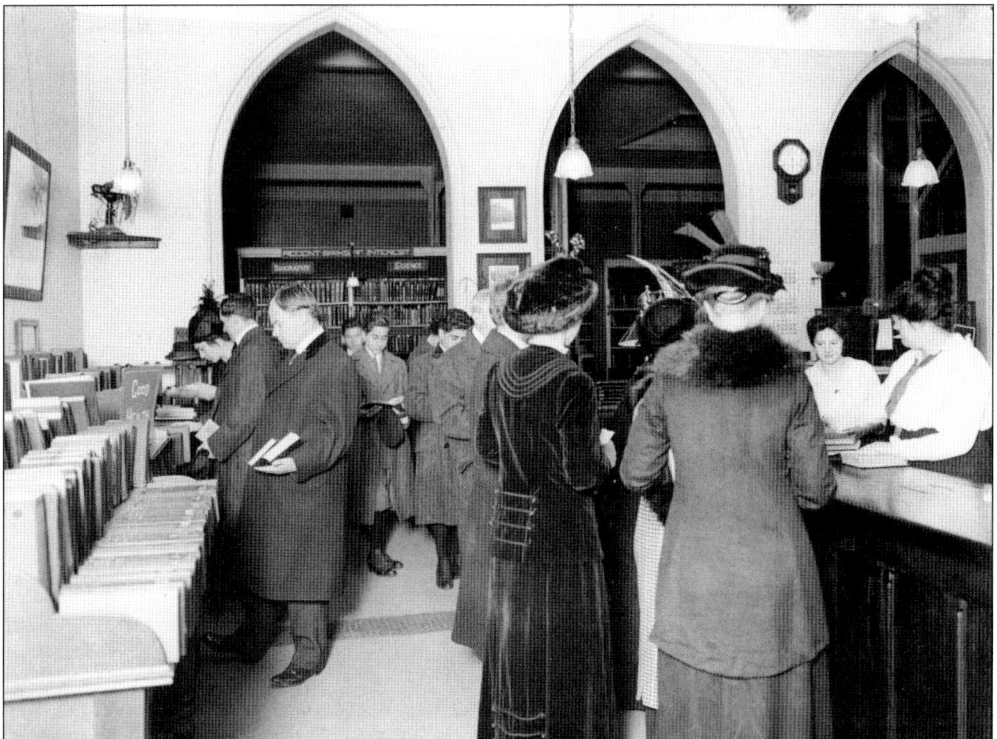

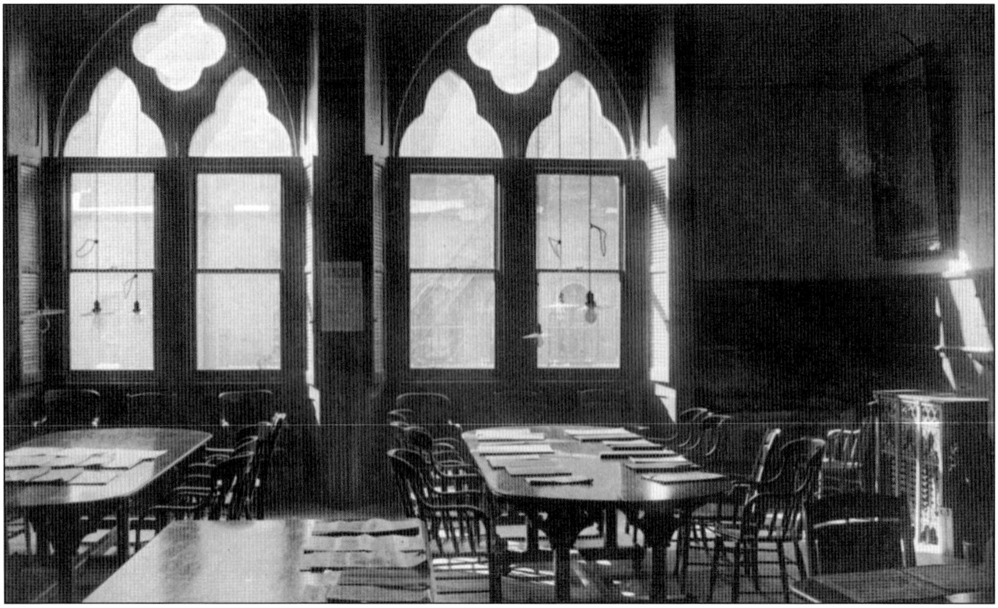

In 1878, the Mercantile Library changed its name to simply Brooklyn Library. These interior views, taken near the turn of the 20th century, give a sense of the reading rooms and shelving layout of the building. The distinctive large windows facing onto Montague Street allowed for natural light during the day. Electric light was introduced to the Brooklyn Library building in 1889, after an upset oil lamp caused a fire in 1882. Once the free Brooklyn Public Library system was established in 1897, memberships at the older institution began to decline. In February 1902, the Brooklyn Library trustees offered the building and its collections to the city. After some negotiation, the two institutions, old and new, merged in 1903. From that point forward, the location was known as the Montague branch of Brooklyn Public Library.

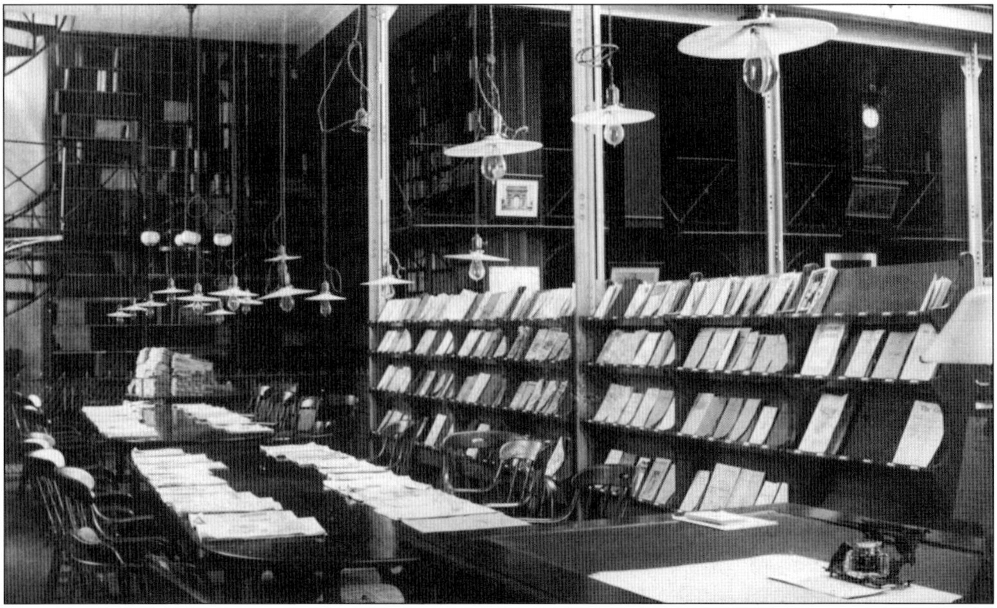

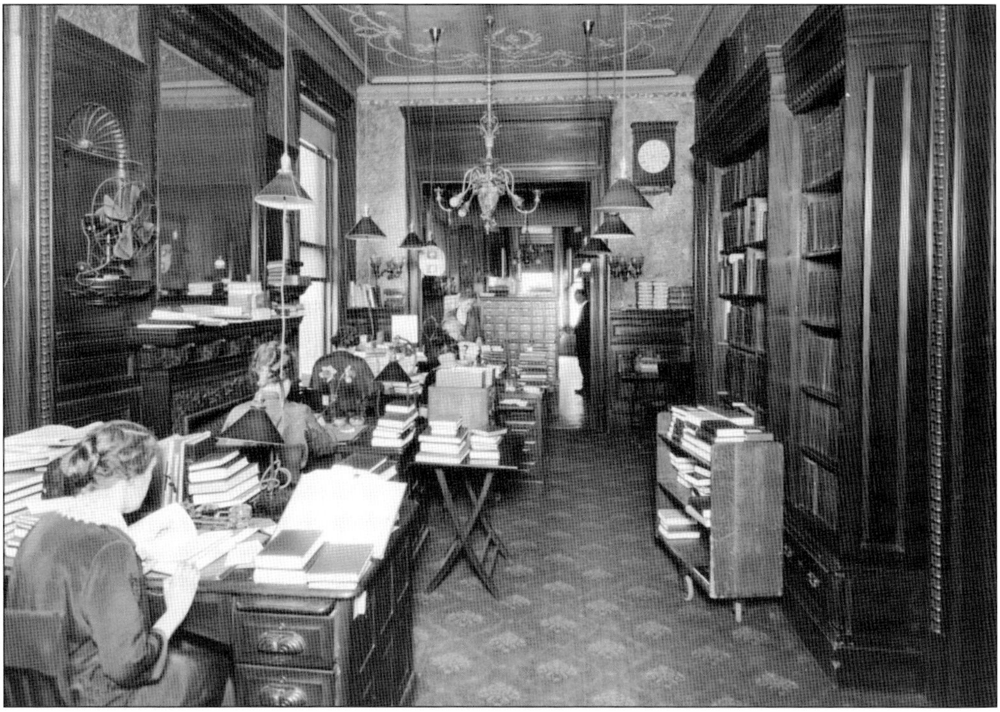

Incorporation into Brooklyn Public Library brought alterations for the building on Montague Street. As the largest library in the still-young network of branches, it housed many processes that served the entire library system. These photographs show processing and catalog rooms in the 1910s. The building began to show its age in the 20th century. By 1926, its elevator was continually broken, making it difficult to transfer books from storage areas to reading rooms. Inventive librarians worked around the obstacle with a "basket system," whereby books were shuttled up and down the building's spiral staircase in buckets attached to ropes.

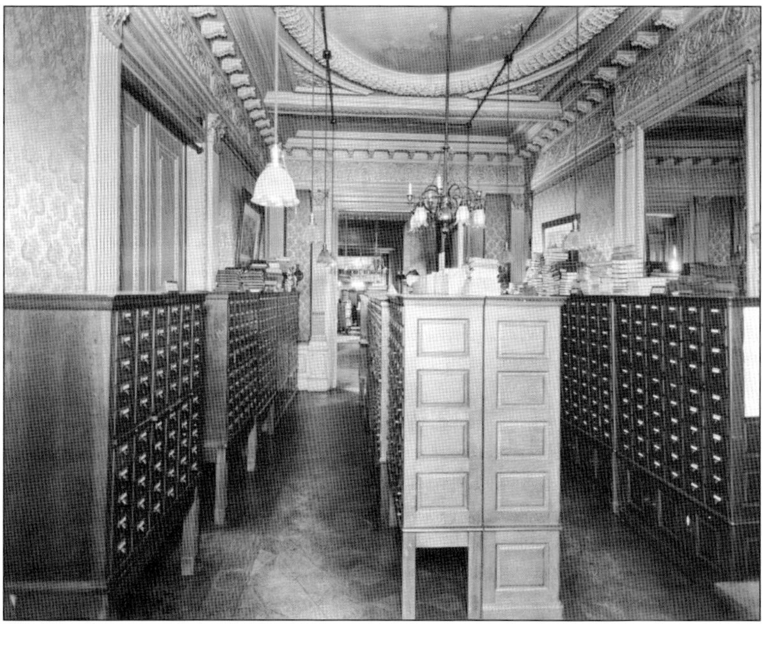

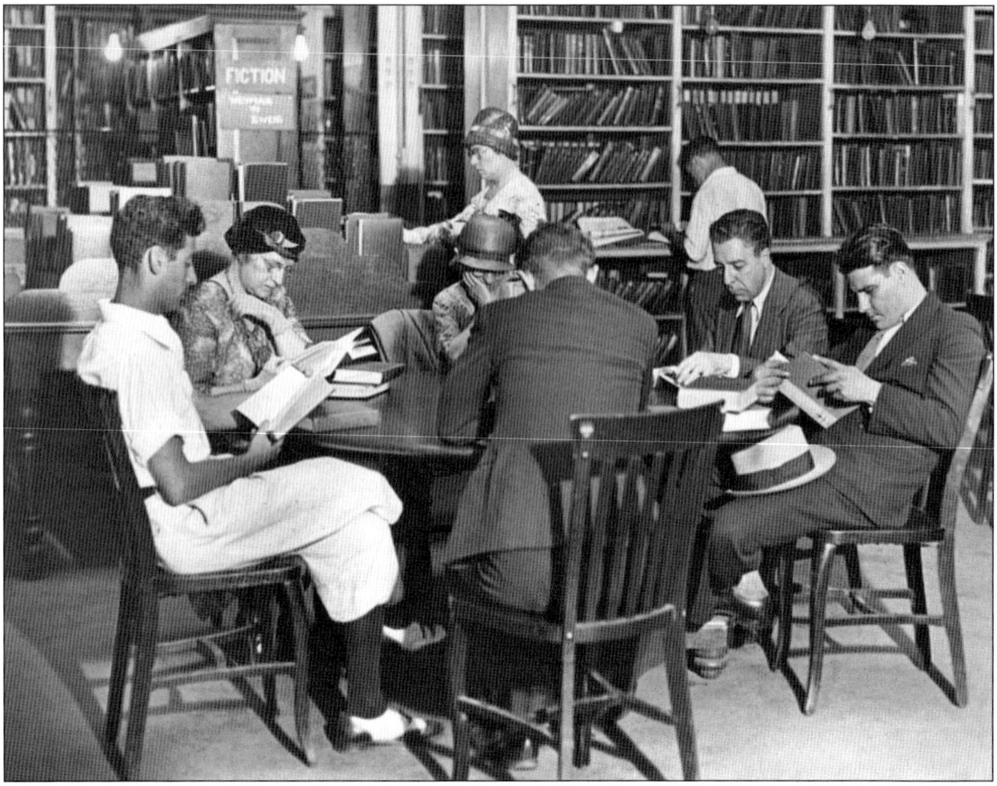

The aging Montague Library became more and more cramped over the years. WPA funds allowed for cleaning and repainting in the 1930s, but a face-lift could not solve the problems posed by overcrowding amid growing collections. Administrators in the building stressed the need for a new central library that could adequately house and process the books for the entire Brooklyn Public Library system.

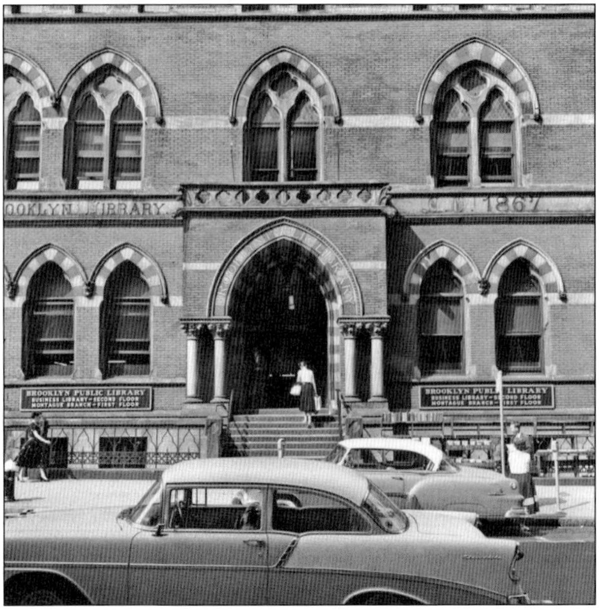

Despite its inadequacies, the Montague branch continued to serve as a de facto central library through the first part of the 20th century. The first floor housed circulating collections, and the second floor was home to reference books—many of them transferred from predecessor libraries like the Brooklyn Athenaeum and the Mercantile Library. In the 1940s, a special business reference library was established and housed here until the building was demolished in 1960.

Two

A Rough Draft

With the budding young Brooklyn Public Library system sprouting up branches all over the borough thanks to Andrew Carnegie's donations, the long-tabled idea of erecting a central library resurfaced. The triangular site at Flatbush Avenue and Eastern Parkway was recommended again in 1904; its proximity to the Brooklyn Institute of Arts and Sciences (today's Brooklyn Museum) and Prospect Park would put it in Brooklyn's cultural hub. The site was approved by the state legislature in May 1905, although the plan was not universally welcomed by architectural and cultural tastemakers of the day. The Brooklyn League, a civic organization founded in 1898, strongly objected to the plan on the grounds that the site was not central, was not accessible, and would damage the aesthetics of Grand Army Plaza. Franklin W. Hooper, director of the neighboring Brooklyn Institute of Arts and Sciences, argued that the new library should be located near Grand Army Plaza, but the specific site in question would prove harmful to the Mount Prospect Reservoir nearby.

The plan moved forward despite these protests. Raymond F. Almirall was appointed as the architect for the project, and along with chief librarian Frank P. Hill and Columbia University professor A.D.F. Hamlin, he embarked on a tour of 25 libraries across Europe to find inspiration. After taking input from librarians across the country, the board of trustees, friends of the library, and the general public, Almirall presented his designs for an impressively domed Beaux-Arts building in 1907. With two main wings extending down Eastern Parkway and Flatbush Avenue, the design was, in the words of the *Library Journal*, "monumental, dignified and refined." Continued protest from the Brooklyn League did not prevent the board of trustees from securing $300,000 from the city's board of estimate to begin construction on the Flatbush Avenue wing in 1910. On June 5, 1912, in a ceremony attended by Borough President Alfred E. Steers, Mayor William J. Gaynor, and other dignitaries, ground was broken on Brooklyn Public Library's central building.

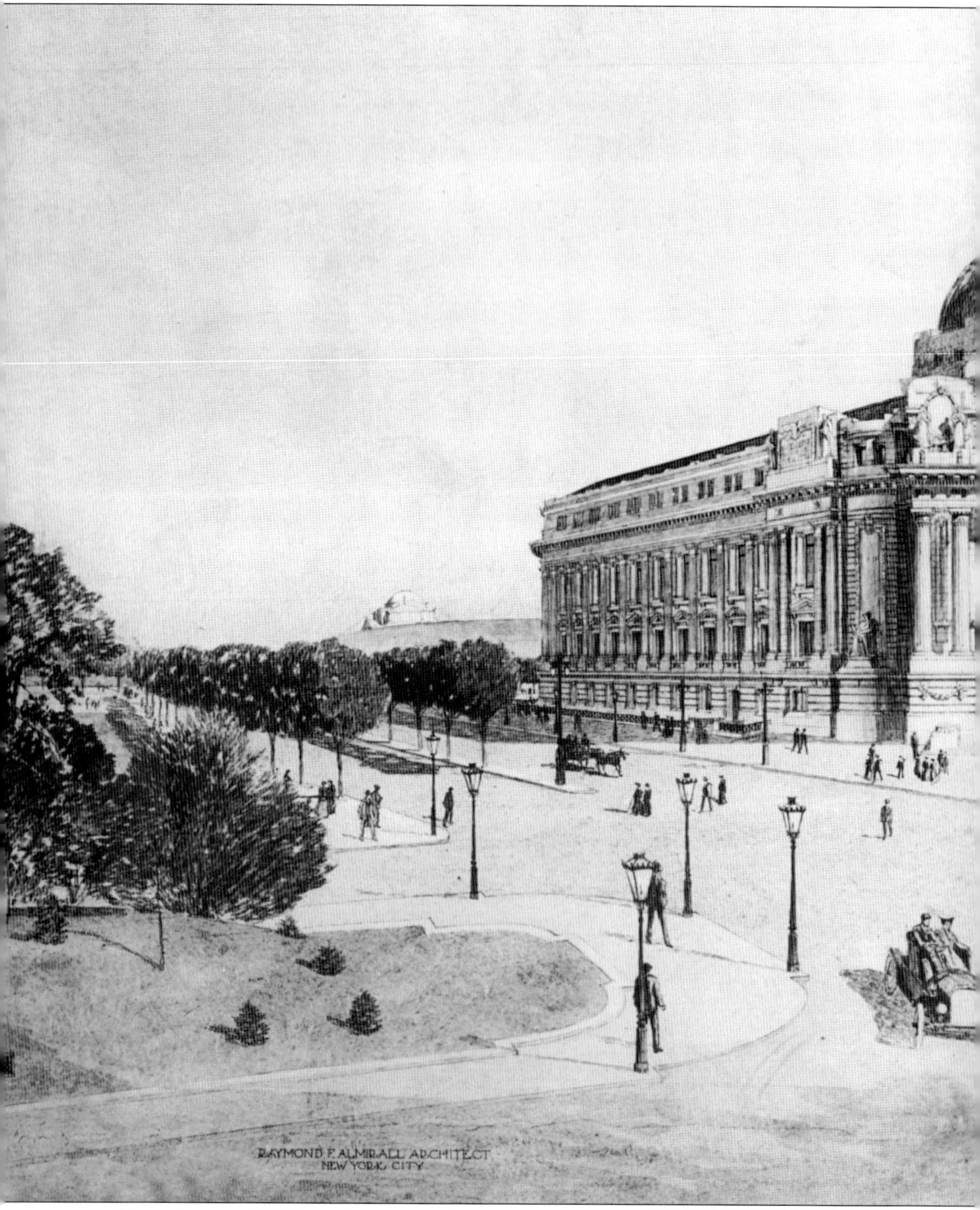

Architect Raymond F. Almirall envisioned an impressive Beaux-Arts library sitting magisterially on the triangle-shaped plot of land at Grand Army Plaza. This type of architecture was popular at the turn of the 20th century and would have produced a library that was congruent with its neighbor, the Brooklyn Museum. Almirall was born in Brooklyn in 1869. After attending Adelphi

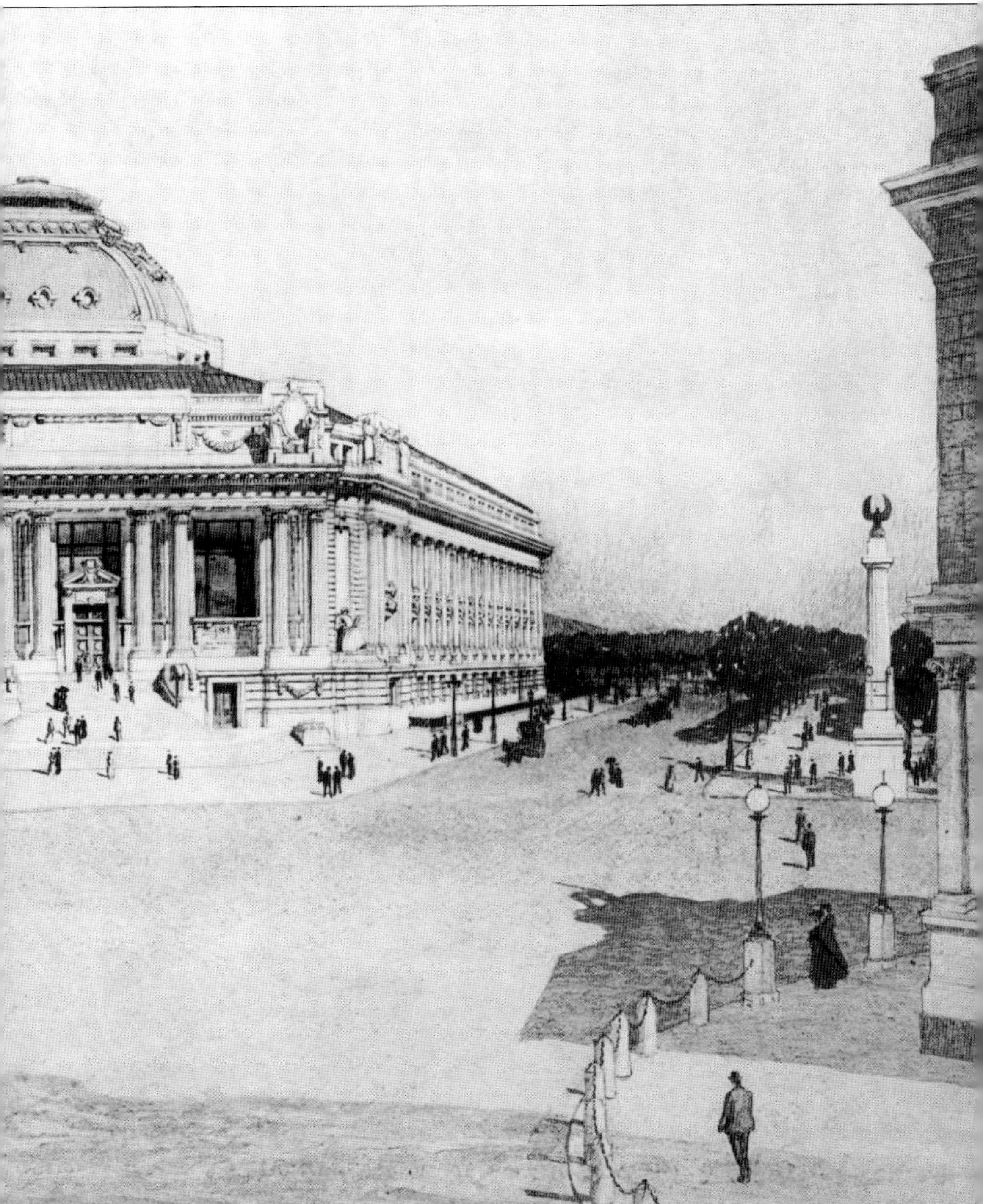

Academy and Cornell University, he went abroad to study architecture at École des Beaux-Arts in Paris. His design for the city hall in Binghamton, New York, was selected by the Jury of Fine Arts to represent the best of North American architecture at the Paris Exposition of 1900.

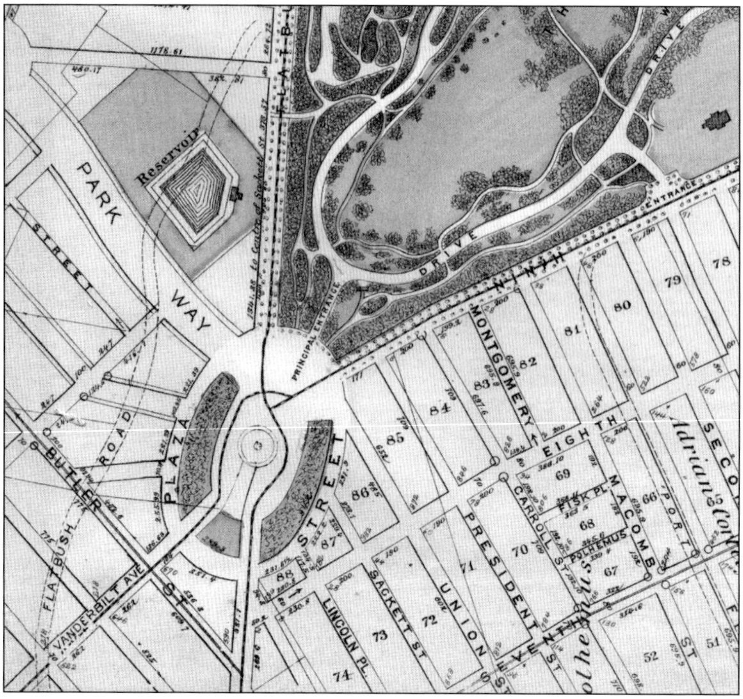

The odd triangular wedge of land that was approved as the library site can be seen in this 1874 map at the intersection of Flatbush Avenue and Eastern Parkway, between the Reservoir, Prospect Park, and the oblong plaza. The Brooklyn League considered the site to be not centrally located and not easily accessible in 1905; they did not foresee subway expansion and population growth that would render the Central Library truly "central."

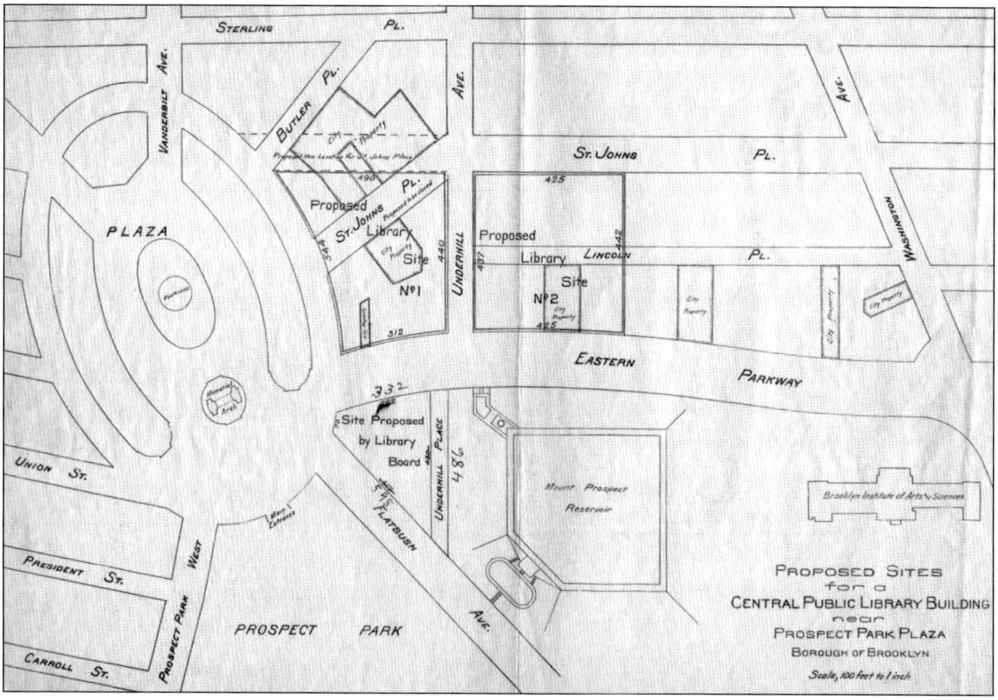

This undated site map shows alternate sites for the library, as well as the triangular location at Flatbush Avenue and Eastern Parkway. Although the author of this particular proposal is unknown, many were opposed to the triangle site. Franklin W. Hooper, director of the neighboring Brooklyn Institute of Arts and Sciences, voiced concerns over the building's proximity to the Mount Prospect Reservoir.

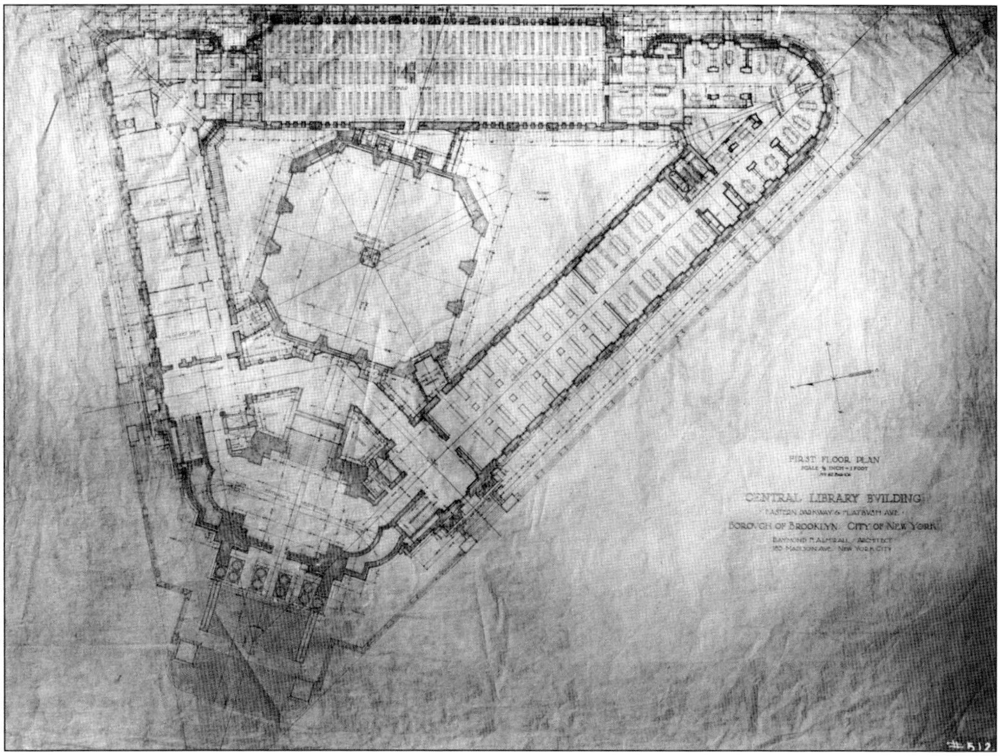

This floor plan submitted by Almirall shows the building filling up the entire plot of land at the top of Prospect Park. The first floor, pictured here, had exhibition space along the Flatbush Avenue wing (right), administrative offices and meeting spaces in the Eastern Parkway wing (left), and stacks for book storage in the back wing, abutting the Mount Prospect Reservoir.

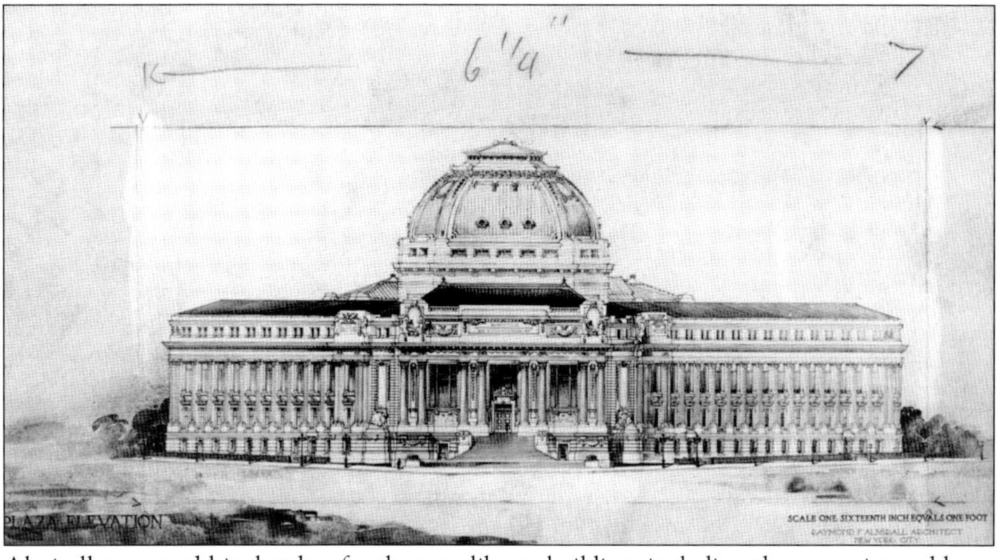

Almirall presented his sketches for the new library building, including the ones pictured here, before former naysayers of the Brooklyn League in March 1907. Addressing the group, he claimed that his proposals could transform the intersection of Flatbush Avenue and Eastern Parkway into "the most beautiful plaza the world has ever known."

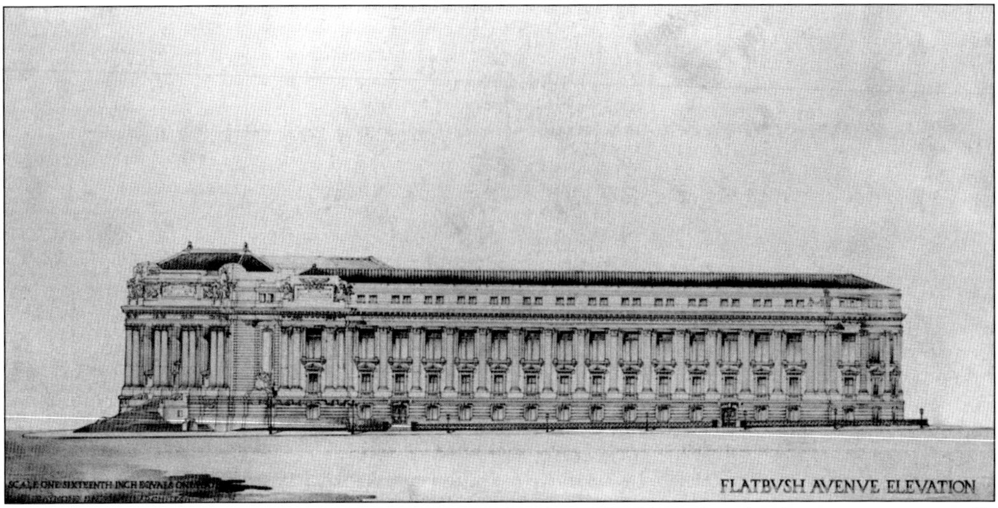

Early sketches show a large central dome adorning the library building, but this feature was eventually scrapped after the Municipal Art Commission found the dome to be "too conspicuous." The architect resubmitted plans to the commission in February 1912, only to have the dome rejected again. This image shows the Flatbush Avenue wing as it would eventually be built—without a dome.

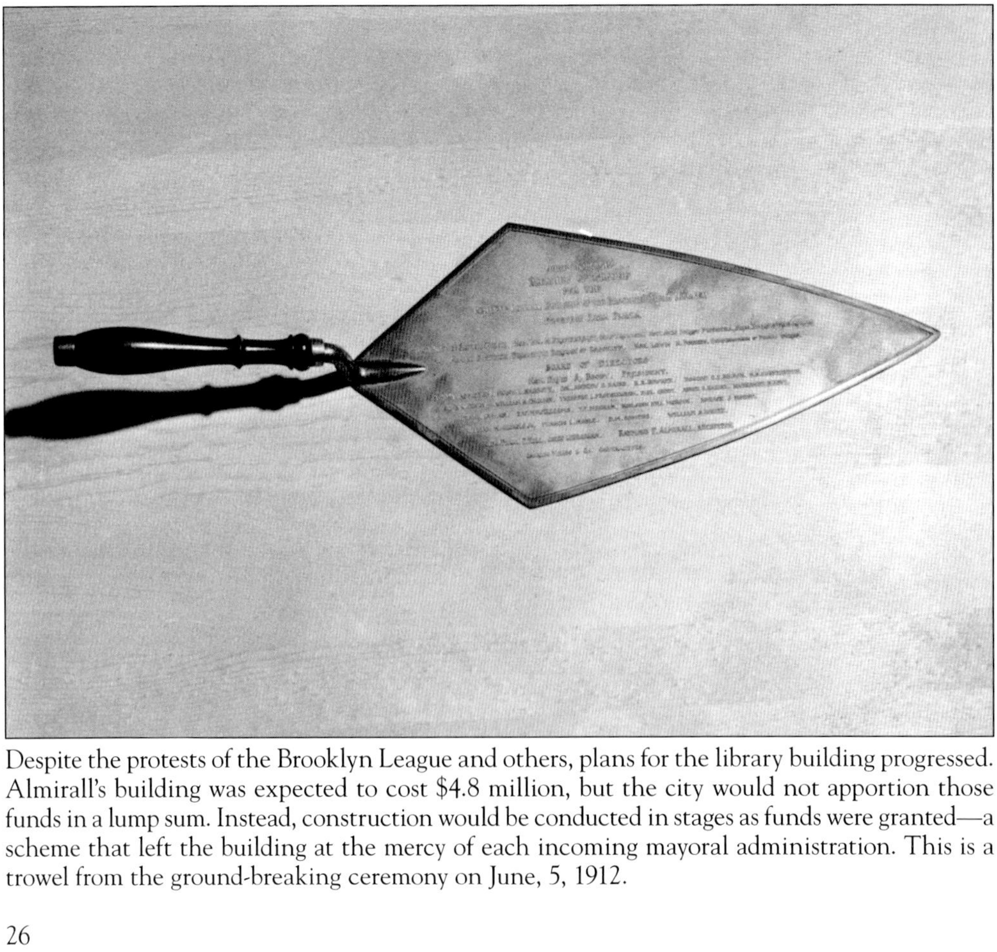

Despite the protests of the Brooklyn League and others, plans for the library building progressed. Almirall's building was expected to cost $4.8 million, but the city would not apportion those funds in a lump sum. Instead, construction would be conducted in stages as funds were granted—a scheme that left the building at the mercy of each incoming mayoral administration. This is a trowel from the ground-breaking ceremony on June, 5, 1912.

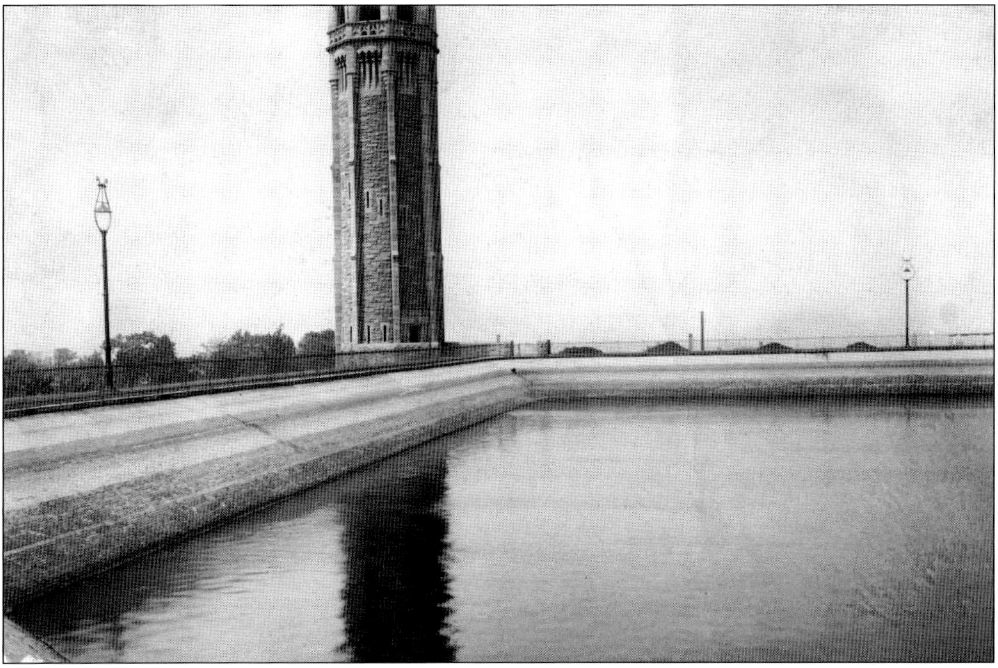

The new Central Library butted up against the Mount Prospect Reservoir, which, with an elevation 28 feet higher than the larger Ridgewood Reservoir, was part of a distribution network supplying water to south Brooklyn. Its distinctive pink granite tower can be seen above presiding over the calm waters of the reservoir, and behind the library construction site in the 1919 photograph below. The tower was built in 1891 and could hold 100,000 gallons of water. Made obsolete by a new network bringing water from the Catskills, the tower was demolished in 1930 after it was determined that library construction would weaken its foundations.

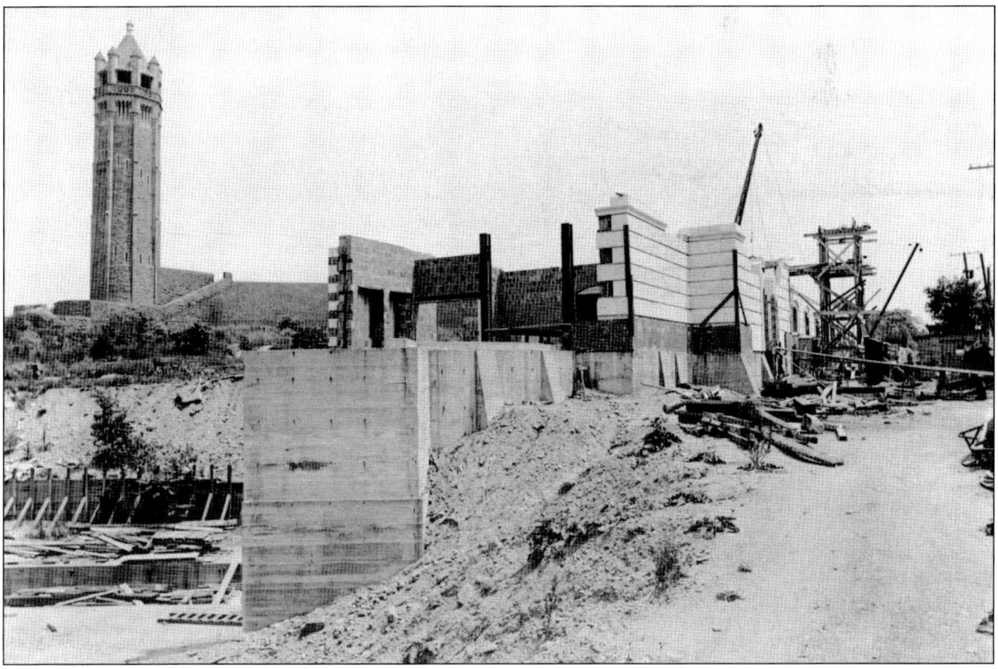

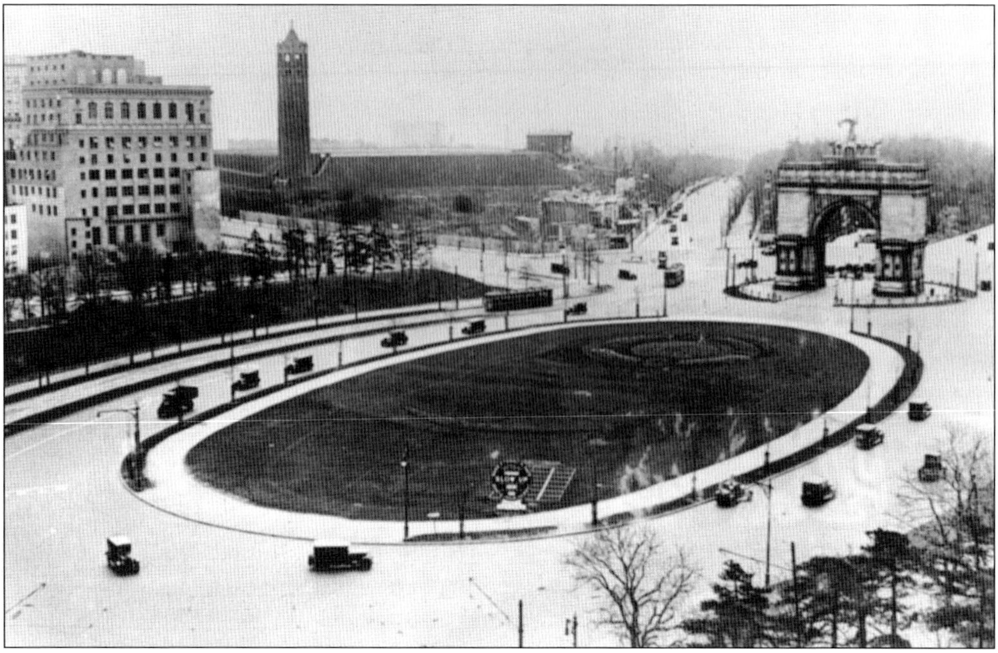

Although the library was originally planned to be completed within five years, securing funding to pay for construction was a constant struggle. By 1915, only the foundations had been completed and lay bare and exposed to the elements. That year, the library's board of trustees requested a lump sum from the board of estimate to speed along the process. They were given enough money to start only the Flatbush Avenue wing of the building. World War I further complicated matters, pushing the issue of a library building to the back of everyone's mind. These photographs (above from 1919 and below from the 1920s) show the Flatbush Avenue wing under construction; it would not be completed until 1929. Seventeen years after the ground-breaking ceremonies, only one third of the library building was constructed.

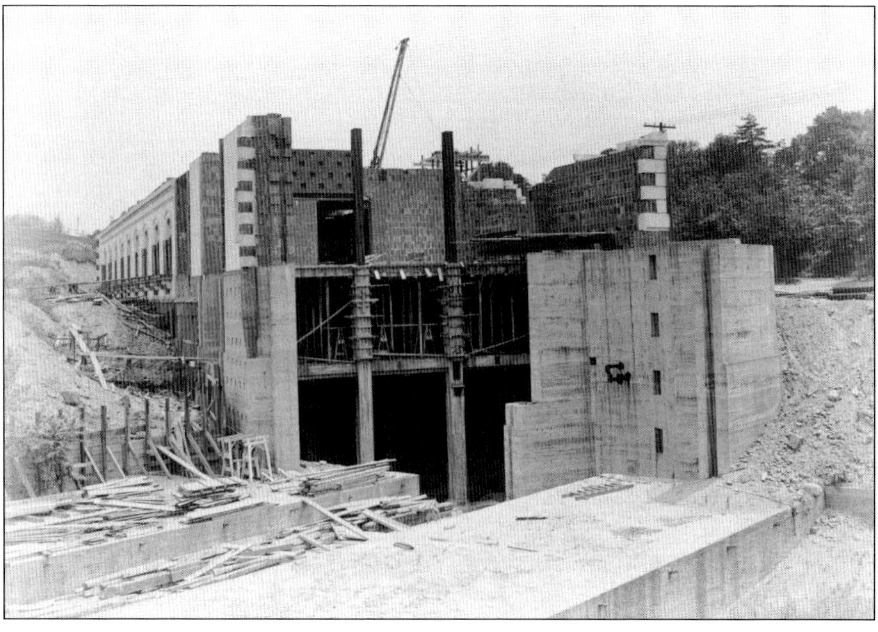

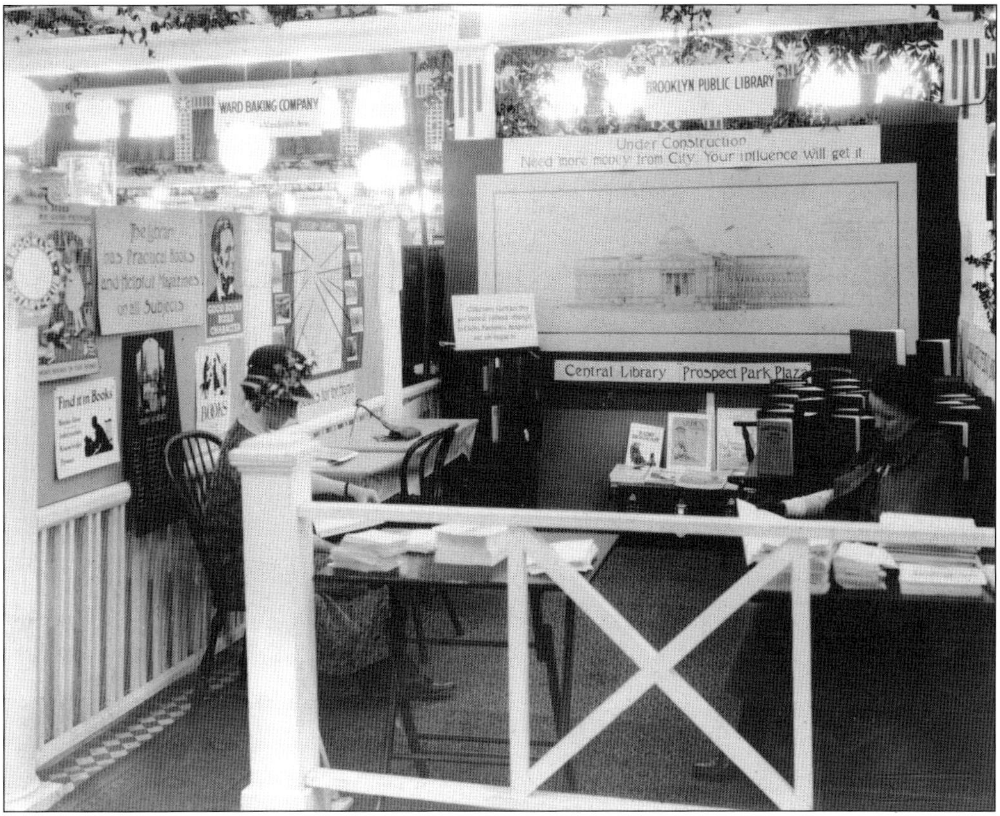

This undated image shows a Brooklyn Public Library booth at a local fair. Of interest is the display at the back, which shows Almirall's grandiose design for the library with the terse words "Under Construction. Need more money from City. Your influence will get it." The troubles with the library construction were very public, and city officials and laypeople alike fueled debate on the topic in the opinion columns of local newspapers.

This image, captioned in the *Brooklyn Daily Eagle* as "Ruins of Brooklyn," was taken sometime after the Mount Prospect Tower came down and shows a scene that was all too familiar through the early 20th century. Just one wing of the Almirall-designed Central Library stood alone and unfinished at the corner of Flatbush Avenue and Eastern Parkway for decades after work had stalled.

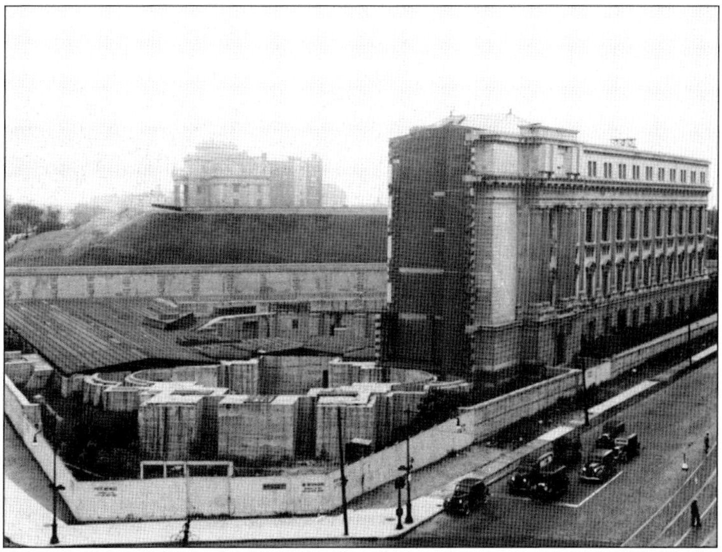

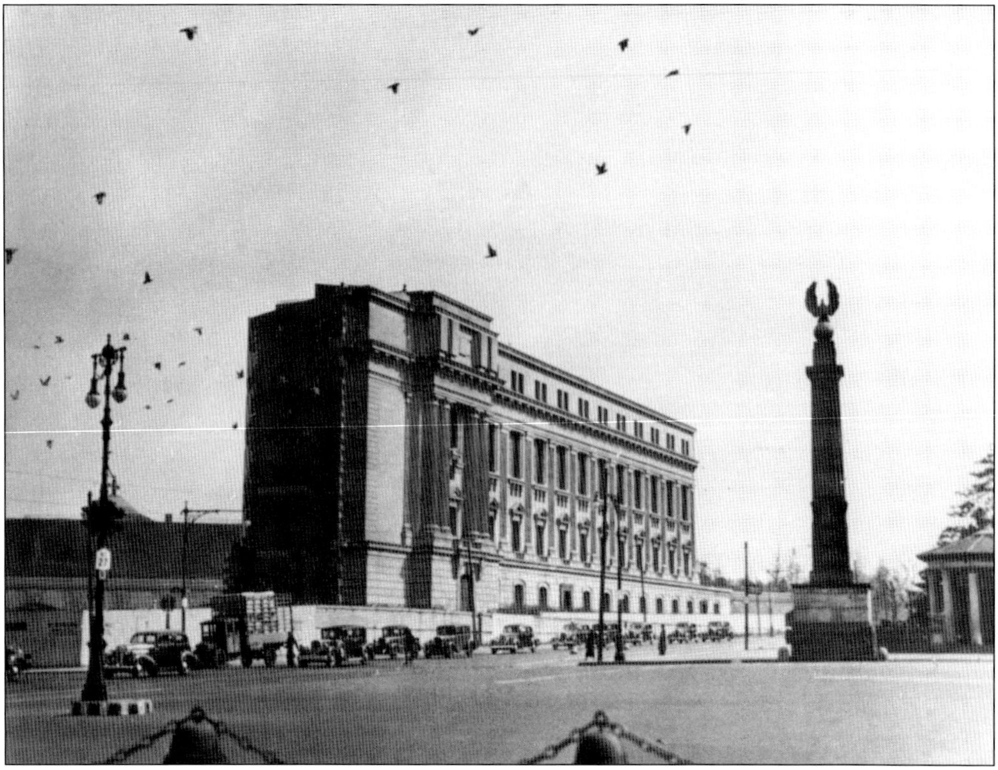

Chief librarian Dr. Frank P. Hill made repeated pleas to the board of estimate to properly finish the Flatbush Avenue wing, at the very least, so that it could be used to store books. More than 250,000 volumes, many from the now historic Mercantile Library collection, were kept at the Montague branch, a decrepit firetrap. Though it appears complete in this undated photograph, the Flatbush wing needed interior work before it could be occupied.

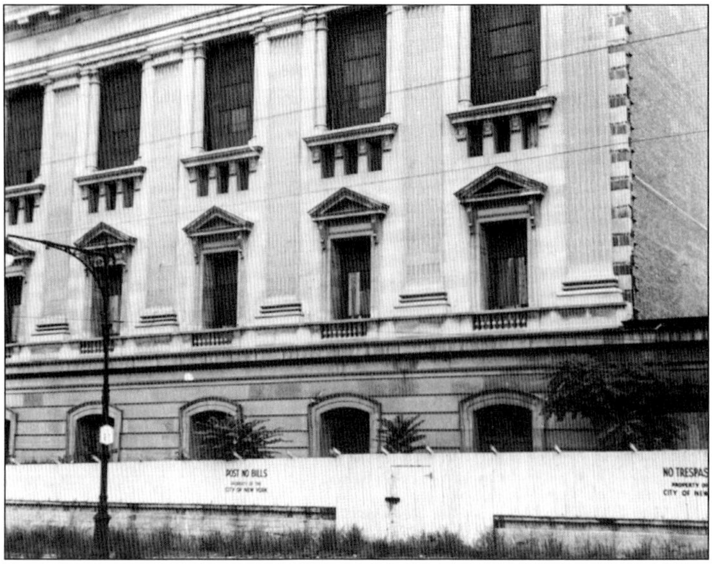

This close-up view of the Flatbush Avenue facade shows boarded-up windows and overgrown weeds facing onto one of Brooklyn's busiest thoroughfares. In 1921, Raymond Almirall, still eager to see his project through to completion, lobbied for a lump sum to finish the building. Mayor John F. Hylan appointed a committee of engineers to estimate the cost of completing the library; they put the total at $11 million.

Three

The Open Book

Ten years after ground was broken, Brooklyn still did not have its central library, and the prospects for finishing the project looked grim. The Flatbush Avenue wing stood alone at the Grand Army Plaza site, alongside the recently dug foundations for the rest of the building. Nowhere near suitable for library patrons, the structure did prove a useful shelter for the local pigeon population. Construction was continually delayed while the library's board tried to scrape together funds to cover costs. Mayor John F. Hylan was not supportive in the unending search for funding; in 1921, he replied to trustee David Boody's fourth request for money by saying, "We are not responsible for that hole in the ground." The unfortunate nickname stuck, and "hole in the ground" became an oft-repeated lament for the sad library structure in local newspapers.

The 1930s brought much-needed change for the gridlocked construction project. Milton J. Ferguson was hired as chief librarian at the beginning of the decade, and Raymond V. Ingersoll was elected as borough president in 1933. These two renewed the fight for a central library, proposing new architects with a fresh vision for the now outdated Almirall design. Alfred Morton Githens and Francis Keally were taxed with the difficult job of creating a new library plan to be built on top of old library foundations, but their vision of a thoroughly modern Art Deco structure was a decisive departure from Almirall's Beaux-Arts building. After finally receiving an inflow of funds from the board of estimate in 1938, construction crews resumed work on the new central library building.

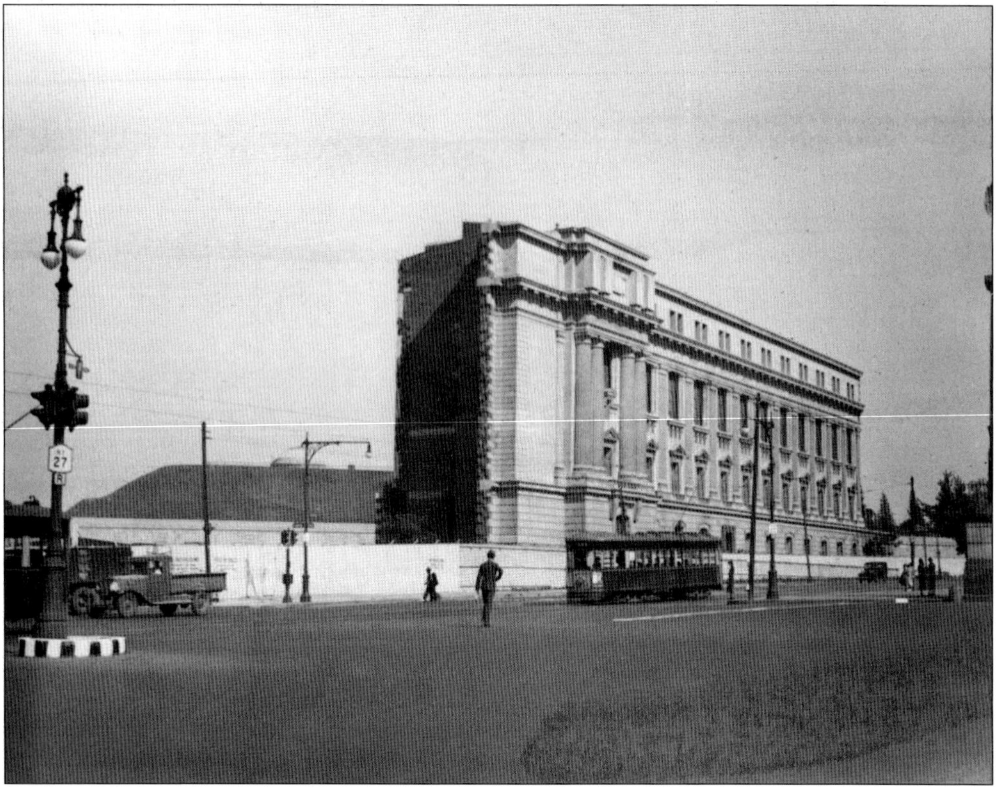

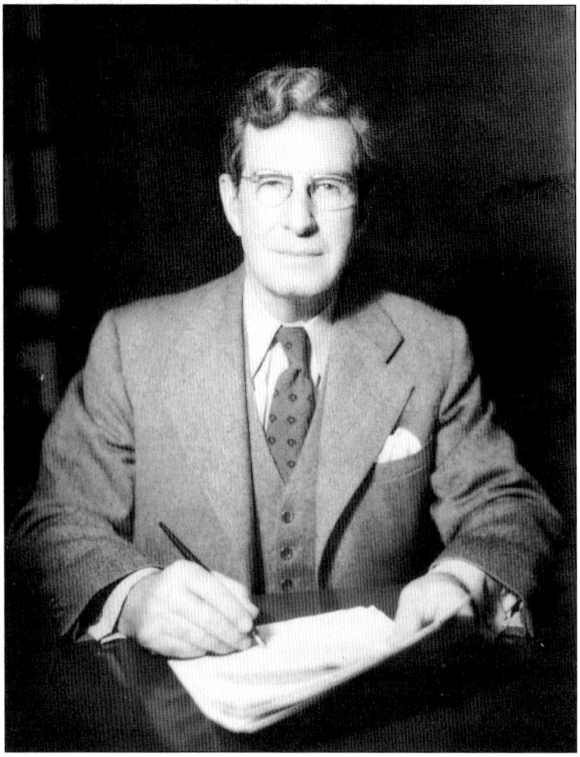

Even though the Flatbush Avenue wing was more or less finished by the end of the 1920s, it was not ready to house staff or collections. The entire nation was suffering through the Depression years, so funding to complete construction seemed out of the question. However, change was in the offing. In 1930, chief librarian Frank P. Hill retired, and Dr. Milton J. Ferguson was hired in his place.

Dr. Ferguson came to Brooklyn by way of California. He had been serving as the California state librarian since 1917, until he was hired away to lead Brooklyn Public Library in 1930. Before that, Ferguson had worked for the University of Oklahoma libraries and had served as president of the library association in that state.

That same year, David Boody died at the age of 92. As the borough's last mayor before consolidation, Boody had closed a chapter in the city's history, and during his years as president of the library's board of trustees, he had tirelessly advocated for a new building. Replacing him was Judge Edwin L. Garvin, pictured here in an undated photograph.

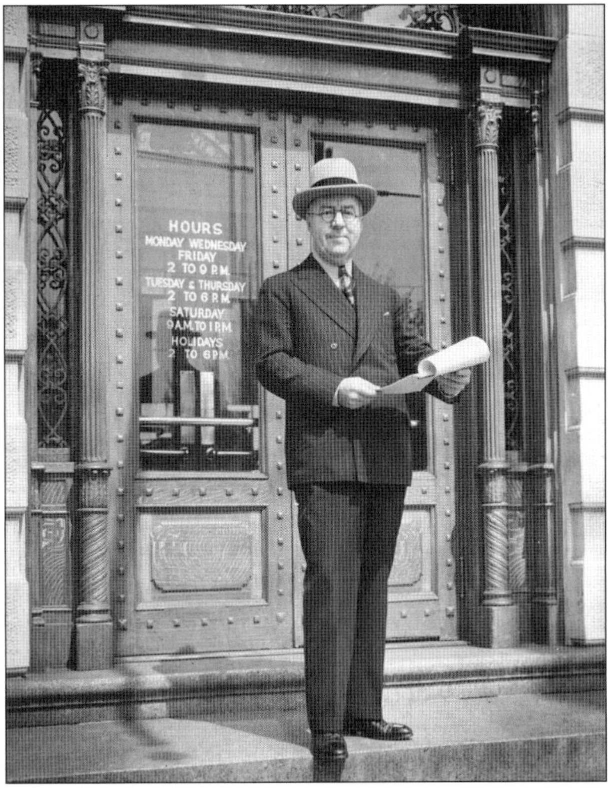

Ferguson and Garvin had their work cut out for them. A full 20 years after ground was broken on the new library site, all there was to show for it was a lone wing along Flatbush Avenue and the dismal hole, pictured here, marking the footprint of a building that seemed unlikely to ever come into being.

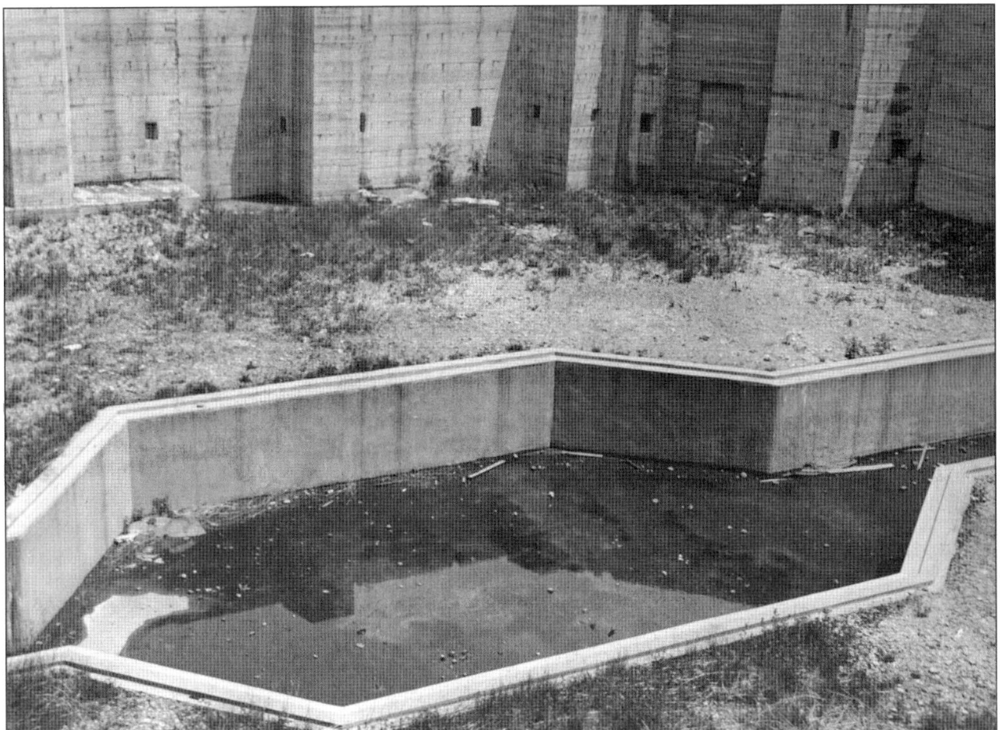

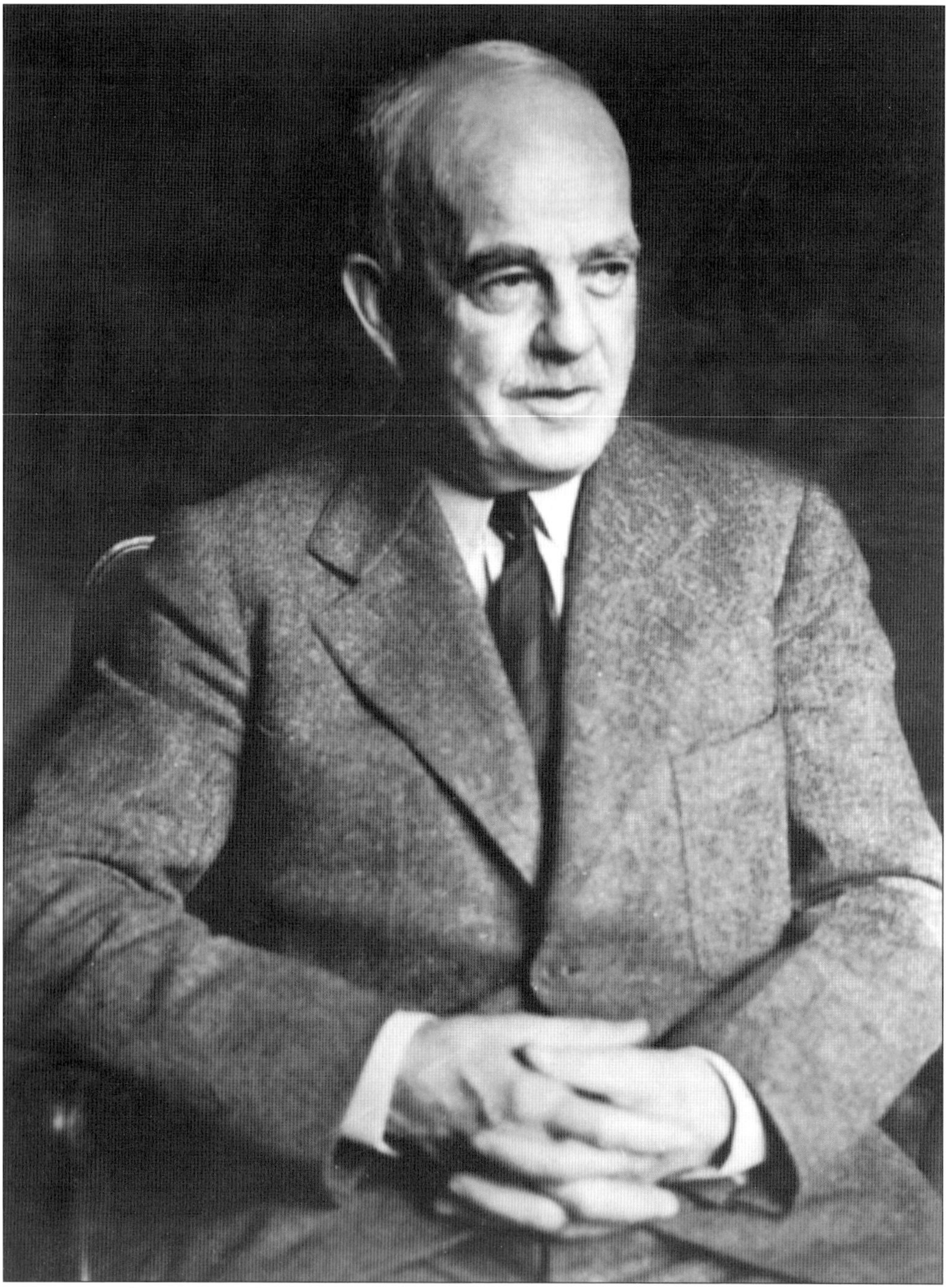

Ferguson and Garvin would soon have an ally in the new Brooklyn borough president, Raymond Vail Ingersoll. As former commissioner of parks in Brooklyn, Ingersoll pledged to secure $9 million from the federal Public Works Administration (PWA), a New Deal initiative, to complete the long-stalled construction project. The plan did not pan out, but Ingersoll remained committed to the cause.

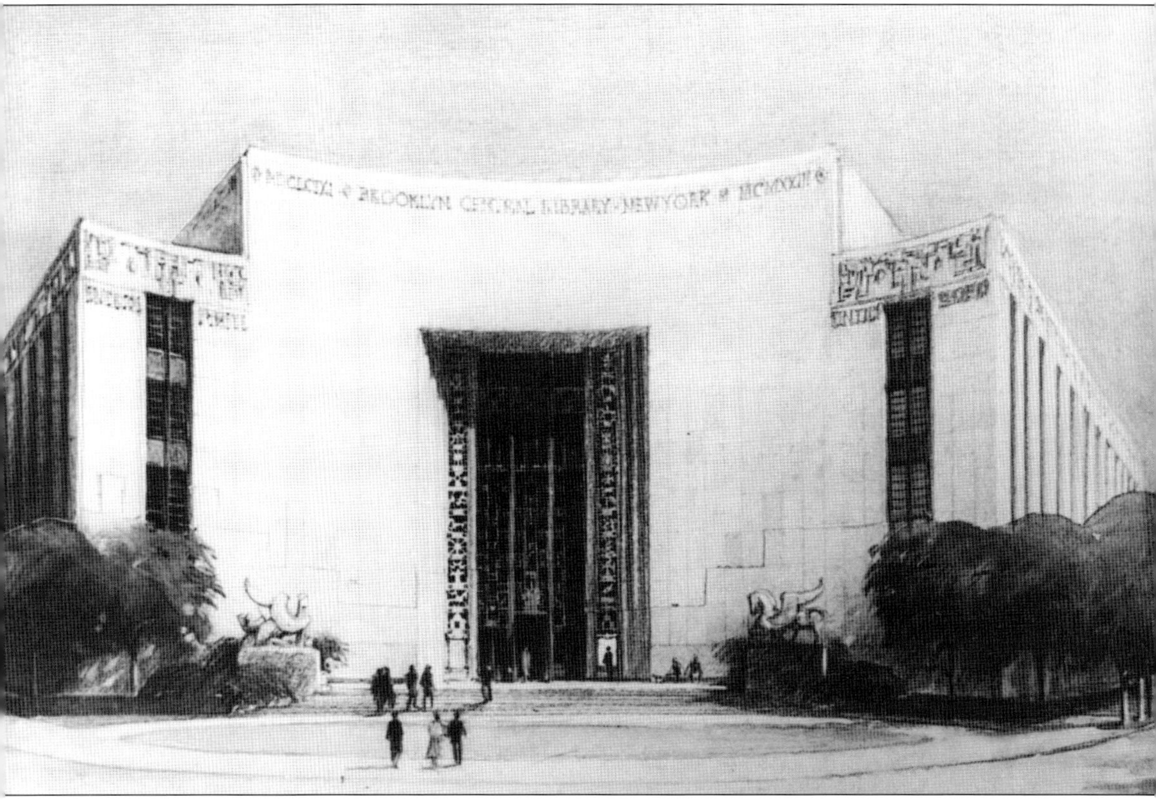

Part of the petition to the PWA involved drafting new plans for Central Library. Almirall's original design would cost a whopping $11 million to complete and had become architecturally outdated by the 1930s. New architects—Alfred Morton Githens and Francis Keally—were brought in to give the project a fresh look. Their new proposal for the building was much more reasonably priced at $2 million. This rendering was created by the architects in 1936 and was based on then current library design trends. Trustee Edwin L. Garvin praised the modern "open plan" of the building designs, which included a large, airy main-floor lobby from which reading rooms radiated outward. The majority of books would be stored in stacks in subbasements so as not to clutter the public spaces. Other libraries in the country had started to adopt this layout, partly because it made buildings more accessible for handicapped patrons.

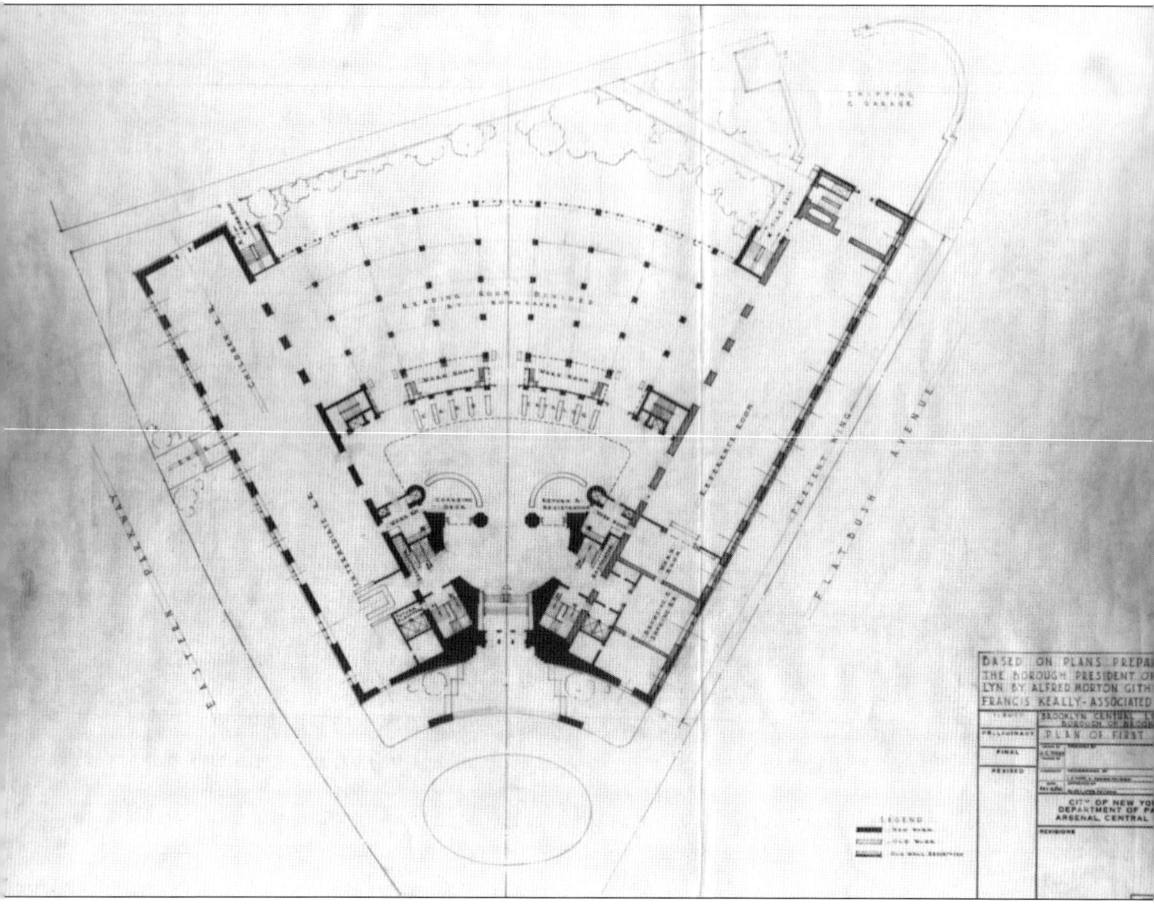

Githens, the older of the two architects, was already well established as a designer of public buildings. Keally was known more as a writer and educator in the field. Together, the two drafted the design pictured here—the library as an open book, its spine curved onto Grand Army Plaza and its "covers" stretched down along Eastern Parkway and Flatbush Avenue. Finally, the winds were turning in favor of building. In March 1937, the board of estimate included a $2 million outlay for the central library in the city's capital budget, to the gratification of Ferguson, Garvin, Ingersoll, and all who had toiled to shepherd the long-stalled project to fruition. In May of that year, the *Brooklyn Daily Eagle* reported, "Dr. Frank P. Hill, chief librarian of the Brooklyn Public Library for two score years before his retirement from that position six years ago, writes from his home in Hartford that he feels a decade younger over news that the central library here (for which he fought vigorously) is at last being built. That makes him 73."

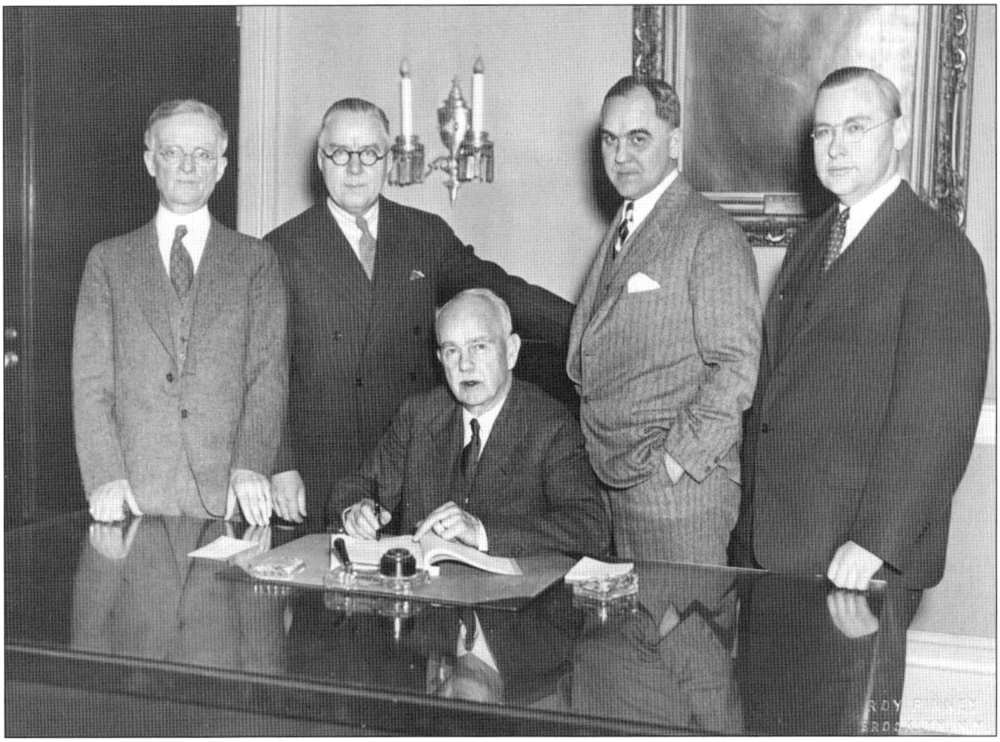

December 29, 1937, proved to be a decisive day in the long, drawn-out battle for a central library. Here, the contracts are signed to complete construction on the building. From left to right are Philip P. Farley, consulting engineer to the borough president; Edwin L. Garvin, president of the board of trustees; Raymond V. Ingersoll (seated), borough president; Francis Keally, architect; and Lauson H. Stone, board of trustees member.

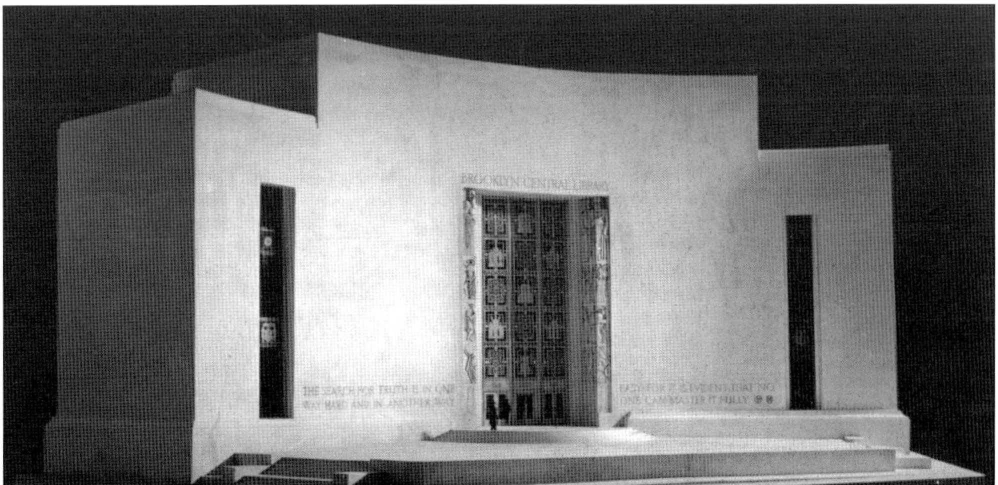

This model was one of three displayed at the WPA's gallery in 1937. It shows a library radically different from Raymond Almirall's Beaux-Arts design, yet also built on its very foundations. Gone are the ornate columns and grand staircases; in their place are unornamented limestone and street-level access.

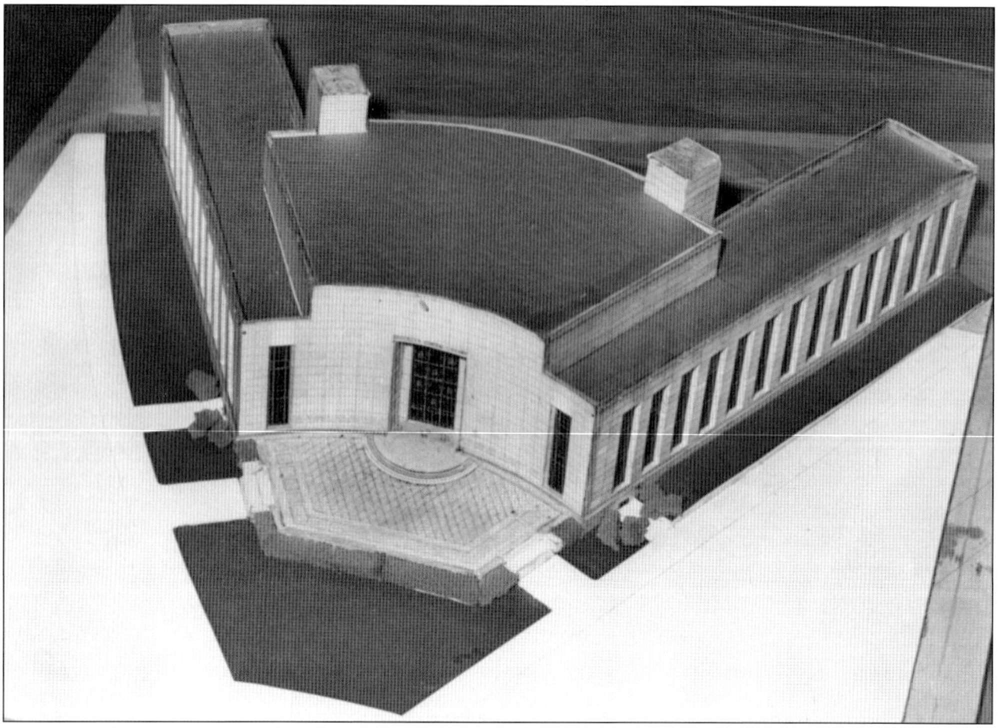

The "open book" aspect of the library's design is best appreciated from above, as these models created by sculptors employed by the WPA indicate. It was not just the exterior that was streamlined in the new plan; efficiency of cost and space were paramount in Githens and Keally's reimagining of Almirall's design. The planned fourth floor was scrapped, as was the grand staircase leading from Grand Army Plaza up to the library's main floor. Modern sensibilities favored an open floor plan and street-level access, and what had been envisioned and constructed as the basement level instead became the first floor.

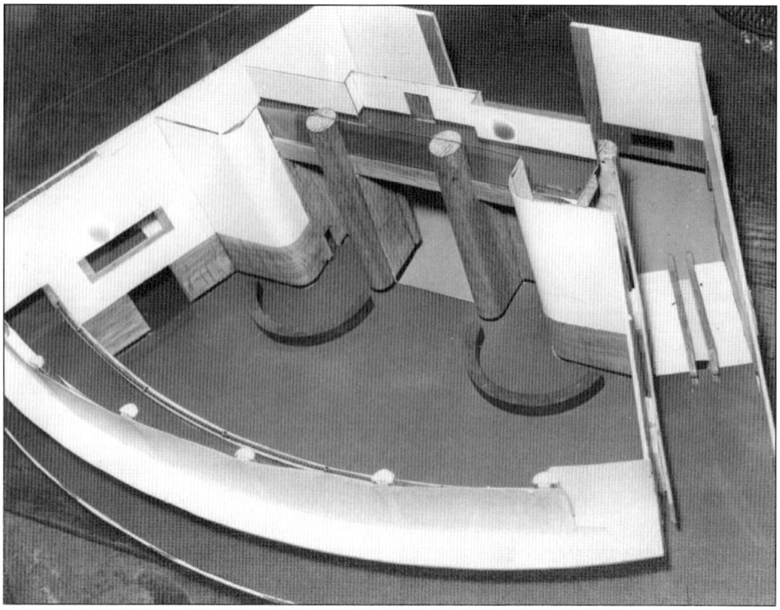

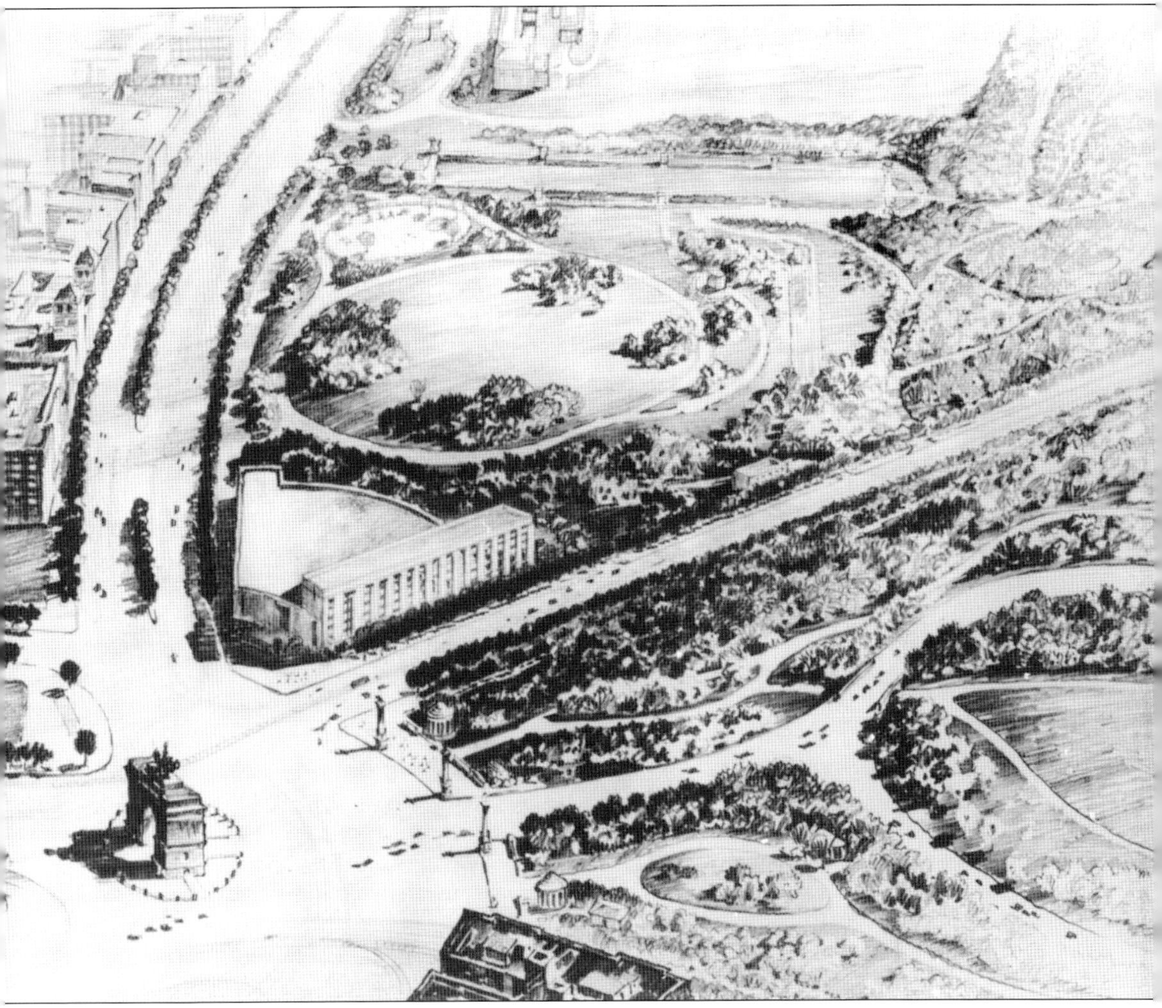

The *Brooklyn Daily Eagle* published this rendering of the plan for the library and its environs in September 1938, recounting the entire history of the construction site in a lengthy article. The Mount Prospect Reservoir is gone; in its place is a public park proposed by parks commissioner Robert Moses. That park, named Mount Prospect for the reservoir it replaced, remains today.

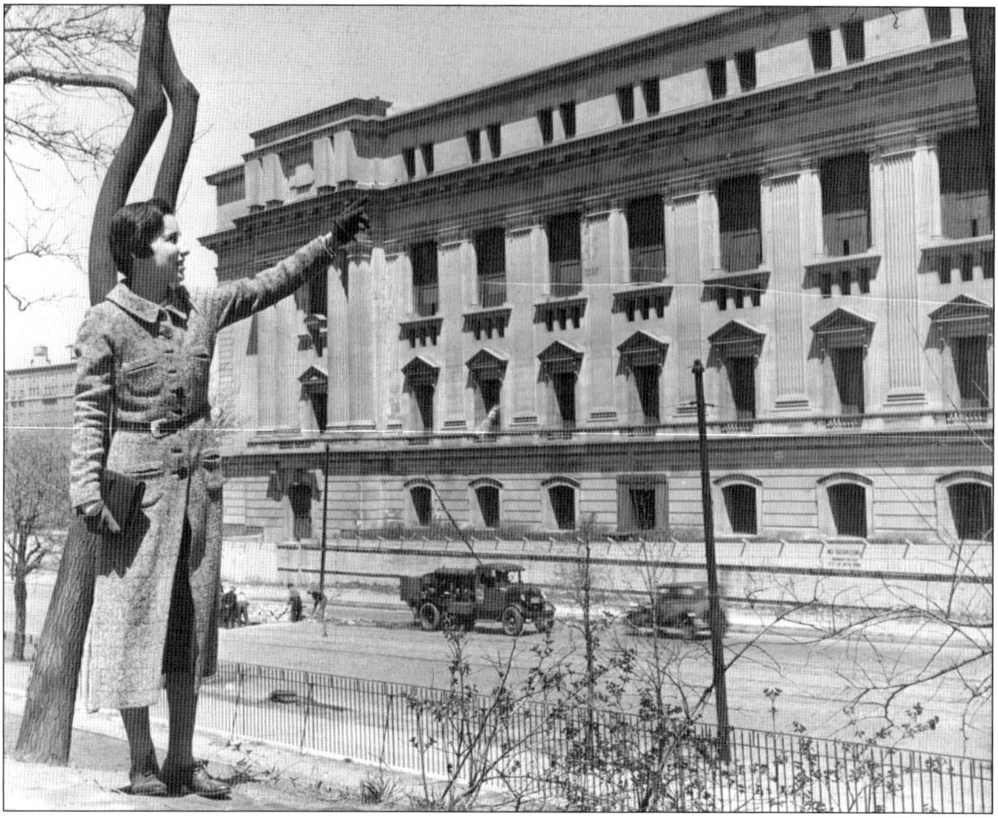

As Jane Woroneck points out in this photograph published by the *Brooklyn Daily Eagle* in 1938, the question of the old Flatbush Avenue wing remained. Chief librarian Milton Ferguson described it to *Eagle* reporters as the "second oldest uncompleted ruin in the world," next only to the Tower of Babel.

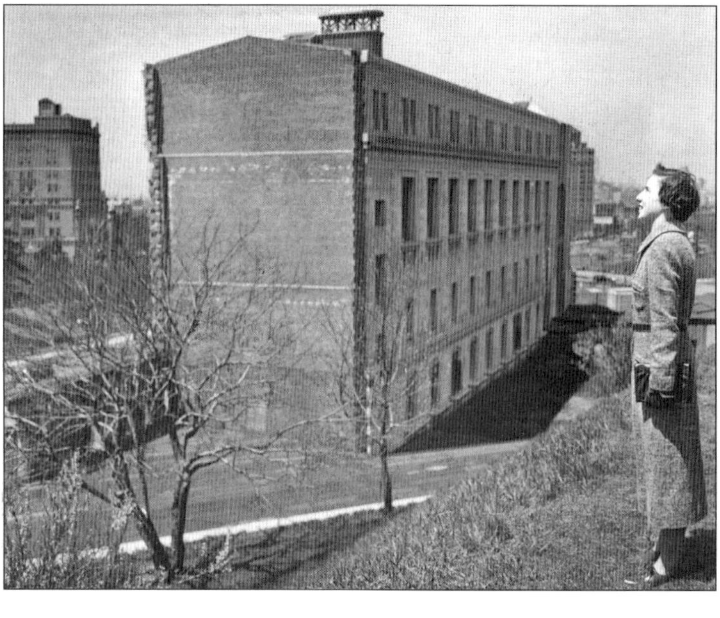

Even though the lone Flatbush wing was widely decried as a ruin, too much public money had been sunk into the building to scrap it entirely. Part of the genius of Githens and Keally's design is that it would repurpose the existing structure to suit the needs of the modernized library.

The *Brooklyn Daily Eagle* might have been exaggerating when, in 1938, it called Central Library the "most expensive pigeon roost in the world," but only slightly. This photograph from that same year bears a handwritten caption: "One of the pigeons which refused to leave nest in old building."

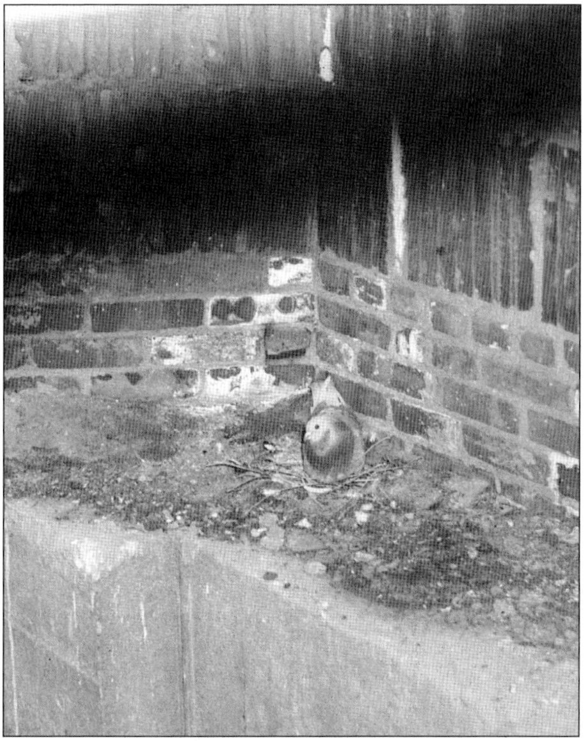

Once the Art Deco designs of architects Alfred Morton Githens and Francis Keally were adopted, workers began dismantling the original Almirall facade of the lone Flatbush Avenue wing. The contracts signed in December 1937 stipulated that work must be completed in 500 days, setting a brisk construction schedule after years of inaction.

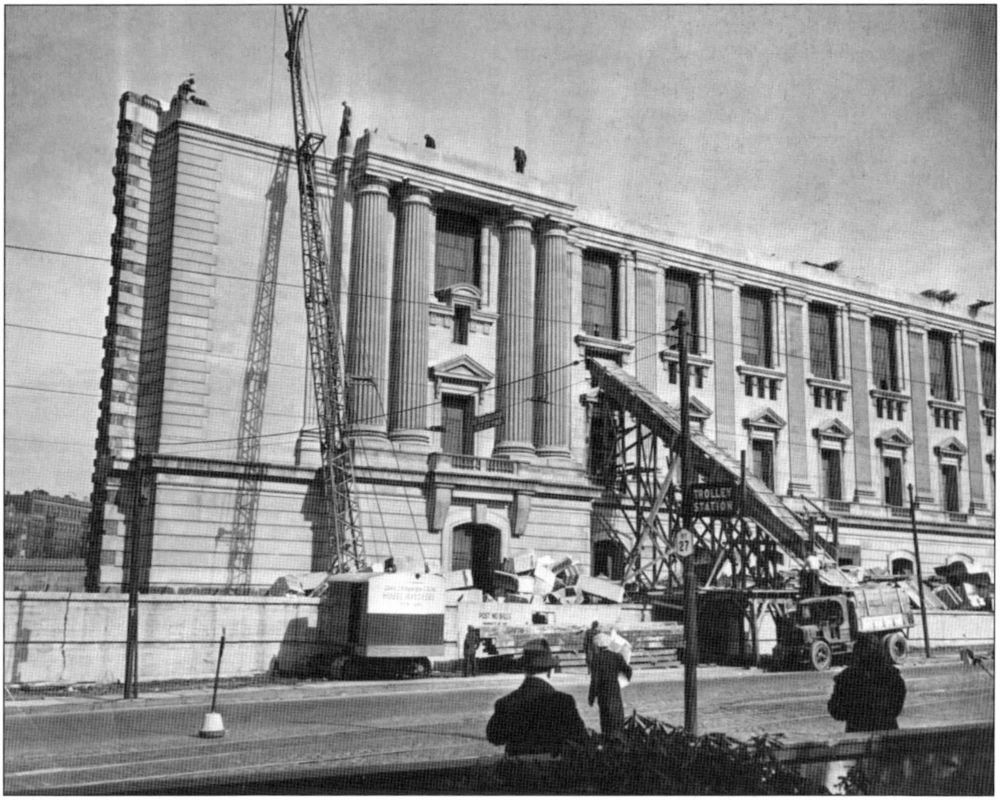

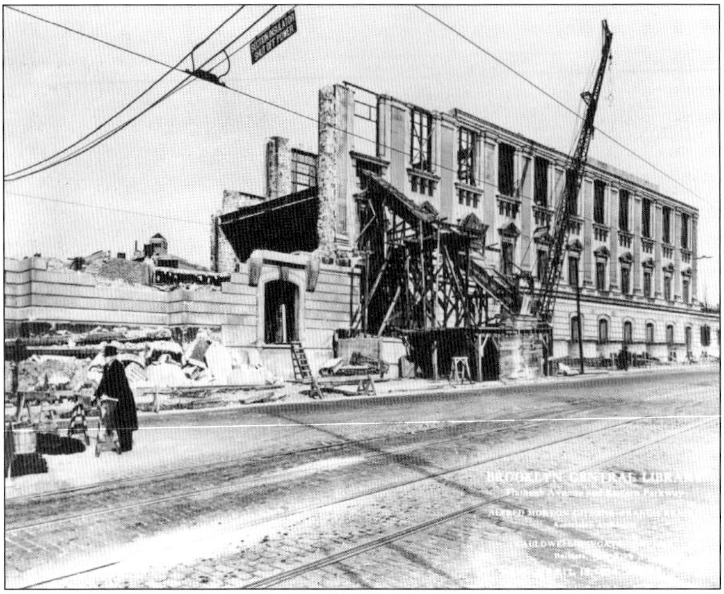

This photograph shows the project a little further along. The complete departure from Almirall's original plan is especially remarkable since Githens and Keally were forced to work with the foundation and wing that had already been built. As Ferguson noted, "The windows of the Flatbush wing were varied in design but all so small that daylight would at no time enable the student to read his books."

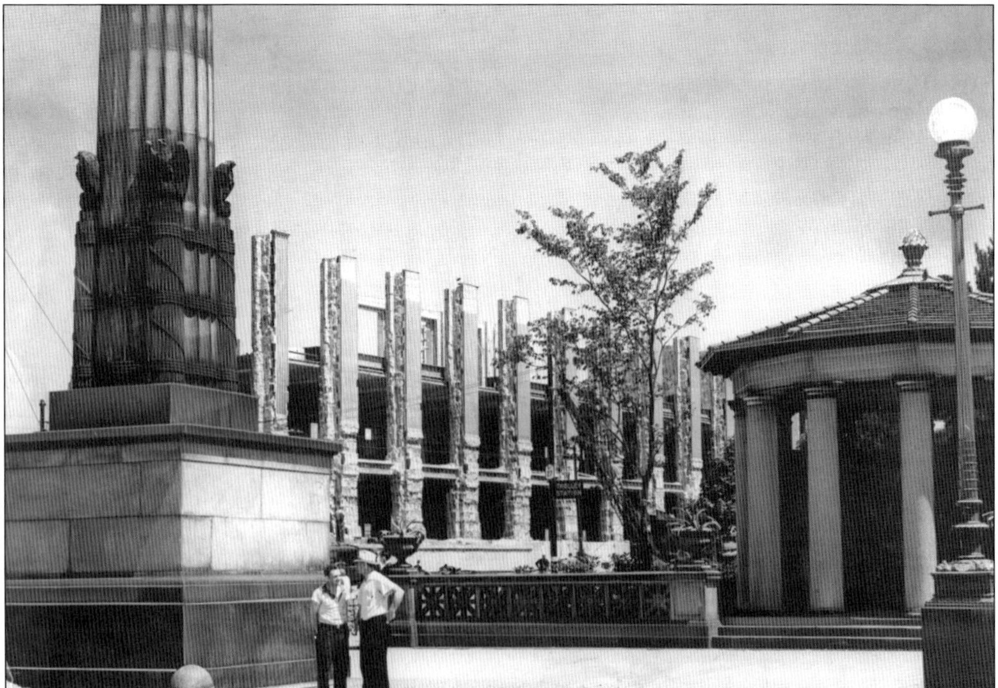

This later construction photograph shows the Flatbush wing as viewed from the entrance to Prospect Park. By stripping the facade, Githens and Keally were able to restore natural daylight to the building. Part of the justification for removing the fourth floor entirely was that the windowsills were seven feet high, giving the rooms "the effect of a jug" in Ferguson's words.

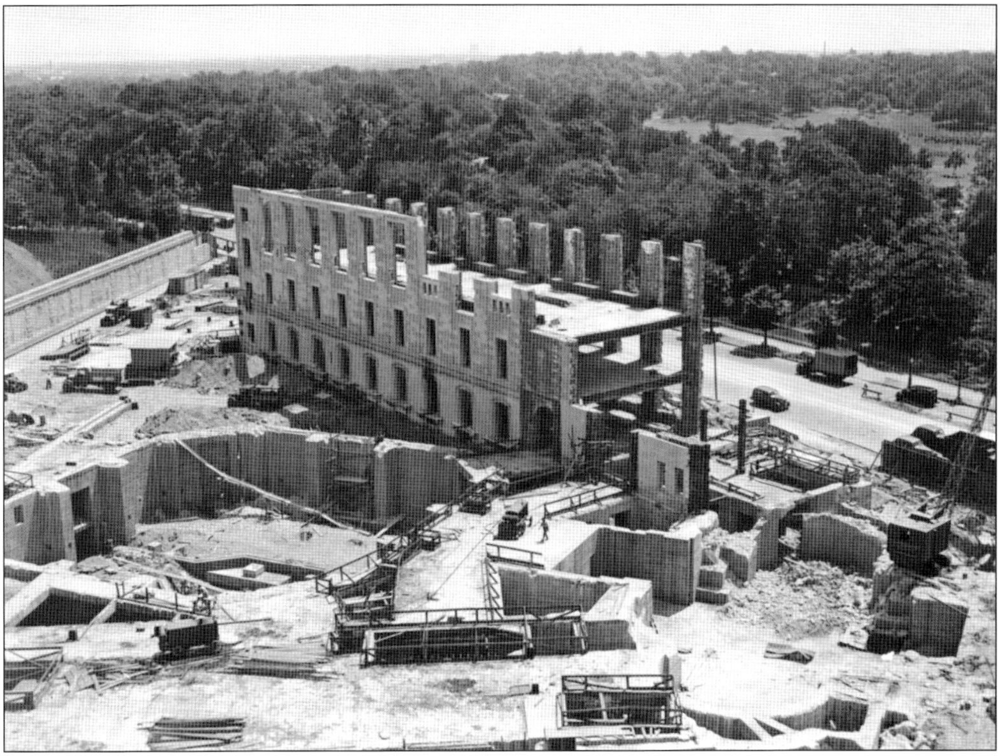

This aerial view, undated but likely from 1938, gives some sense of the scope of the project. While the cut-stone facade was removed from street-facing sections of the Flatbush Avenue wing, the inward-facing wall of the building was left largely untouched. Those who enter the library's back parking lot today can get some sense of Almirall's vision.

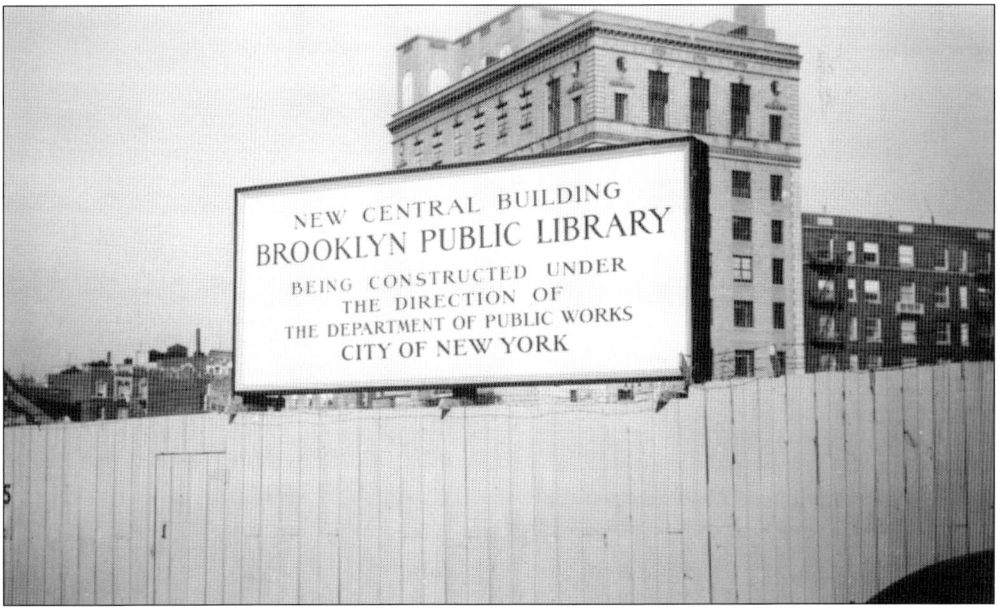

A new sign was proudly hoisted above the tall fence surrounding the site of the old ruin. Although undated, this image is most likely from 1938, when construction work was resumed.

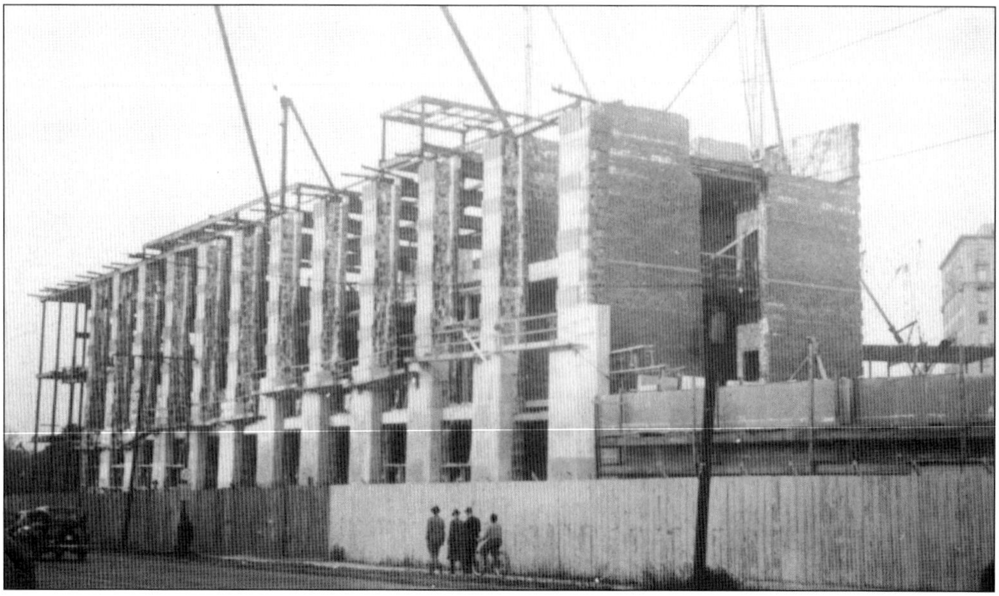

These photographs, taken just five weeks apart in late 1938, indicate how quickly the Almirall facade was replaced by Githens and Keally's austere Indiana limestone. The effect is striking; although contemporaneous, the photographs appear to be from different eras entirely due to the stark difference between the architectural styles. The disparity was well captured by chief librarian Milton Ferguson when he wrote about the project: "When I came to Brooklyn in 1930 and had the opportunity to examine [Almirall's] plans and to inspect the work that had been done, I was unhappy. I felt that the proposal to spend up to $15 million on this structure would result in a monument not a functional library building."

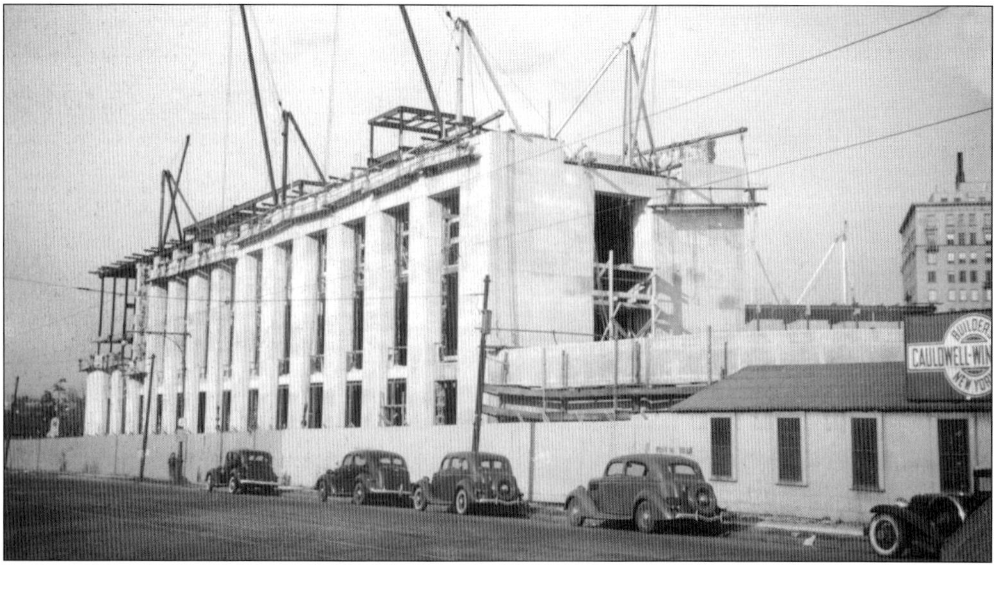

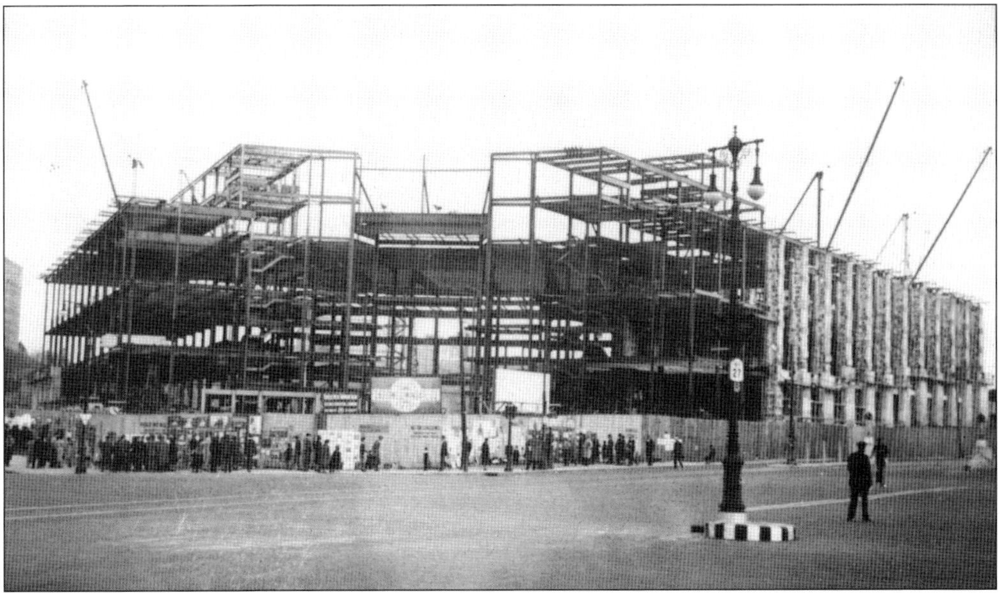

The steel framing of the library building began to rise above the tall wooden fences that surrounded the construction site, drawing curious observers through the fall of 1938 and into 1939, when these photographs were taken. Far from a "monument," the new library taking shape would reflect modern trends in architecture. The front of the building was reconfigured to follow the curve of Grand Army Plaza rather than jut into it. In October 1940, critic Lewis Mumford wrote in the *New Yorker*, "The bright limestone walls, the handsome, bowed-in front of the central mass glittering with gold, the good proportions, the absence of dreary columns, all create a sense of happy expectation."

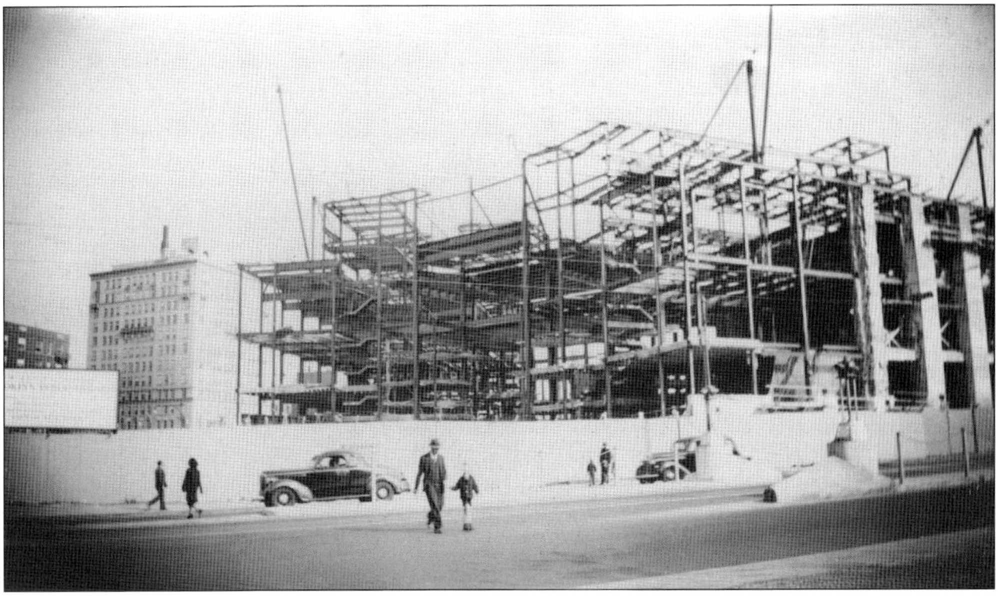

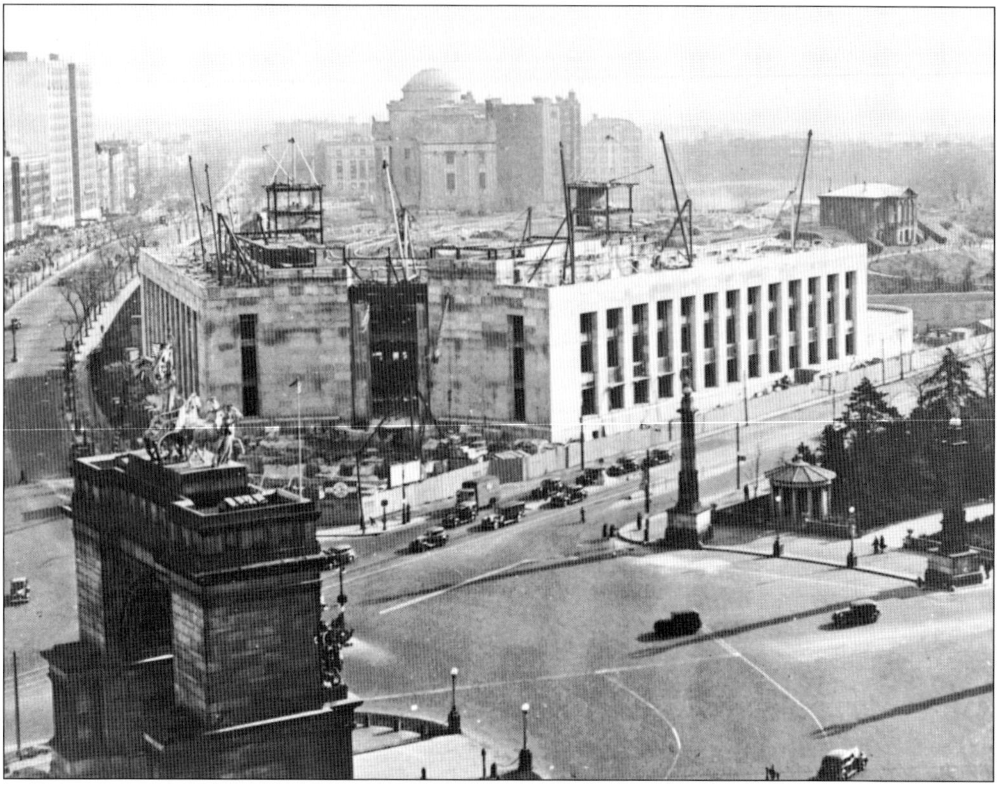

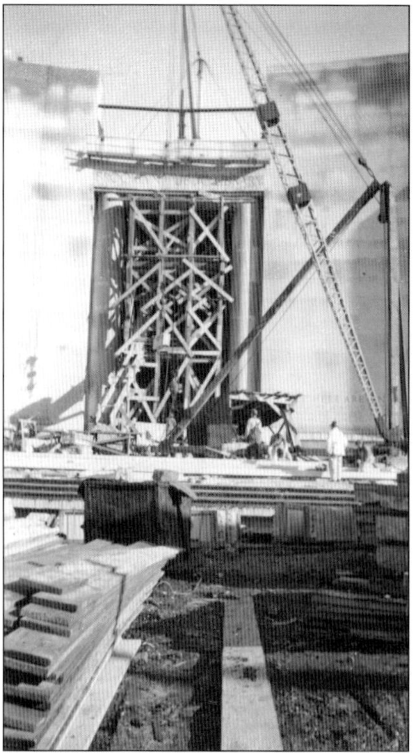

This photograph from 1938 shows the shell of the building nearing completion and finally taking its place among the other architectural landmarks of Grand Army Plaza. Brooklyn Museum can be seen in the background, with the Soldiers and Sailors Memorial Arch in the foreground.

Scaffolding and cranes mar the view of the soon-to-be impressive entrance grille, pictured here in late 1938. Mumford noted that in addition to this grand entrance were two other means of entering the library: "If you can't climb steps you enter on the side, at ground level, and are taken up in an elevator. . . . If you are a book from a branch library, you enter by way of the handsome delivery quarters in the rear."

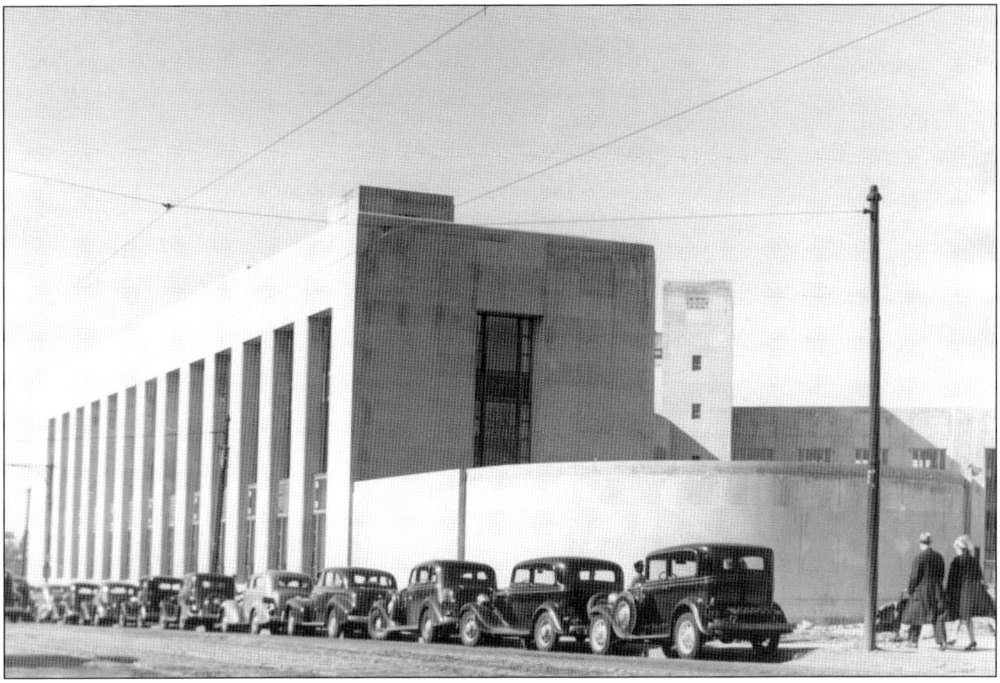

These views show the rear portions of the library as construction neared completion. Above, the curved portion of the Flatbush Avenue wing on the left was a shipping and parking garage, built to handle the flow of books circulating to Brooklyn's branch libraries. Below, the curved back wall of the library—the fanning pages of the "open book"—is evident, as are the third-floor glass blocks intended to flood the Grand Lobby with light. Immediately behind the library was a grassy courtyard; eventually, a rose garden would be planted there. The garden has since been removed, and the area is now a parking lot.

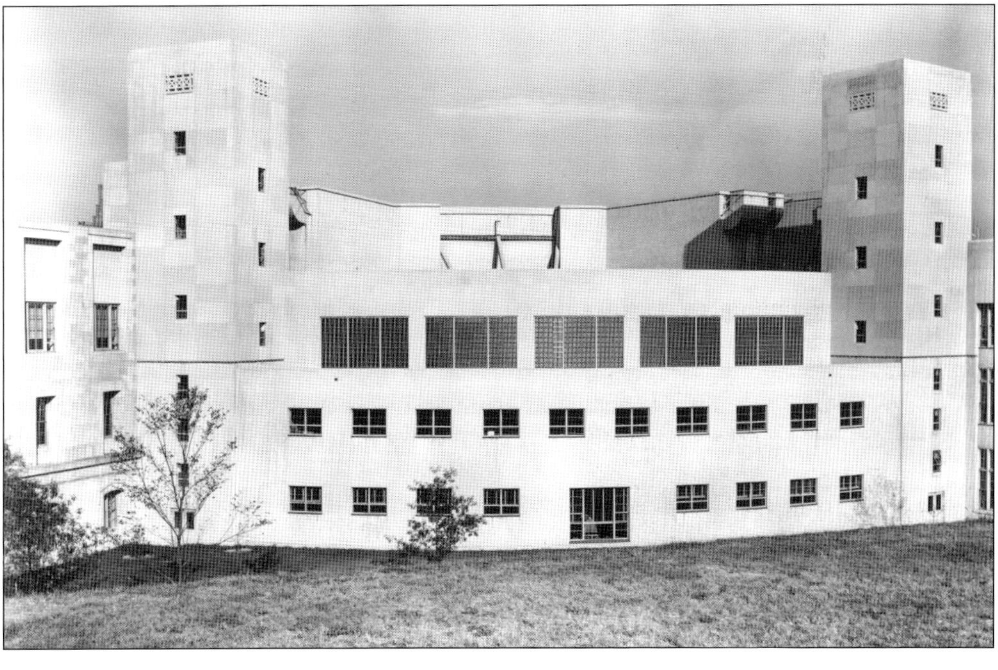

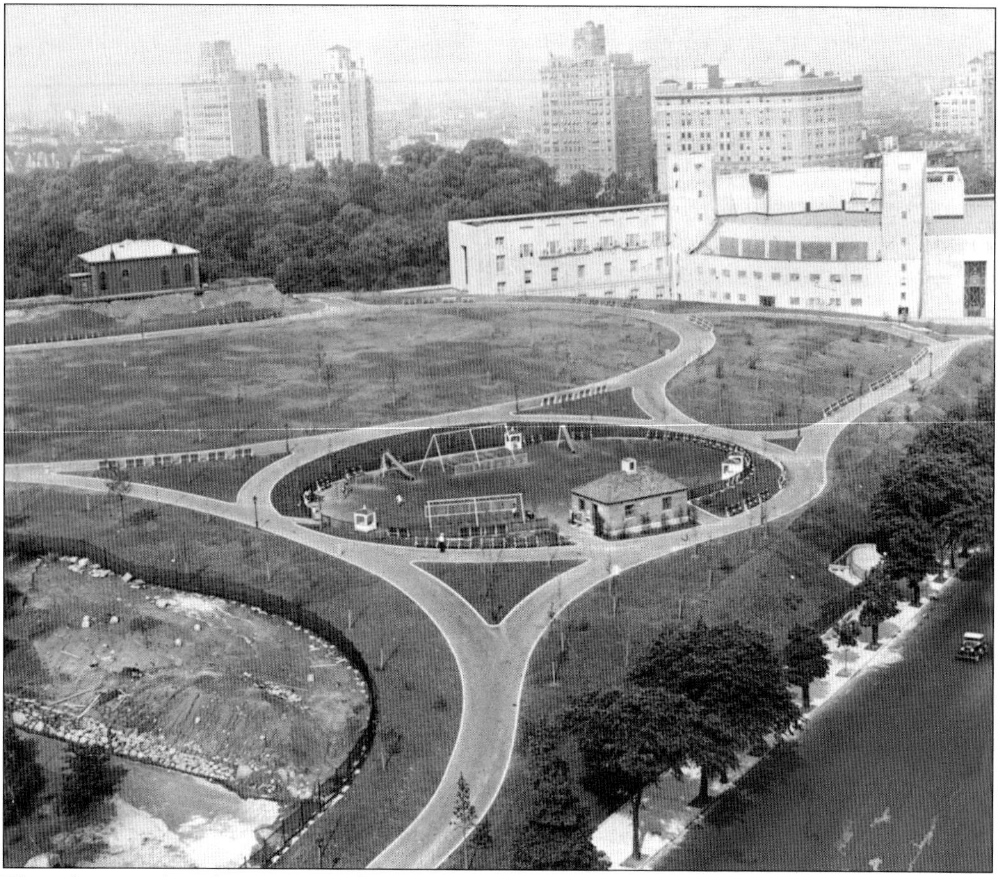

This photograph, taken in 1939, shows the rear of the library from Mount Prospect Park. The caption reads, "Atop Mount Prospect [Park], the eight-acre old reservoir site has been transformed into a play area. New library is in background." Parks commissioner Robert Moses had acted quickly to have his playground built on the site of the former reservoir.

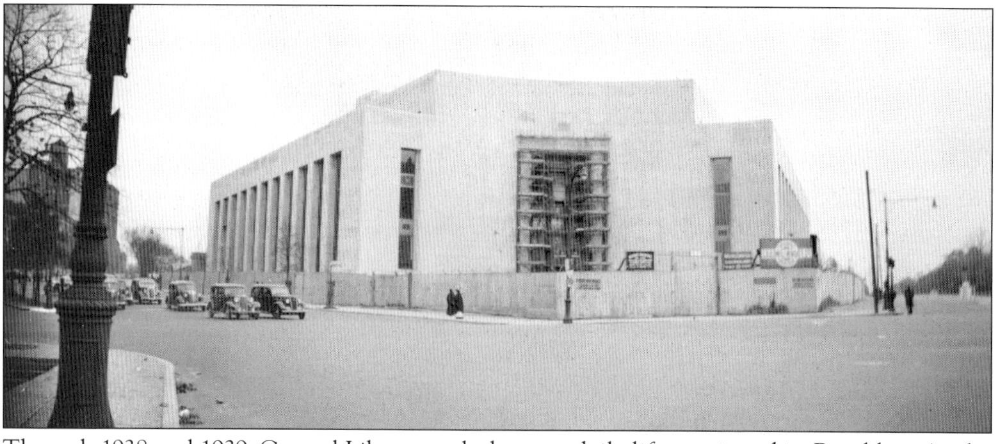

Through 1938 and 1939, Central Library took shape as daily life continued in Brooklyn. As the decade drew to a close and the new one opened, local newspapers began reporting more optimistically about the long-hoped-for Central Library. What had been an eyesore, a "ruin," and a "hole in the ground" instead became an integral part of modern Brooklyn's educational and civic life.

Four

Turning the Page

As the 1930s drew to a close, Brooklyn's Central Library was finally taking shape as the Art Deco landmark it would become. Despite the many concerns and delays that had dogged the building since its inception, popular opinion seemed to be rallying around the impressive new structure that rose above Grand Army Plaza. The *Brooklyn Daily Eagle* closely followed the progress of construction, regularly publishing images of the emerging library and heralding its facilities as part of Brooklyn's revival even before it was finished. Mayor Fiorello La Guardia visited the building in December 1939 when it was three-quarters completed, declaring its design to be "most beautiful and appealing." Art critic Lewis Mumford offered praise for the building in the October 19, 1940, issue of *The New Yorker* magazine, finding its Grand Lobby "unexpectedly exhilarating" and declaring that, compared with other large libraries in the area, "Brooklyn's new one is tops!"

The library opened tentatively at first, offering a preview and informal ceremony in its Children's Room on February 1, 1941, after a final push from new borough president John Cashmore to move the debut forward. The official dedication would follow nearly two months later, on March 29, 1941. Over 1,500 guests attended the ceremony to mark the completion of a civic project more than 35 years in the making.

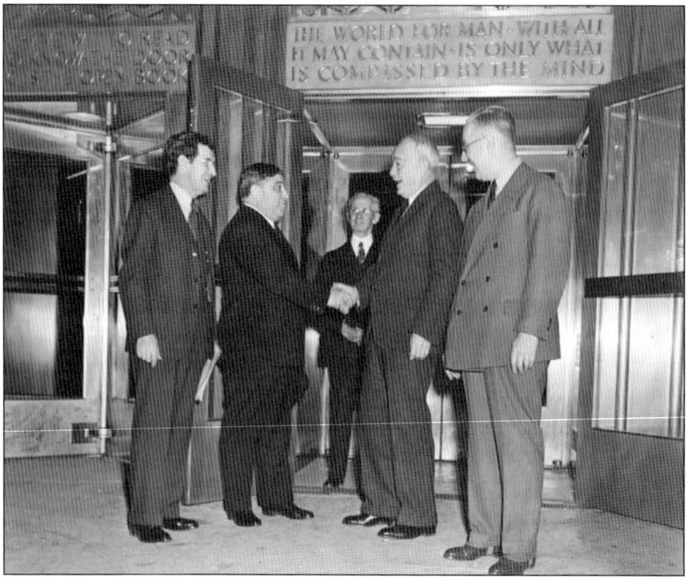

New York mayor Fiorello La Guardia toured the new Central Library as the building neared completion in December 1939. He is shown here in front of the library's distinctive doors, shaking hands with Borough President Raymond Ingersoll. Just months later, in February 1940, Ingersoll died of pneumonia. La Guardia named the new library the Raymond V. Ingersoll Memorial Library in his honor.

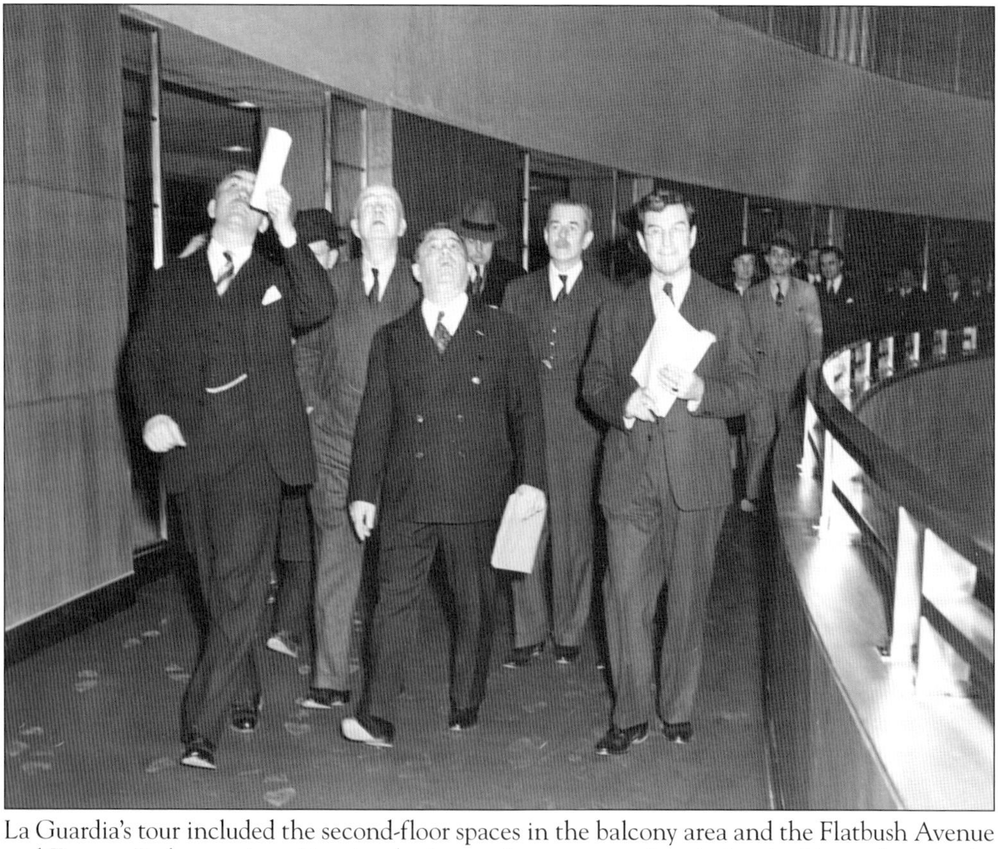

La Guardia's tour included the second-floor spaces in the balcony area and the Flatbush Avenue and Eastern Parkway wings. Despite the impressive amount of work that had been done in the last two years, the library still lacked the necessary funding to complete these sections of the building. Also lacking in late 1939 were sufficient funds for Central Library's workforce and maintenance crew.

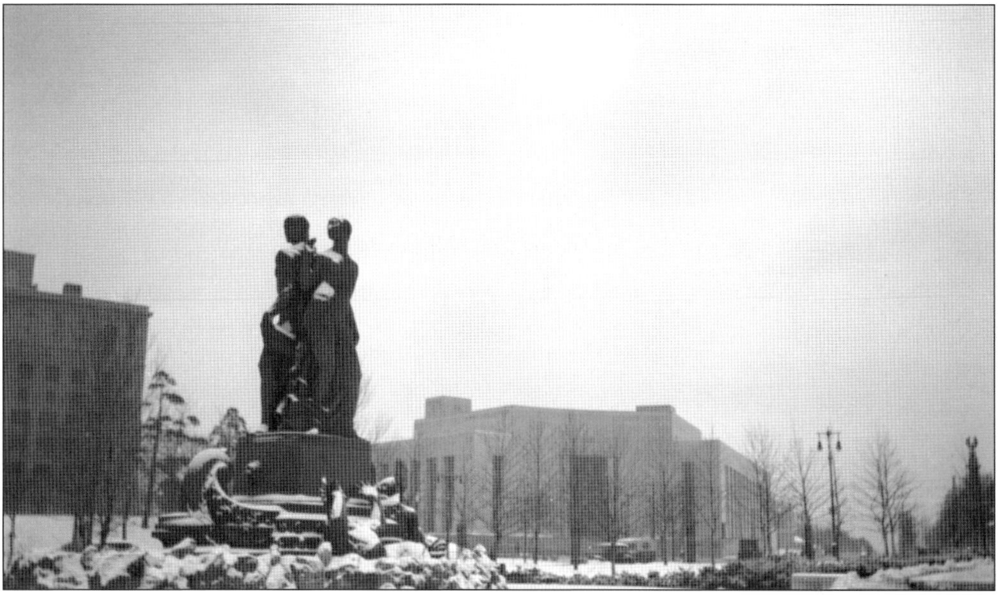

After decades of dashed hopes, the library was finally almost ready to open to the public. The last of the fences enclosing the construction site came down in February 1940, and from the outside, the building looked ready to go. By its completion, the building had cost $5 million and had been designed to hold as many as two million volumes.

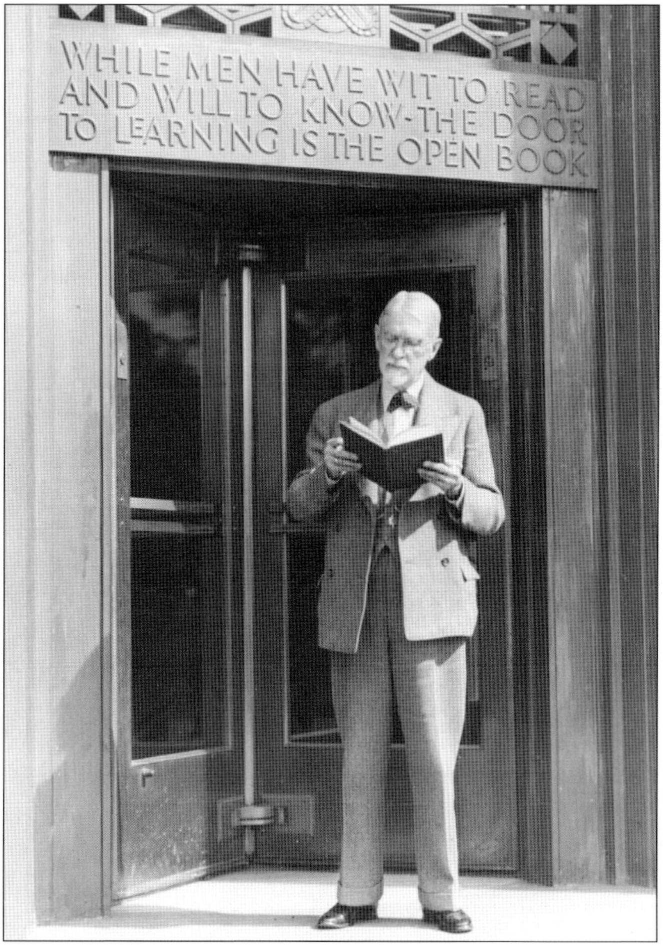

Roscoe C.E. Brown, a trustee since 1908, became board president in 1940, replacing Judge Garvin. Brown wrote many of the inscriptions that adorn the facade of Central Library, including the one he is pictured with here at the main entrance door.

More of Brown's inscriptions appear carved into the Indiana limestone facade flanking the front door. The one above is to the left of the main entrance. The photograph from 1958 shows the inscription to the right of the main entrance. The presence of people gives a sense of the large scale of the engravings.

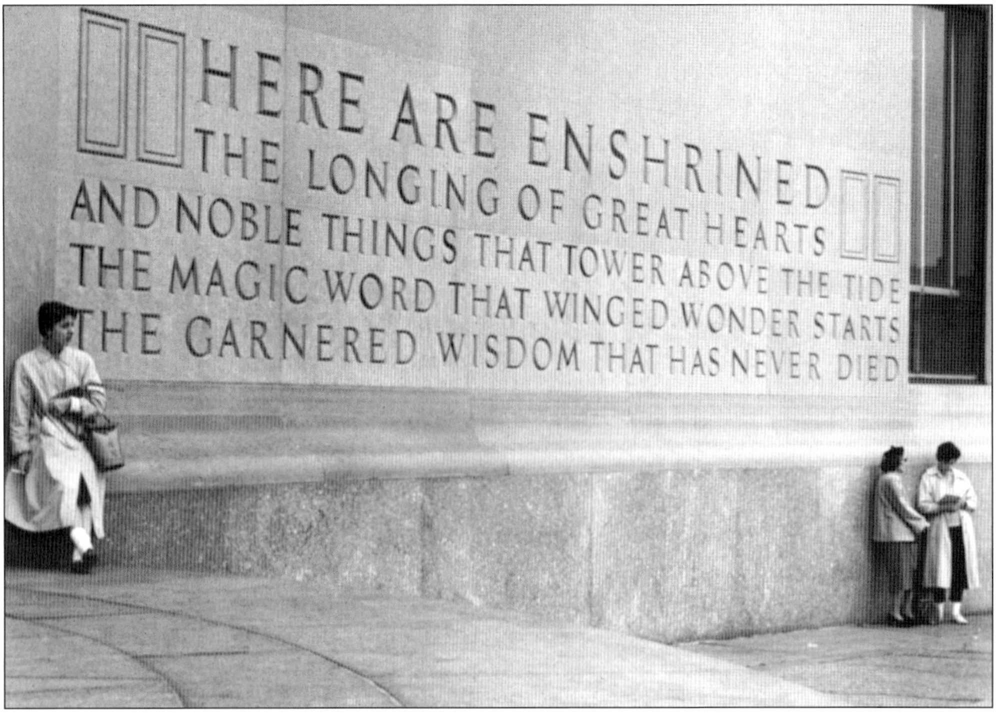

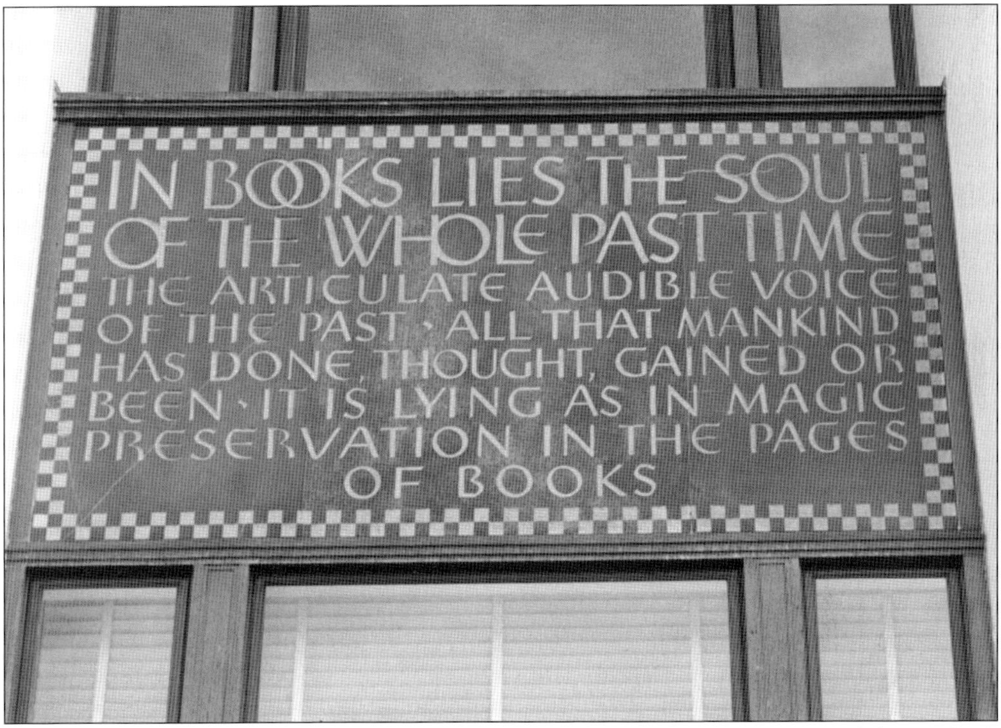

The windows along the Flatbush Avenue wing were outfitted with large granite slabs in which inspiring literary quotes were etched. The one above is from Scottish historian and essayist Thomas Carlyle. The verse below came from Scottish poet Alexander Smith.

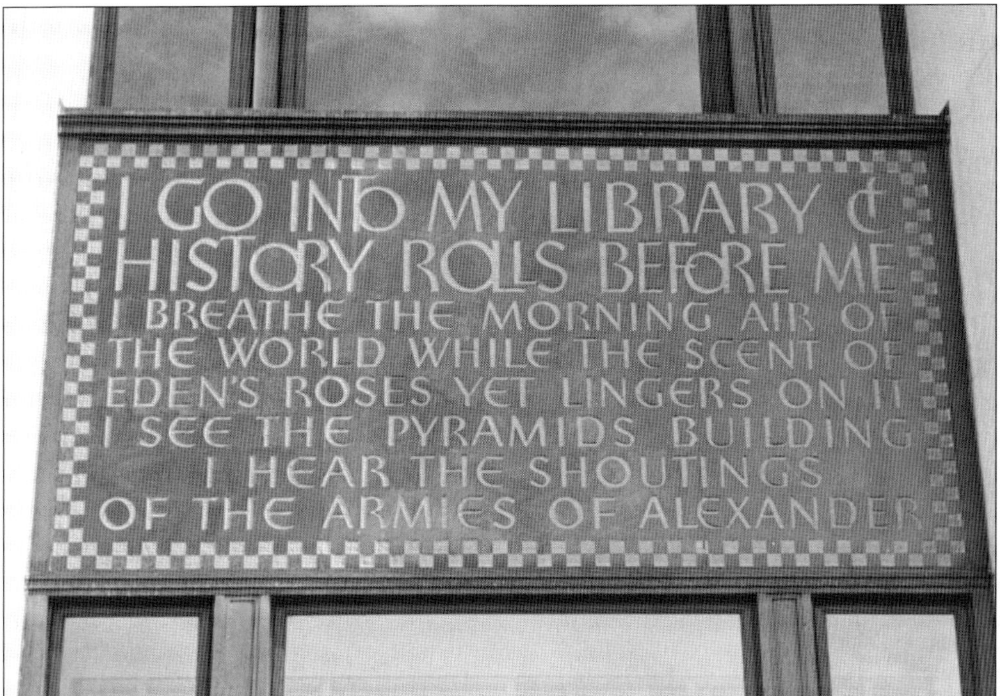

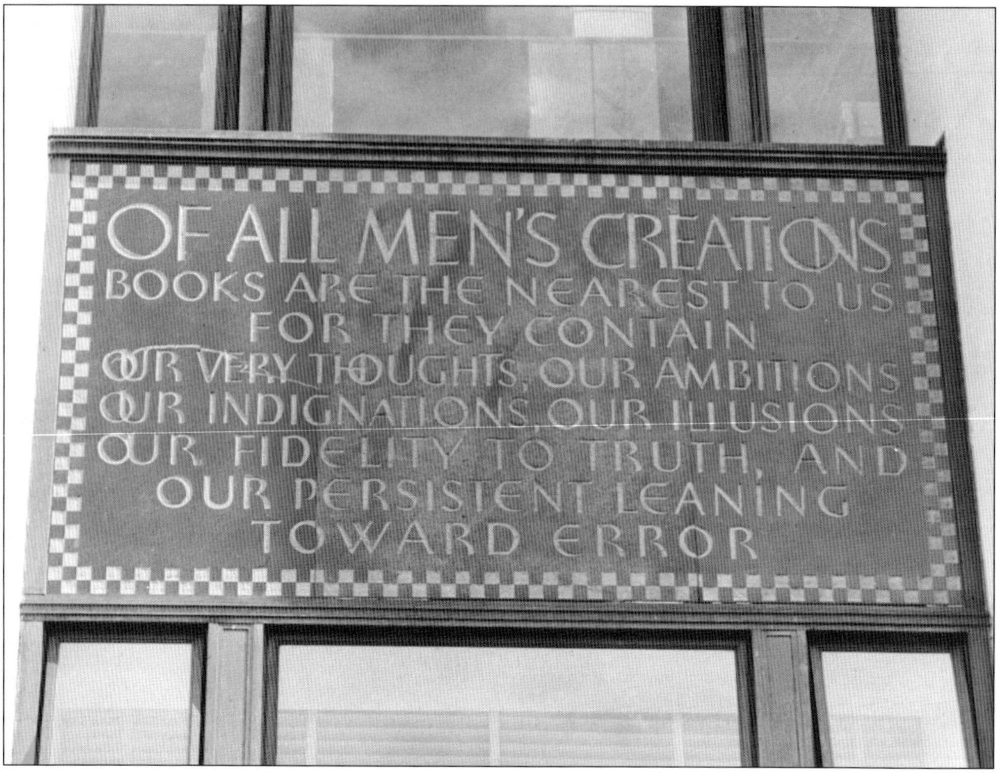

This text was written by Joseph Conrad, author of *Heart of Darkness* and other classics.

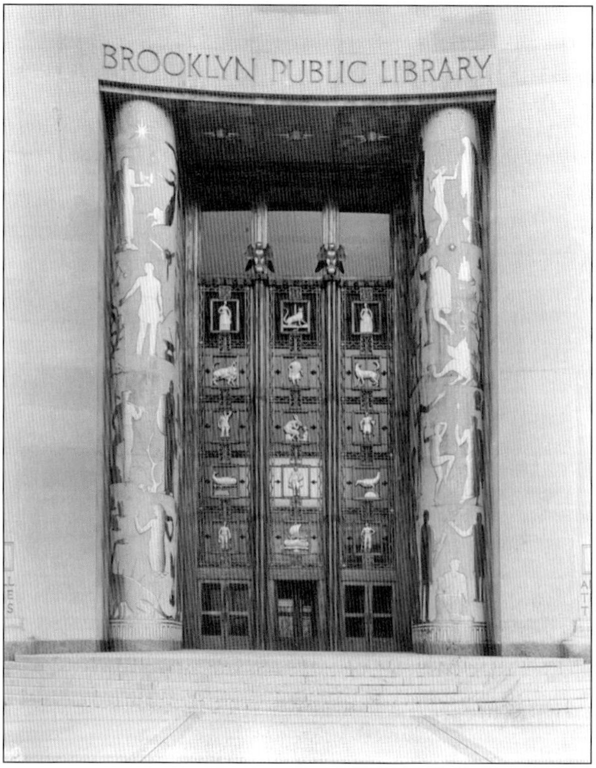

The most impressive feature of the new library building was its towering gold-plated entrance. Sculptor Carl P. Jennewein created the two columns covered in gold figures, representing art and science, and Thomas Hudson Jones designed the central grille, featuring characters from American literature. Details on this iconic structure can be found in chapter eight.

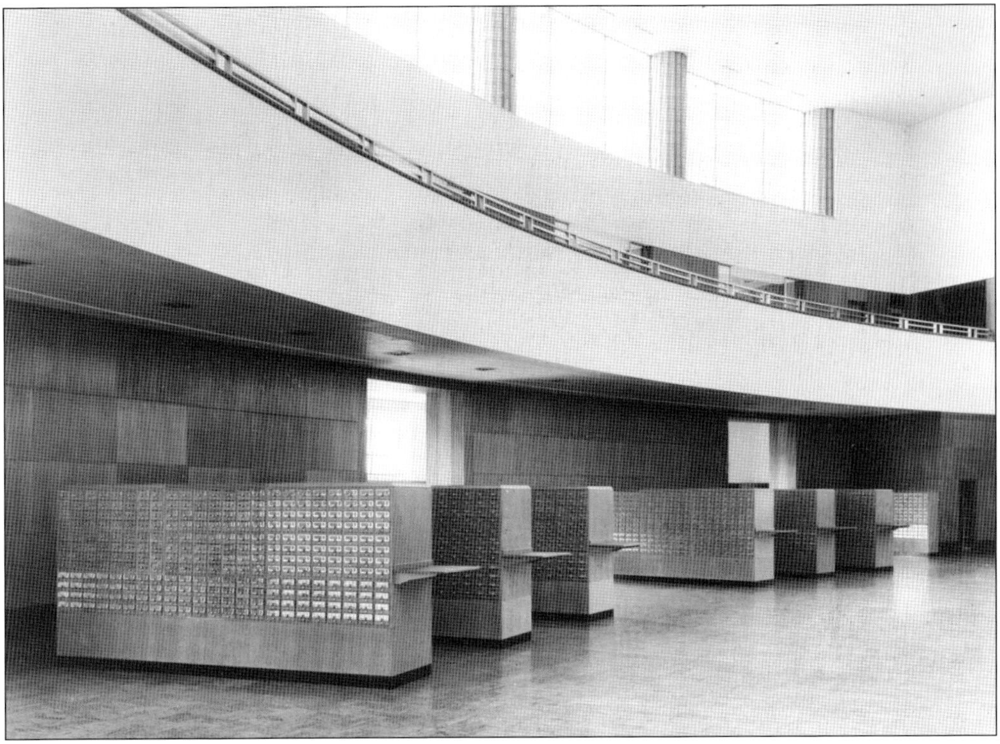

These photographs show Central Library's interior lobby and public spaces at their most pristine, before book carts and muddy feet would scuff the floors and before the general wear and tear of thousands of daily users would take its toll. As Ruth Ferguson, wife of chief librarian Milton J. Ferguson, wrote in an unpublished manuscript titled *The "Hole in the Ground" That Became the Central Building*, the lobby, originally called the Circulation Hall, "owes its beauty partly to its spaciousness and partly to the oatmeal and honey tones of the walls and the white oak panels, and the green ceiling with its star-like lights."

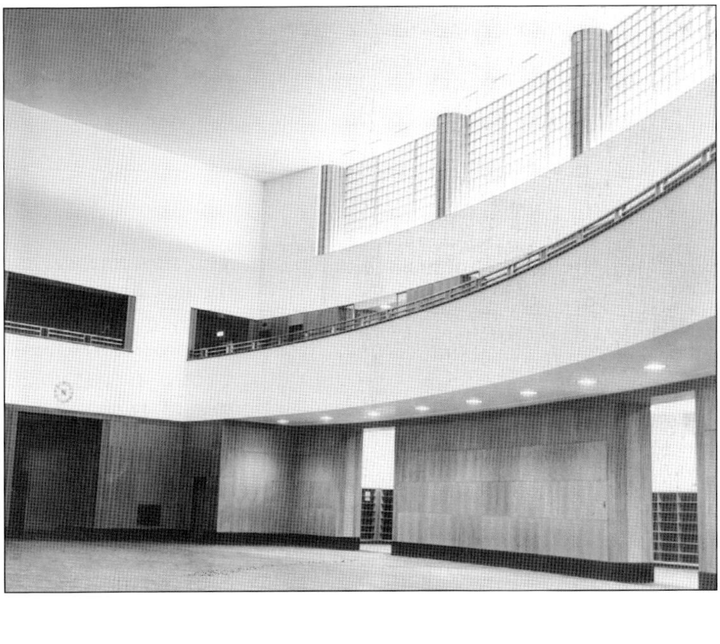

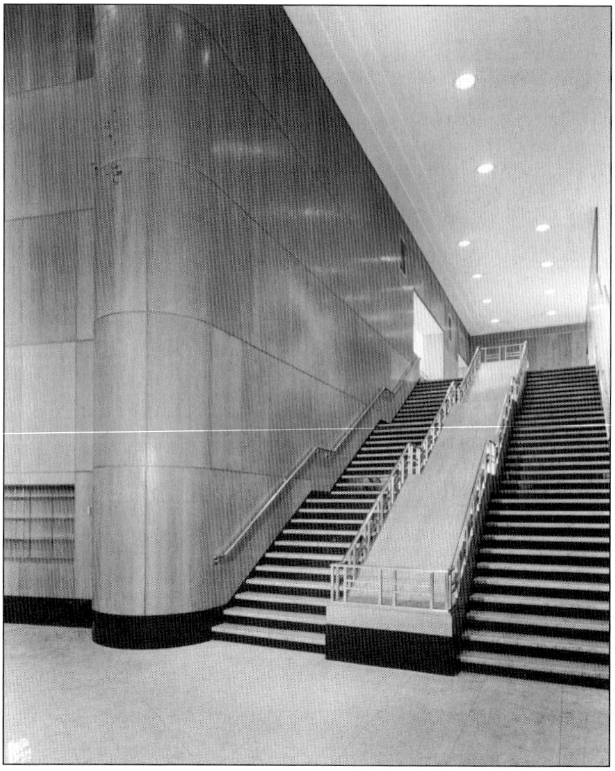

Although the stairways leading up to it were impressive, the second floor of the library was not ready for public use when the building opened in 1941. Modern-day users of Central Library will note that, in their earliest incarnation, the stairways did not have escalators running up the middle as they do now. Escalators were part of the original plan for the building, but funding could not be secured to install them.

This unassuming shelf-lined room is actually a steel vault tucked away behind a locked door in the Trustees' Room. It was designed to house the library's most rare and valuable materials—first edition books that would not circulate. Known among staff as the Treasure Room, it still houses special collections today.

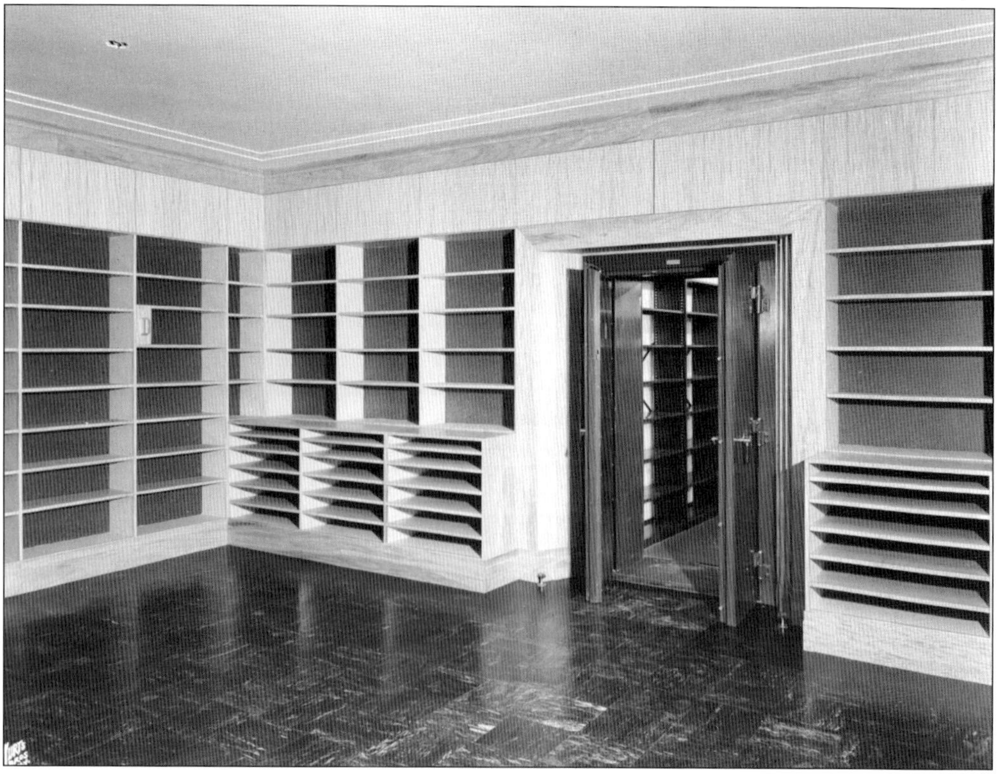

The wood-paneled foyer is the first sight that greets visitors entering through Central Library's main doors. On the right panel, carved into the woodwork, is a tribute to the trustees who brought the building project to completion. Included in this list are then president Roscoe C.E. Brown and past presidents Edwin Garvin and David Boody, as well as the full board as it stood in July 1940. Also inscribed are the names of New York mayor Fiorello H. La Guardia, comptroller Joseph D. McGoldrick, and Borough President John Cashmore. Milton James Ferguson is listed as chief librarian, with his predecessor Frank P. Hill appearing as consultant. The panel remains in the Grand Lobby today.

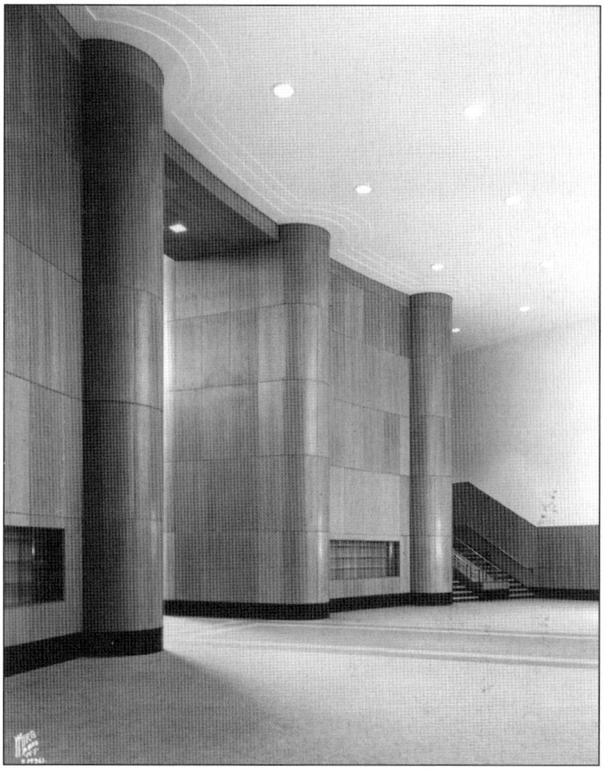

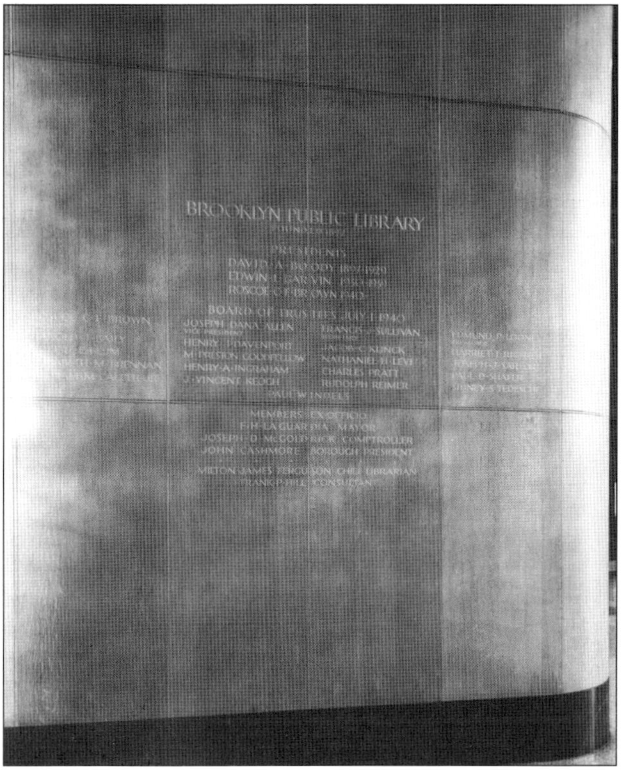

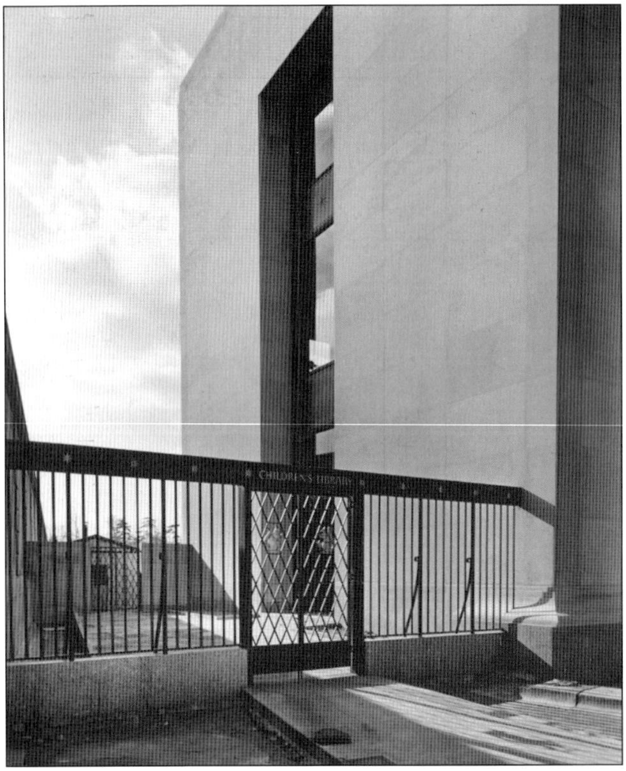

These views show the entrance and main reading floor of the Children's Room on Eastern Parkway. Long, low benches were installed under the windows looking out on the street to accommodate daydreamers and readers alike. The glass-partitioned balcony above the main reading room was used for story hours. When the library first opened in 1941, a wall separated the children's and young adult areas from the rest of the building. They were given their own entrance on Eastern Parkway, decorated with fanciful wrought-iron squirrels. This area remains the Youth Wing today, although the structure has been remodeled to allow young ones free access to the entirety of the Central Library building.

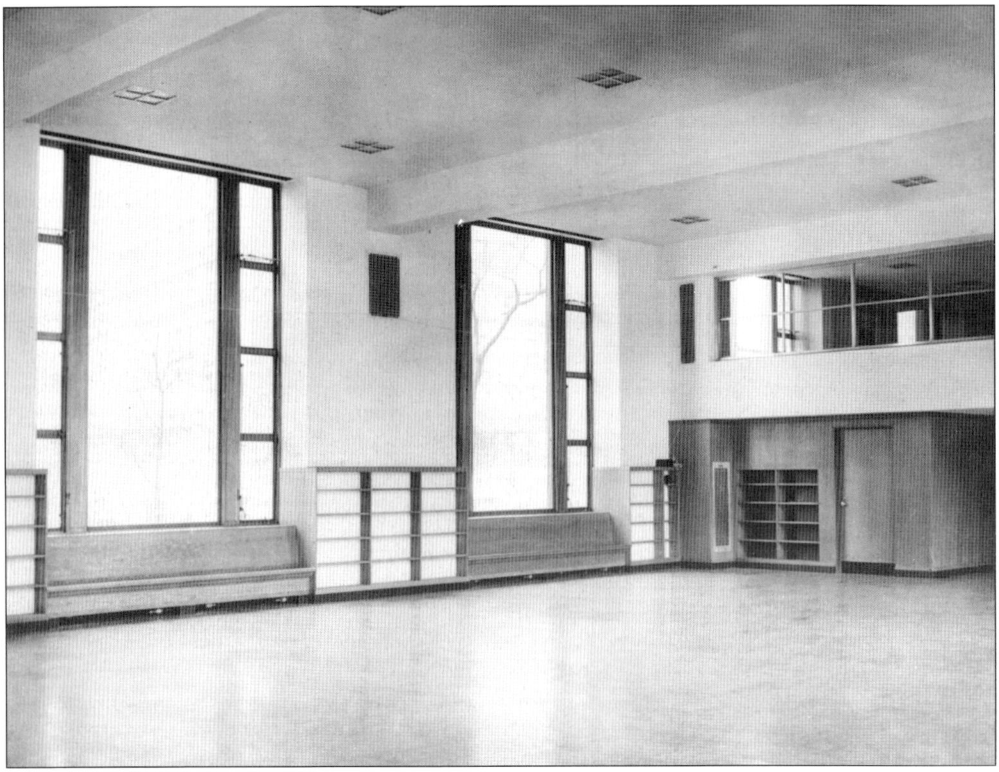

Pictured here is the chief librarian's office as it appeared when the library opened in 1941. Ruth Ferguson wrote, "The Chief Librarian's office, overlooking the Plaza . . . is a room of great richness and great simplicity, too, with its black walnut panels and the picturesque Chinese mural over the fireplace. It leads into a small study, a private little gem of a room, done in teakwood."

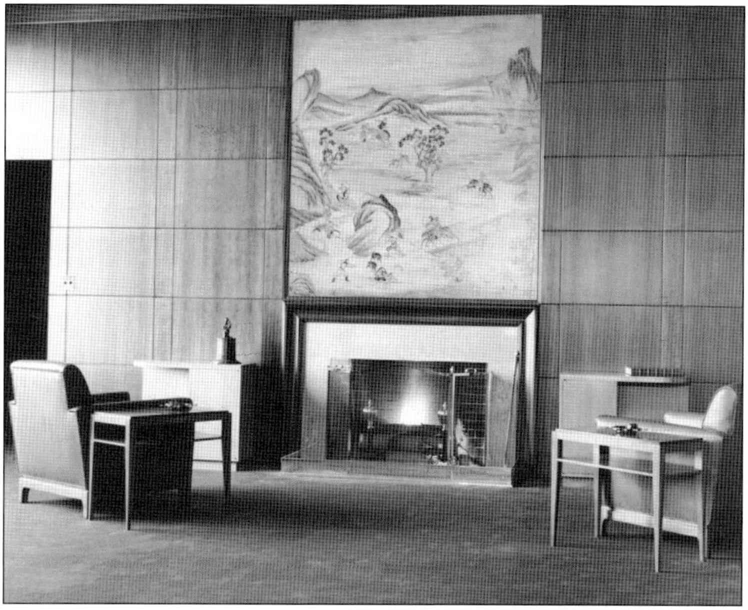

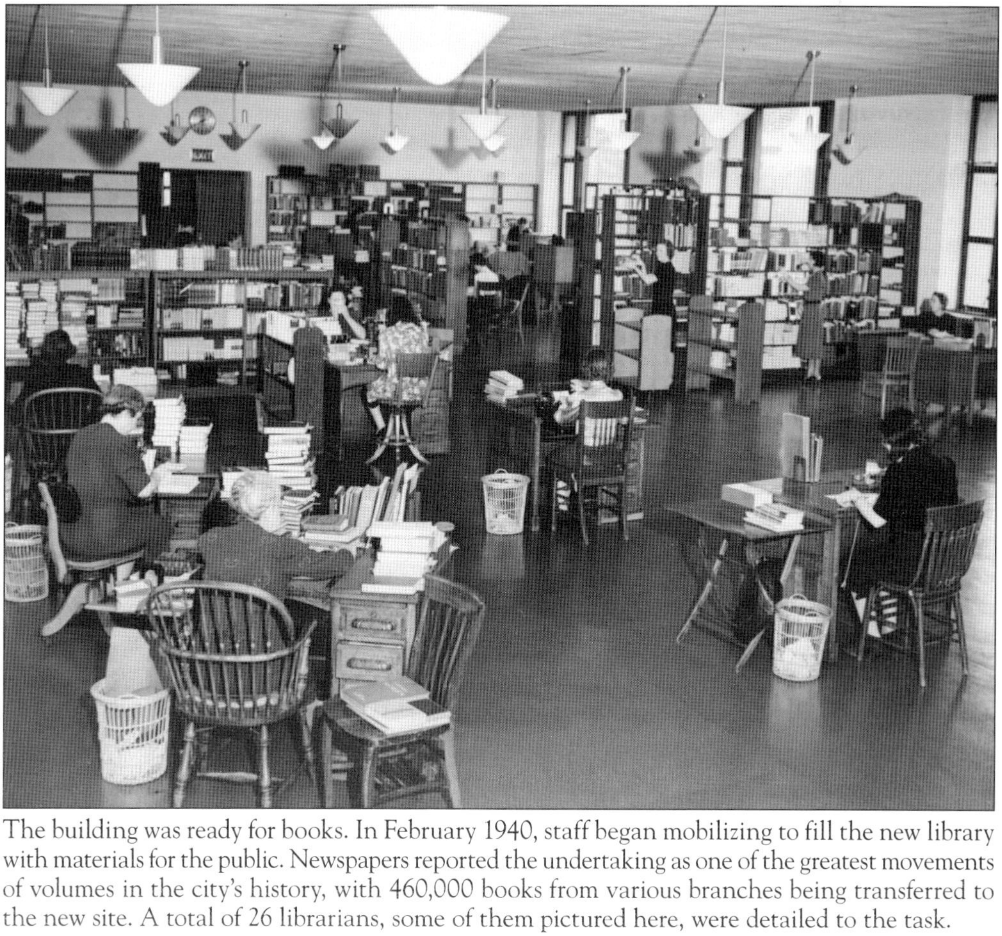

The building was ready for books. In February 1940, staff began mobilizing to fill the new library with materials for the public. Newspapers reported the undertaking as one of the greatest movements of volumes in the city's history, with 460,000 books from various branches being transferred to the new site. A total of 26 librarians, some of them pictured here, were detailed to the task.

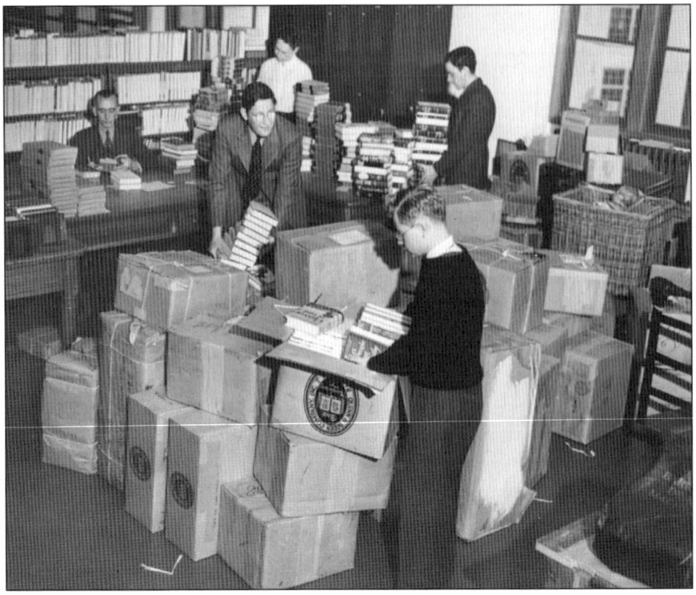

While some volumes had been kept at the Carroll Park, City Park, and Prospect branches (today's Carroll Gardens, Walt Whitman, and Park Slope branches, respectively), the great majority of the new library's collection—360,000 books—was shipped over from the decrepit Montague branch. Activity at the Montague branch would scale down significantly, with its top two floors closing to the public. A special business library would eventually open at that location.

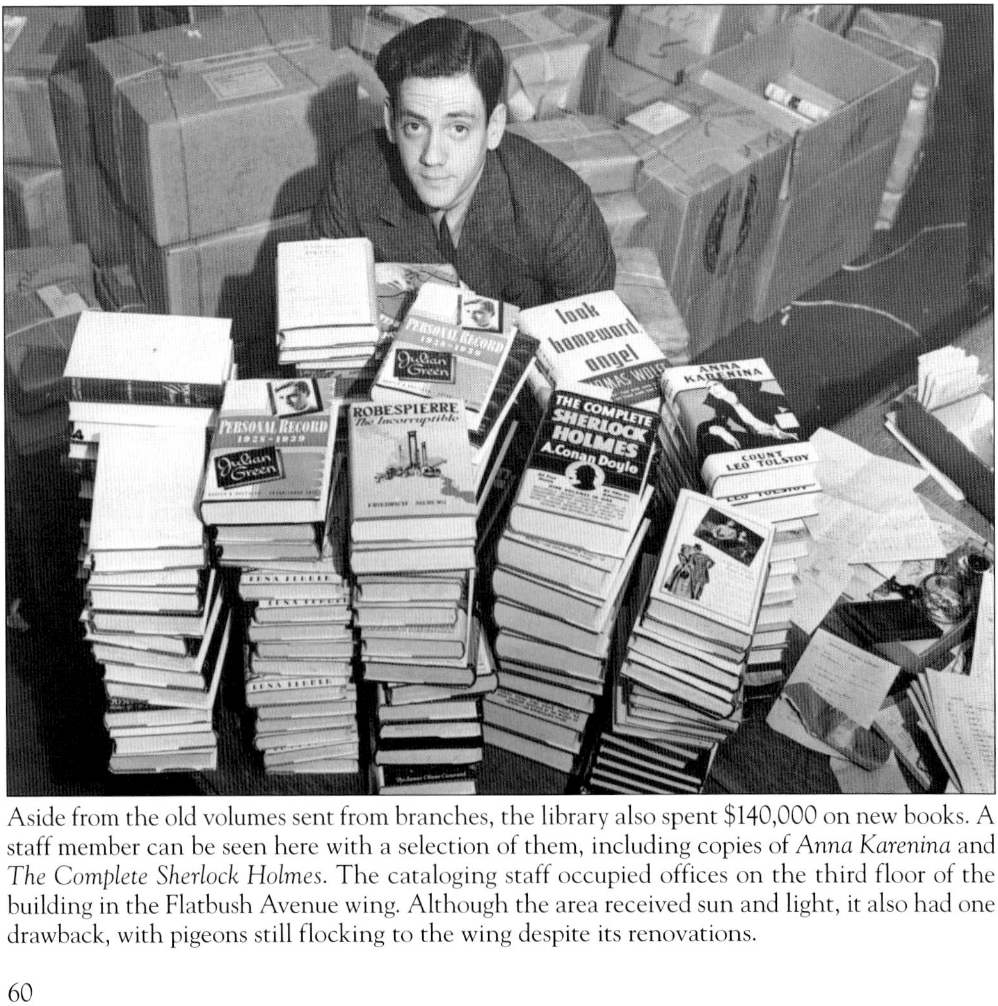

Aside from the old volumes sent from branches, the library also spent $140,000 on new books. A staff member can be seen here with a selection of them, including copies of *Anna Karenina* and *The Complete Sherlock Holmes*. The cataloging staff occupied offices on the third floor of the building in the Flatbush Avenue wing. Although the area received sun and light, it also had one drawback, with pigeons still flocking to the wing despite its renovations.

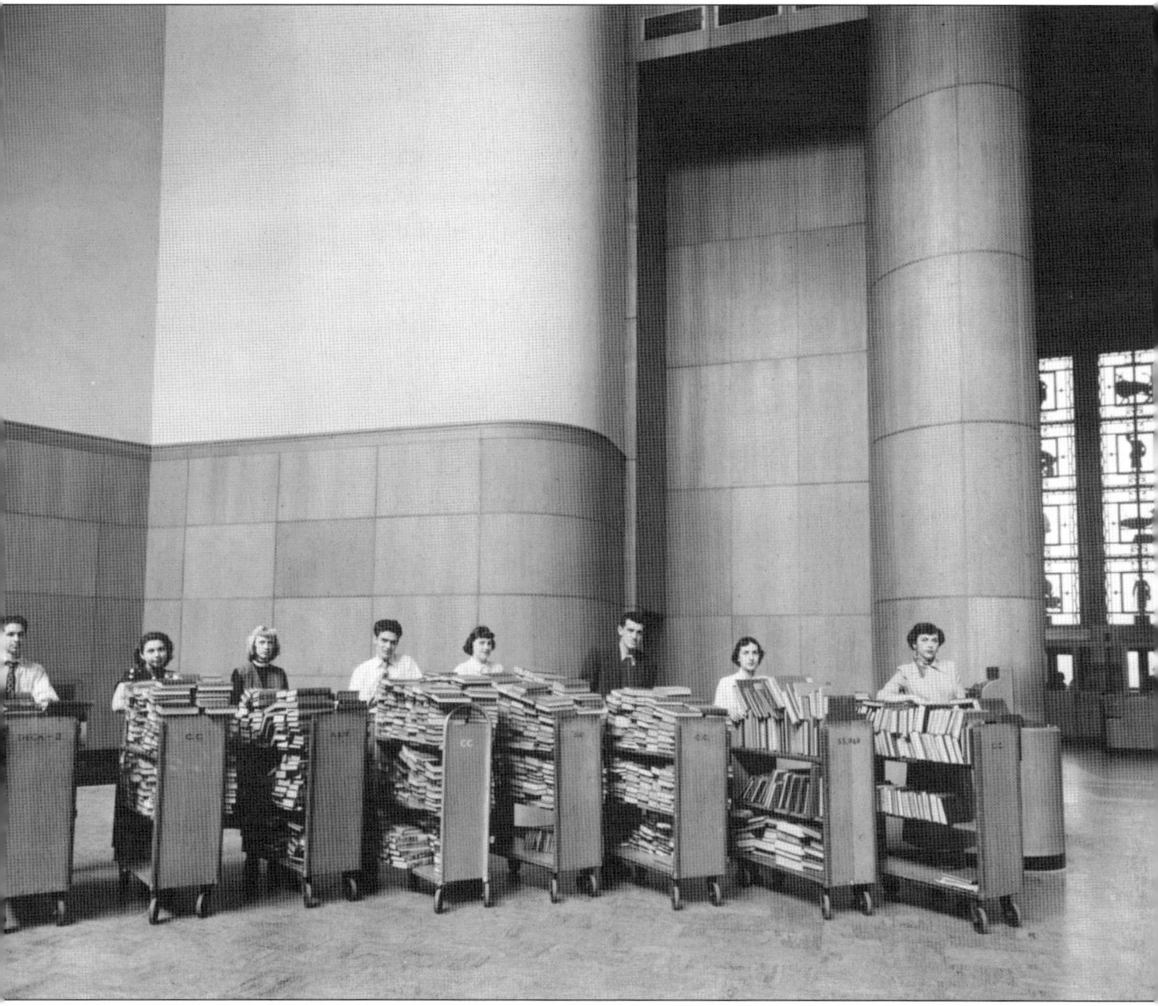

As Central Library came closer to its debut, more staffers were brought in to prepare the building. By October 1940, there were 170 people working in the building, in addition to an extra 30 WPA employees. These clerks push carts laden with books to be shelved. In the new library's floor plan, the first floor of the Flatbush Avenue wing housed books in five subject divisions: history, travel, and biography; social science; science and industry; language and literature; and art and music. Shelves rather than walls formed the partitions between these divisions, allowing for the area to be more flexible as collections grew or contracted. More books were stored in subbasements below the public space of the Grand Lobby. These could (and still can) be called up from storage upon request.

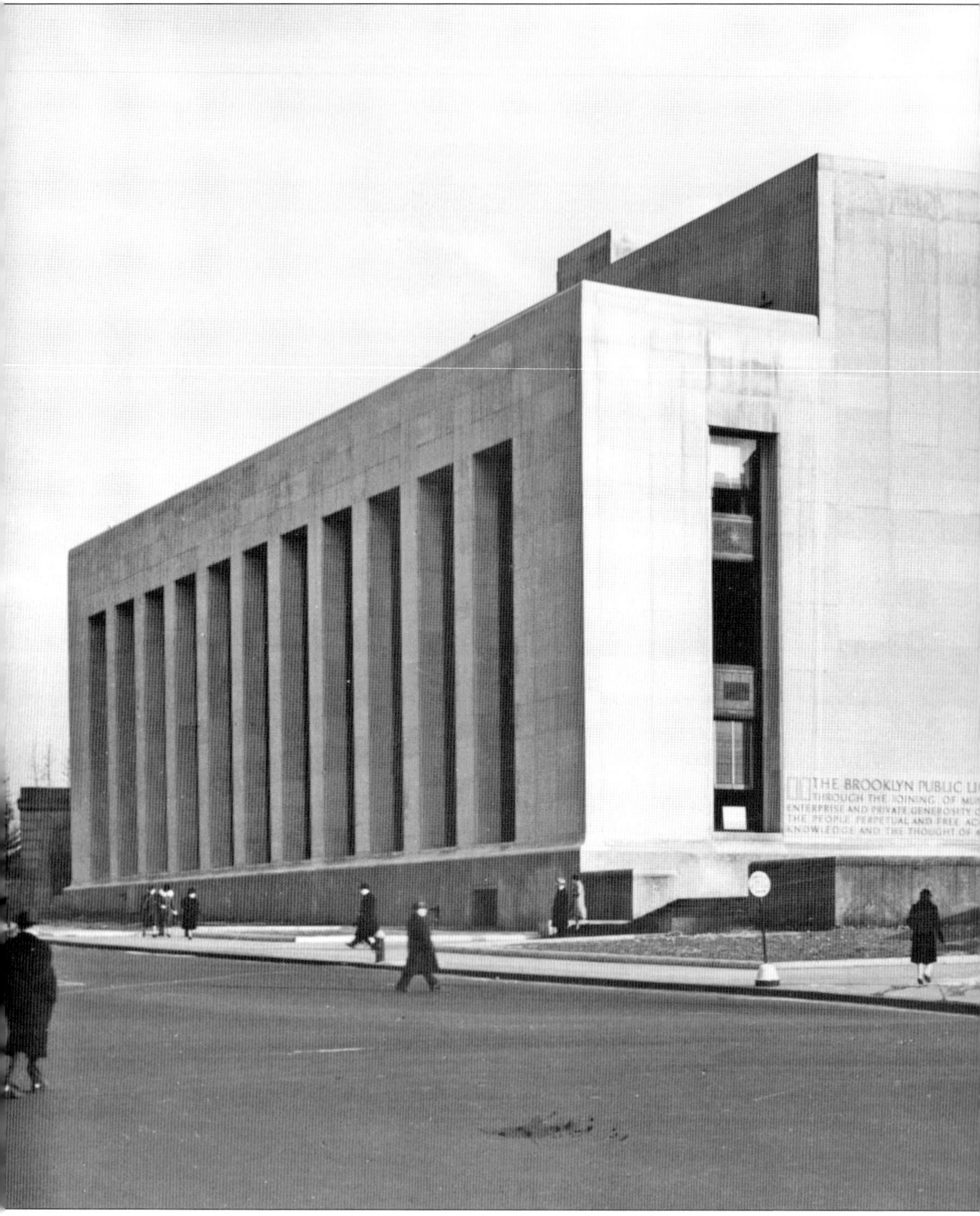

Anticipation was growing, and through the fall of 1940, the public clamored for the long-awaited library to open. Thanks to a last push from Borough President John Cashmore, the Central Circulating Room and Children's Room opened to the public on February 1, 1941. This was a "soft opening," with little fanfare and only limited media coverage. According to the *Brooklyn Daily Eagle*,

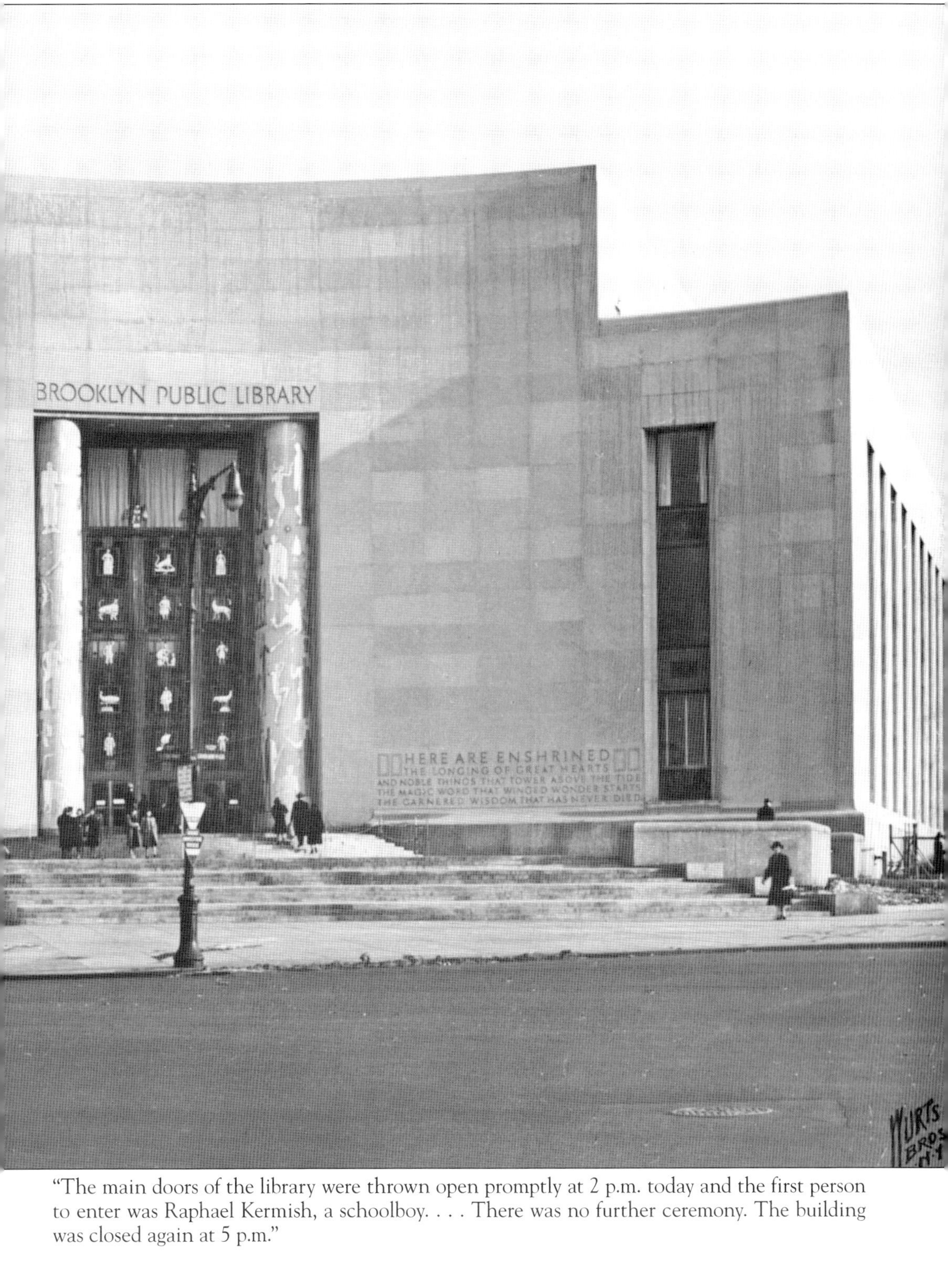

"The main doors of the library were thrown open promptly at 2 p.m. today and the first person to enter was Raphael Kermish, a schoolboy. . . . There was no further ceremony. The building was closed again at 5 p.m."

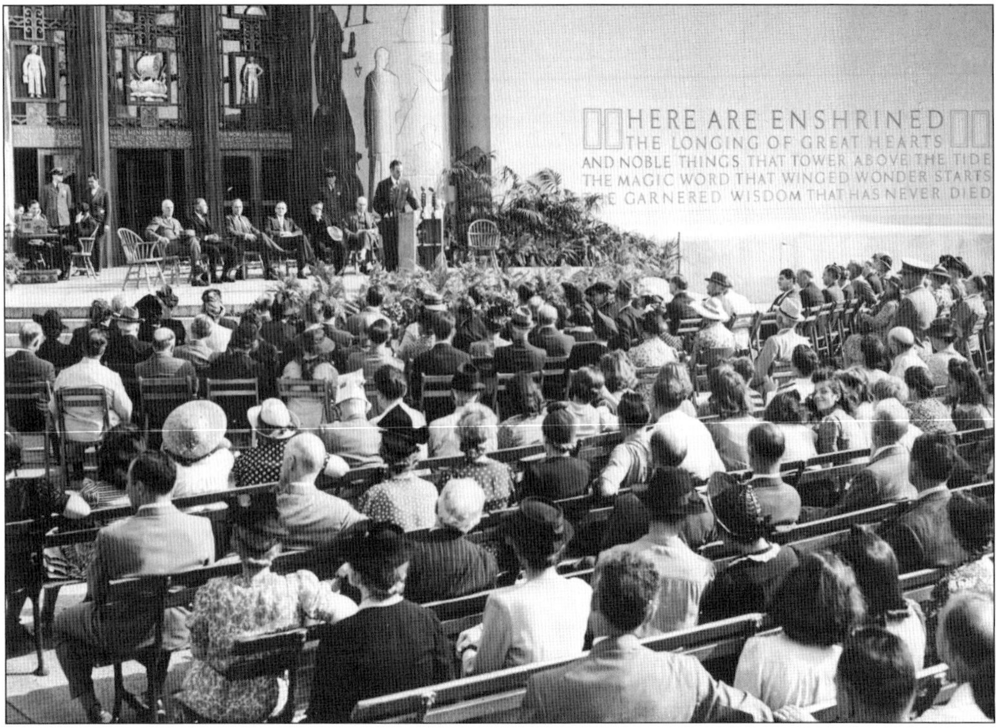

The official opening ceremonies for the completed Raymond V. Ingersoll Memorial Library were held on March 29, 1941, with 1,500 guests in attendance. A band provided entertainment, along with speeches by Mayor La Guardia, Borough President Cashmore, chief librarian Ferguson, and other dignitaries. Special tribute was paid to Ingersoll, who had not lived to see the satisfying culmination of his efforts over the past several years. La Guardia said, "The original sitdown strike was staged by him, in my office, when he persisted and persisted that this library be completed." Cashmore directed a plea for further funding to the mayor, saying, "Everything would be fine if the $350,000 in the capital outlay budget, still needed for the library, were granted." Although the library was open, it was far from complete, with its second floor unfinished and shuttered.

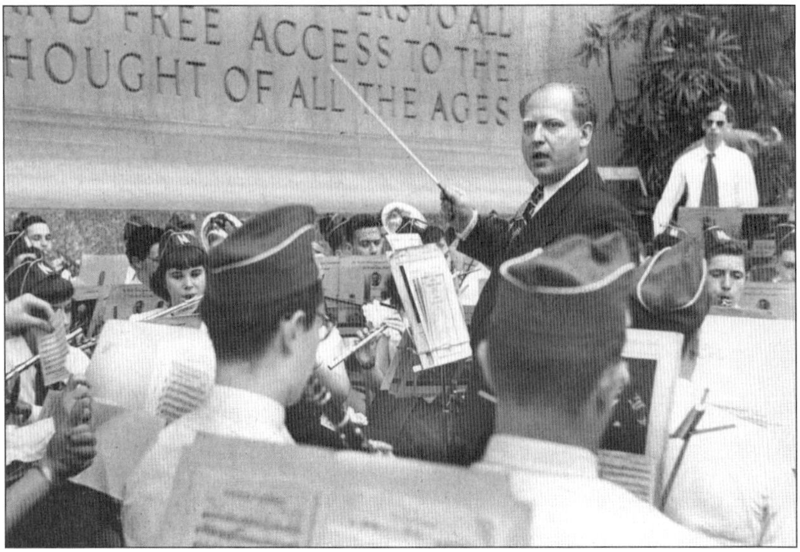

Five

The Plot Thickens

After decades of waiting, Brooklyn finally had a library worthy of its growing population. But even though the "open book" was open for business, there was much work left to be done. The entire second floor of the building remained unused and closed to the public until well into the 1950s. For years, it was a raw, unfinished space used by staff carpenters to repair broken furniture from library branches. The third floor, also mostly off-limits, housed the many cataloging and processing staff members who prepared books that circulated throughout the system.

If the library is indeed an open book, the trend in the past 75 years has been cracking open that tome ever wider. Renovations have been ongoing through the decades, adapting the now landmarked building to current trends and technologies of library science. While information still flows freely throughout the structure, the means of accessing it have changed drastically. Banks of microfilm reader machines once lined the wall of the Popular Library, allowing readers to browse newspapers and periodicals. Today, those largely obsolete machines have been replaced by long desks with laptop plug-ins so that users can read the news digitally. Art critic Lewis Mumford noted the lack of meeting rooms in the building when it first opened in 1941; today, the public can use their library cards to reserve a room in the Info Commons. Even though Central Library's glorious Art Deco structure and its vast Grand Lobby continue to impress after 75 years, the spaces within have drastically changed and will continue to adapt to the needs of Brooklyn's public.

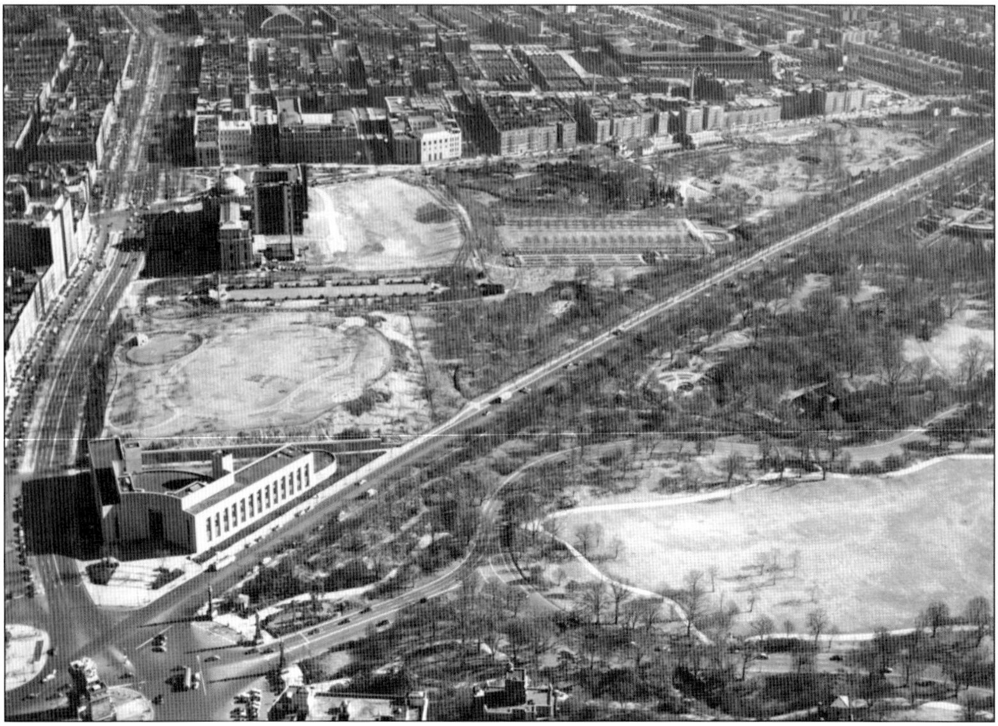

This aerial photograph, taken in January 1952, shows the library within the wider context of its environs. Prospect Park's Long Meadow stretches out to the west, and Mount Prospect Park is immediately behind the library, with the Brooklyn Museum farther down Eastern Parkway. Ebbets Field can be seen at upper right.

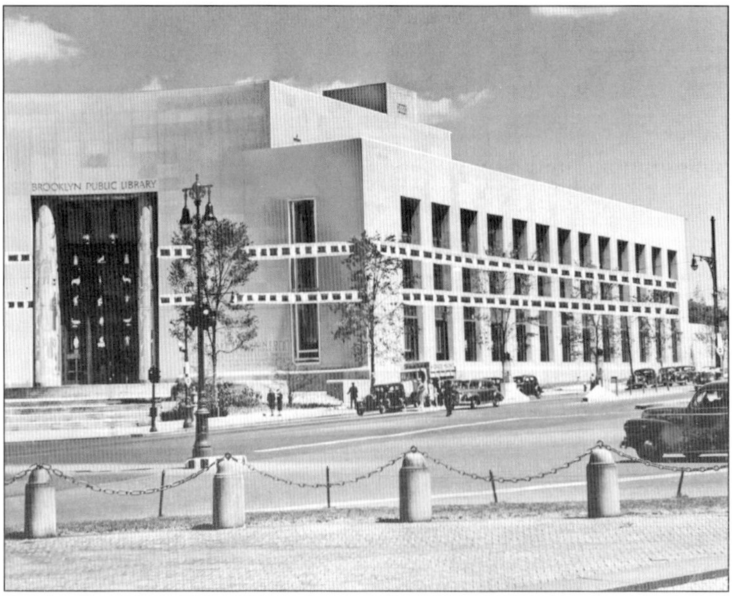

Even after the library opened to the public in 1941, work was not yet completed, and the facility could not keep up with public demand. This retouched photograph ran in the *Brooklyn Daily Eagle* in 1948. The space between the dotted lines, which encompassed the entire second floor, marks areas that remained closed to the public a full seven years after the library opened.

The library's second floor would remain inaccessible to the public for another 14 years after the building opened. The rope barrier that prevented visitors from ascending to the upper floor was temporarily removed in February 1951 for an exhibit on the mezzanine level celebrating the US Army Signal Corps. Members of the Signal Corps are pictured here in uniform with library trustees Henry J. Davenport (left) and Gregory Weinstein.

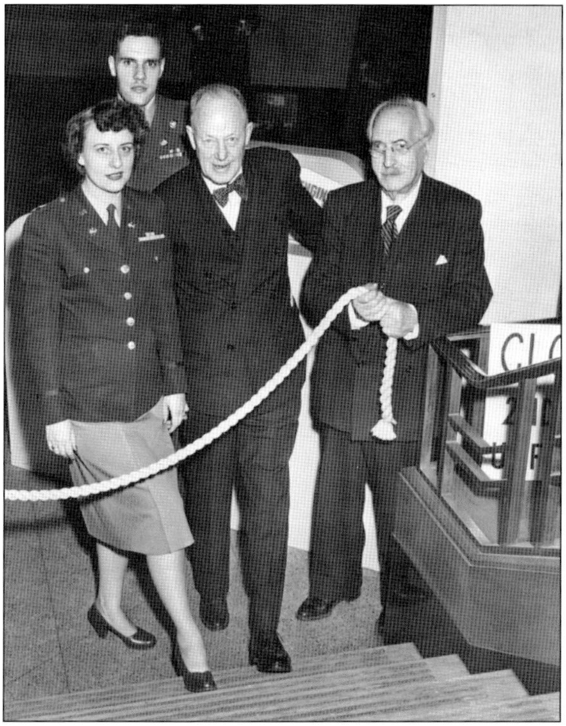

Gregory Weinstein poses again, ceremoniously lifting the rope that barred access to the stairs. A simple sign at the base of the stairs forbade curious patrons from venturing up to the second floor. Exhibit cases were also sometimes set up at the base of the stairs to discourage explorers.

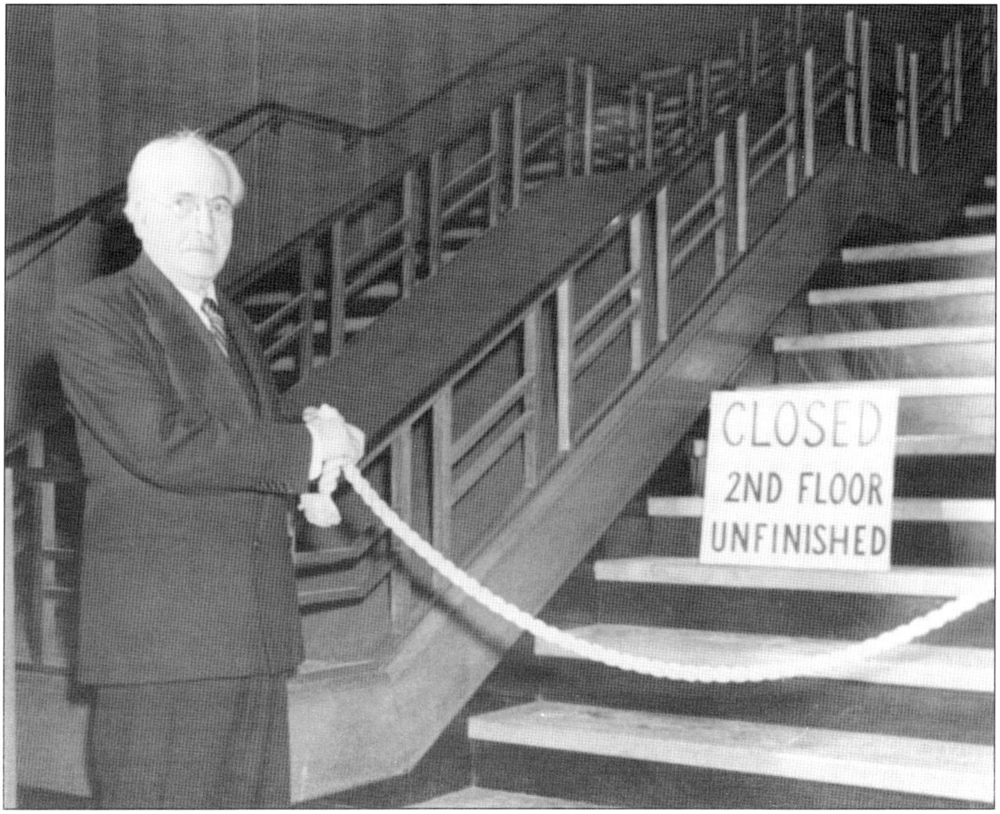

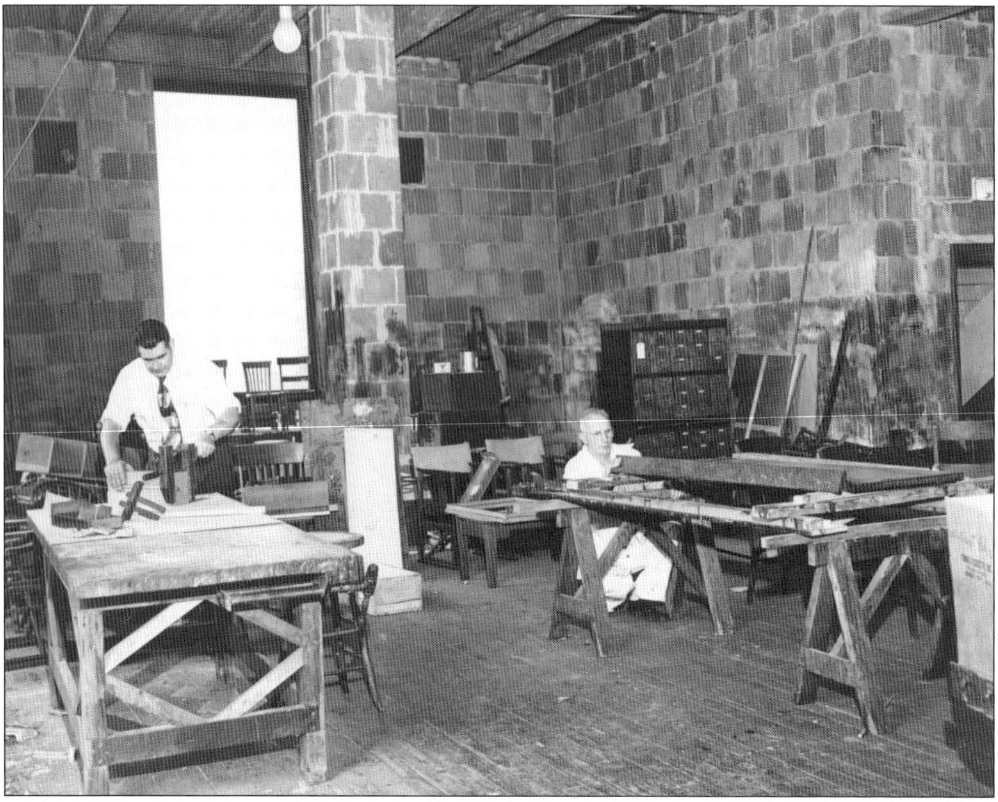

Originally intended to serve as a space for books and reading desks, this unfinished corner of the Flatbush Avenue wing of Central Library's second floor was used as a workshop for the branches throughout the Brooklyn Public Library system for several years. This photograph was taken by a *Brooklyn Daily Eagle* staffer in September 1952, as library leaders again found themselves begging for funds to finish construction.

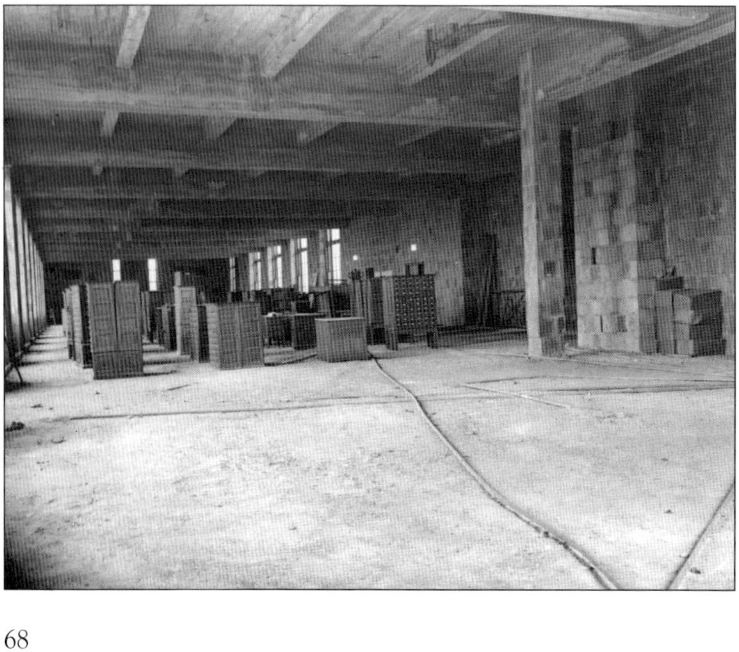

Other spaces on the unfinished floor were being used for storage. This photograph from the same series shows card catalogs, shelving, cabinets, and tables sitting unused in Central Library, possibly waiting to be refurbished by carpentry staff before being distributed to branches.

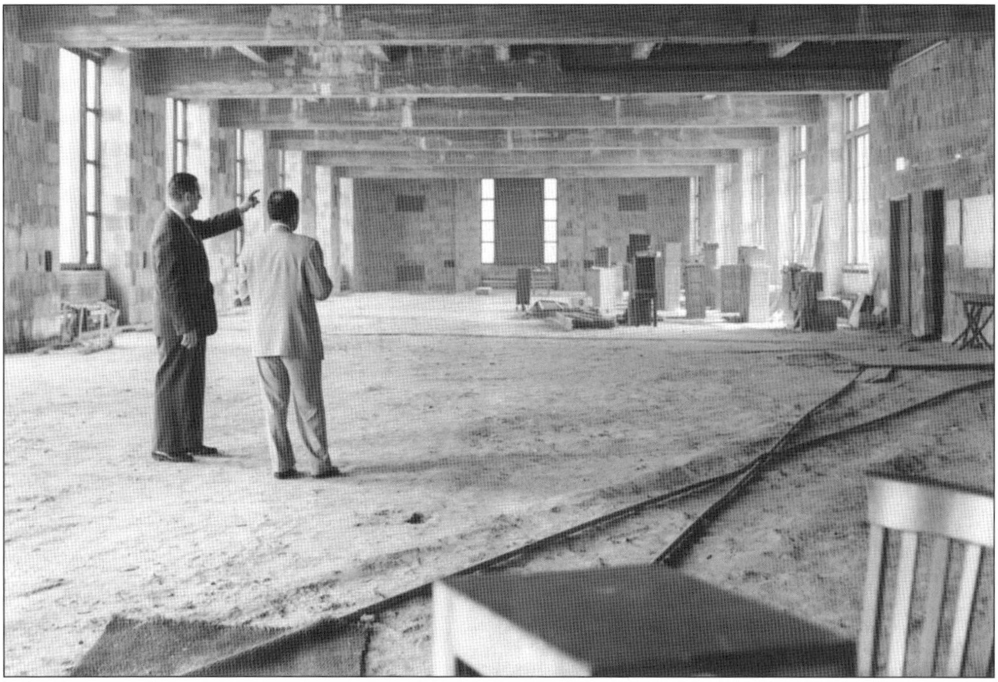

Blueprints for the second floor and basement were completed in 1945, but as was often the case, funding could not be secured to follow through on the plans. The situation was improving after World War II ended, and in December 1952, contracts amounting to $1 million were awarded to renovate the library's unfinished spaces. In these images from 1952, chief librarian Francis St. John (who replaced Ferguson in 1949) gives a tour of the still-raw portions of the Flatbush Avenue and Eastern Parkway wings.

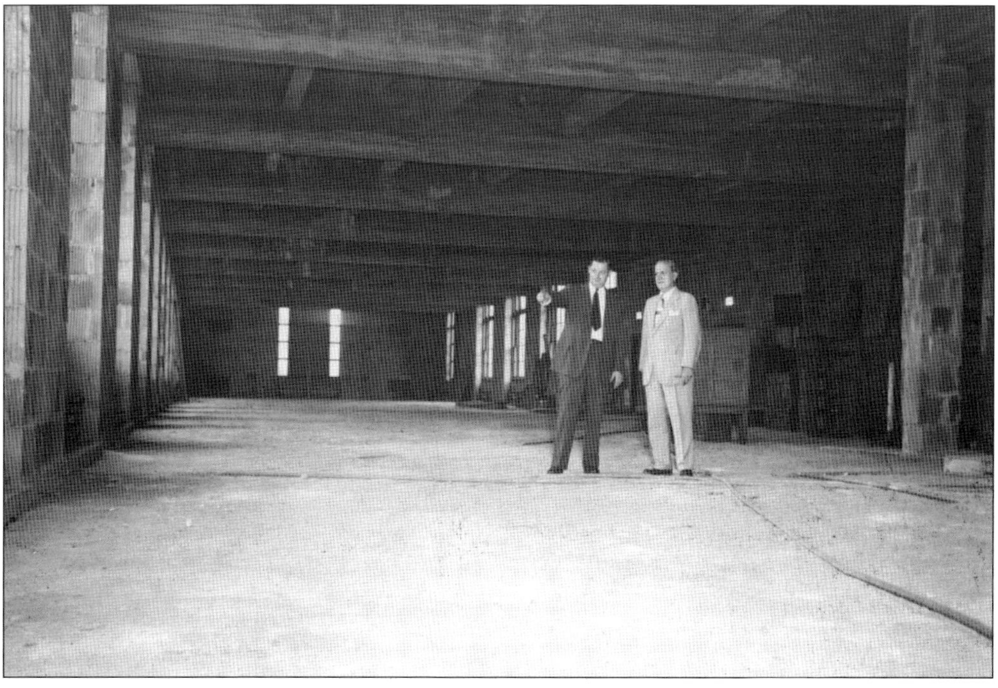

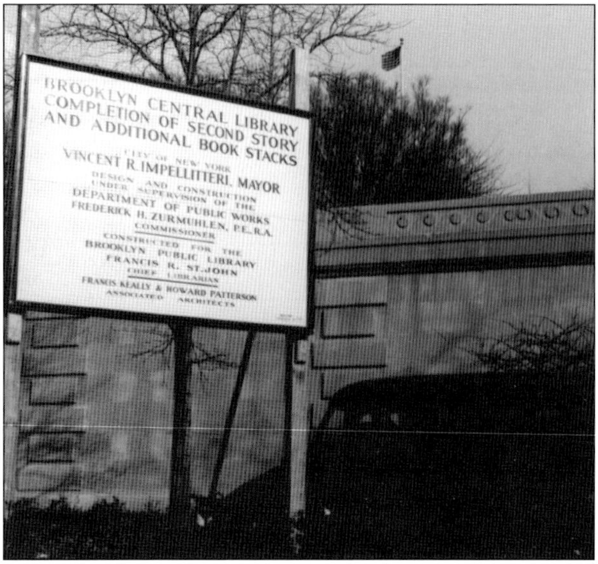

This billboard went up shortly after funding was secured late in 1952, announcing that completion of the second floor and basement level was under way. By this point, Vincent Impellitteri had replaced La Guardia as mayor of New York. Architect Francis Keally contributed to the construction project as well.

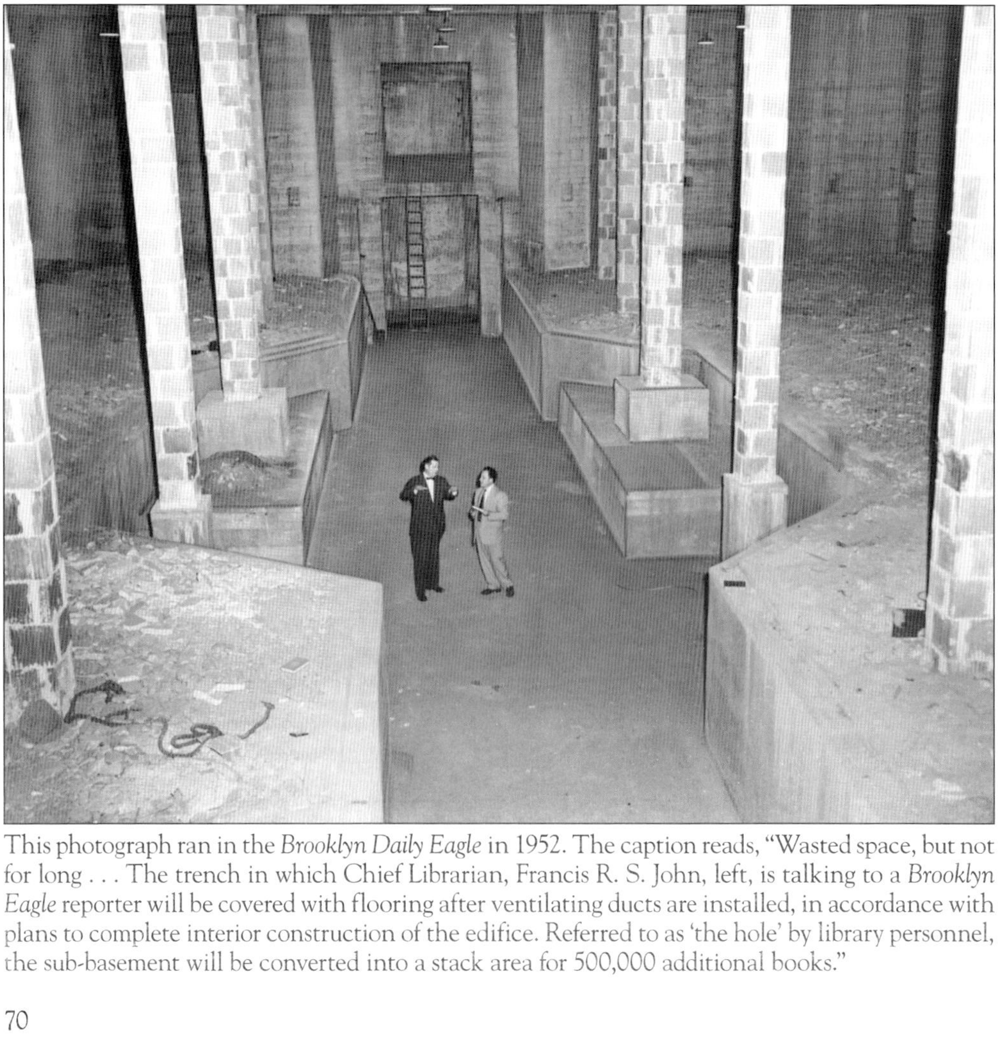

This photograph ran in the *Brooklyn Daily Eagle* in 1952. The caption reads, "Wasted space, but not for long . . . The trench in which Chief Librarian, Francis R. S. John, left, is talking to a *Brooklyn Eagle* reporter will be covered with flooring after ventilating ducts are installed, in accordance with plans to complete interior construction of the edifice. Referred to as 'the hole' by library personnel, the sub-basement will be converted into a stack area for 500,000 additional books."

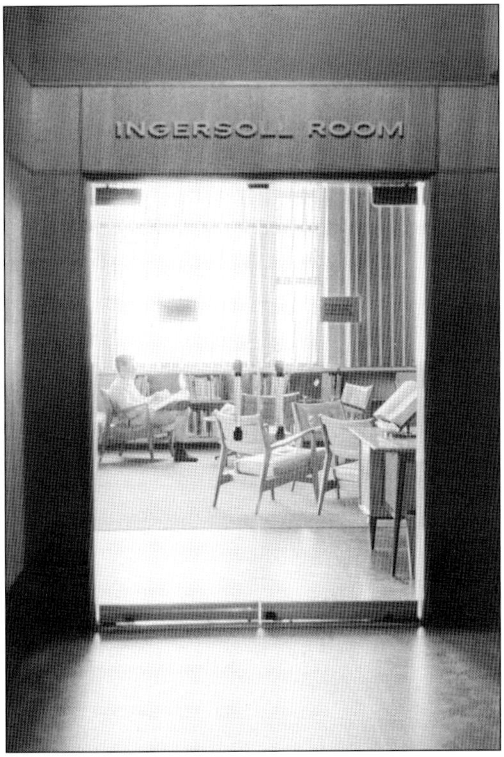

In 1955, the second floor finally opened for public use. Additionally, the library opened a new Ingersoll Room on the north end of its Eastern Parkway wing. "A browsing room for discriminating readers," as the photograph on the right is captioned, the Ingersoll Room offered a more relaxed and informal browsing experience. To meet the growing demand for children's and young adult literature, the Youth Wing now occupies the entire first floor of the Eastern Parkway wing.

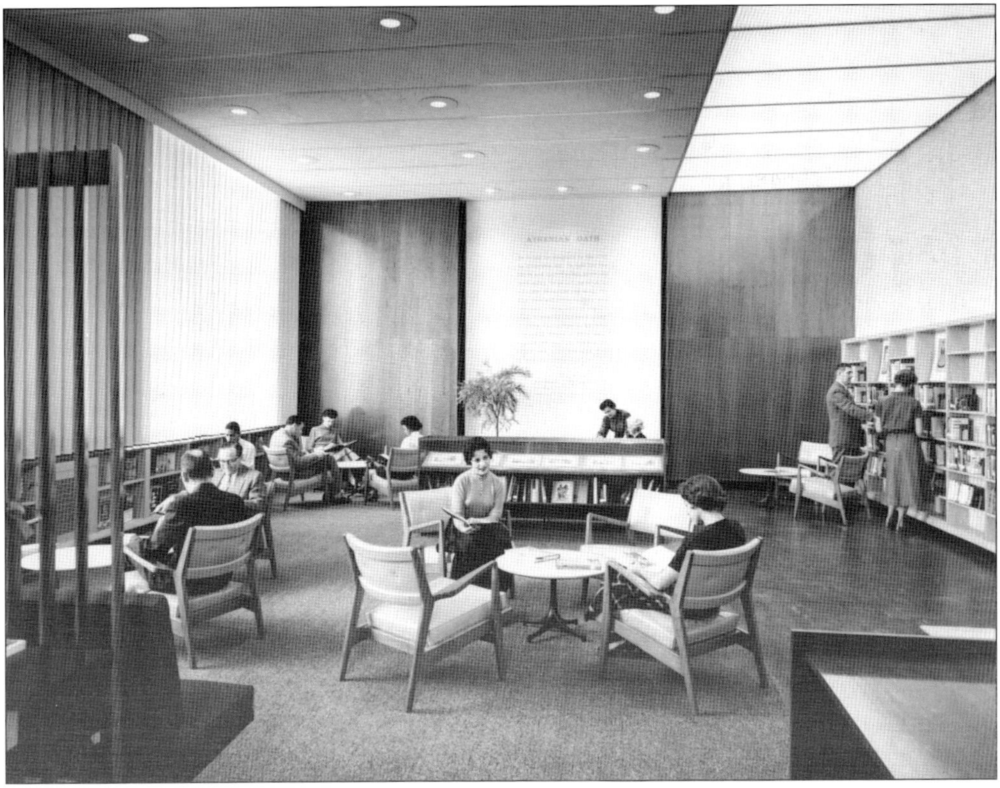

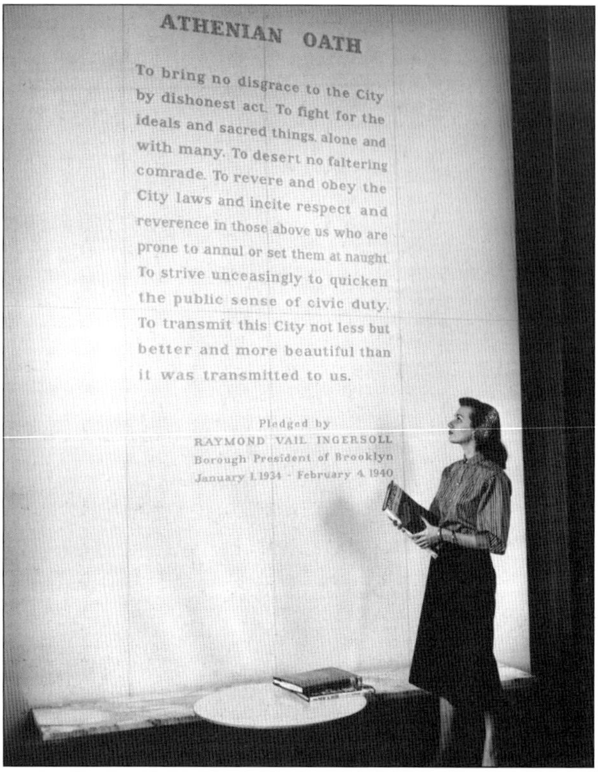

One wall of the Ingersoll Room, pictured from two angles in these photographs, featured a large inscription of the Athenian Oath, which Ingersoll pledged when he took office as borough president in 1934. It reads, "To bring no disgrace to the City by dishonest act. To fight for the ideals and sacred things alone and with many. To desert no faltering comrade. To revere and obey the City laws and incite respect and reverence in those above us who are prone to annul or set them at naught. To strive unceasingly to quicken the public sense of civic duty. To transmit this City not less but better and more beautiful than it was transmitted to us."

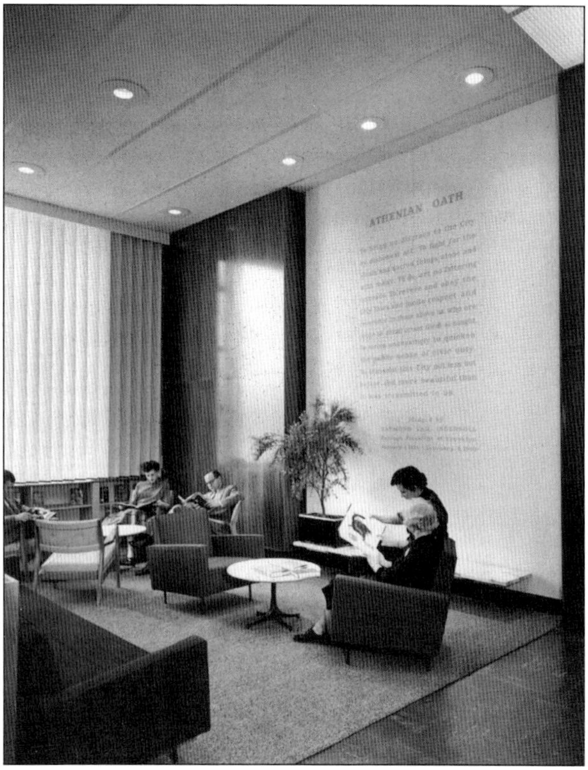

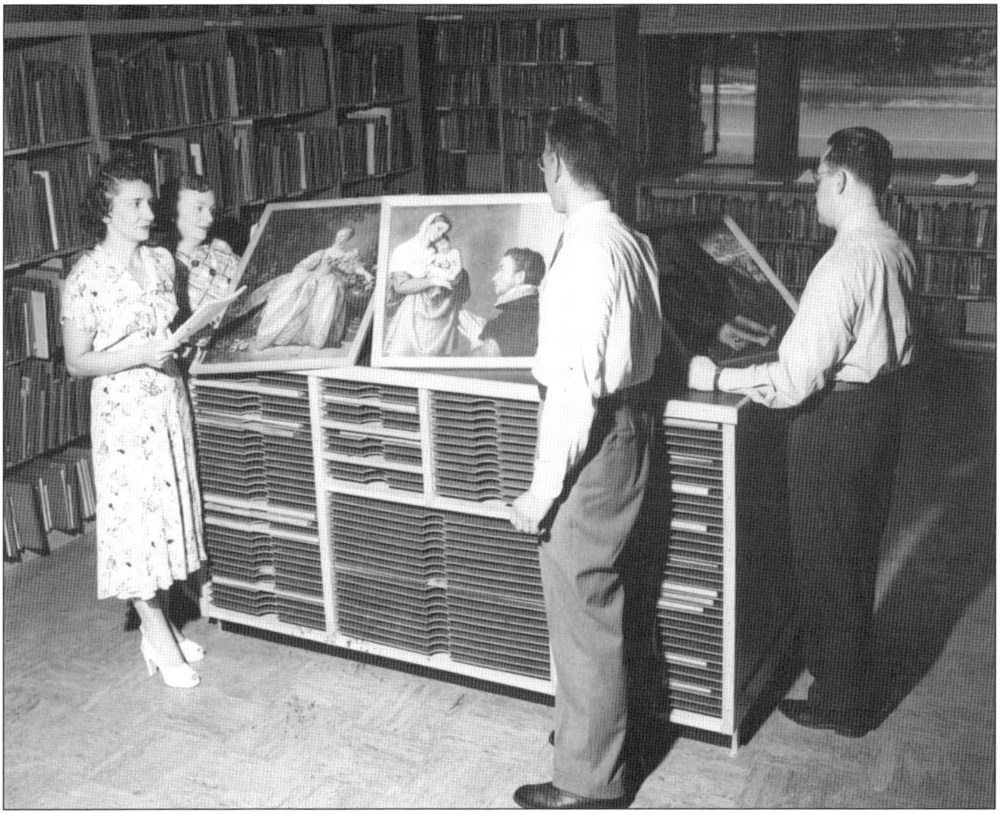

Innovation at Central Library was not limited to the building's infrastructure; services would shape the future of the building as well. One area of growth was in the art and music departments. In 1948, the library began loaning framed art reproductions for patrons to hang on their walls at home, temporarily. The prints were stored in flat files, as shown here.

New technologies also brought change to Central Library. This photograph from the 1950s shows a librarian checking out books for a patron using a photograph charge machine. Replacing handwritten records of library loans, the machines ushered in an era of automated loaning technologies, which have continued to evolve. Today, circulation records are completely digitized, and self-check machines allow patrons to check out their own materials.

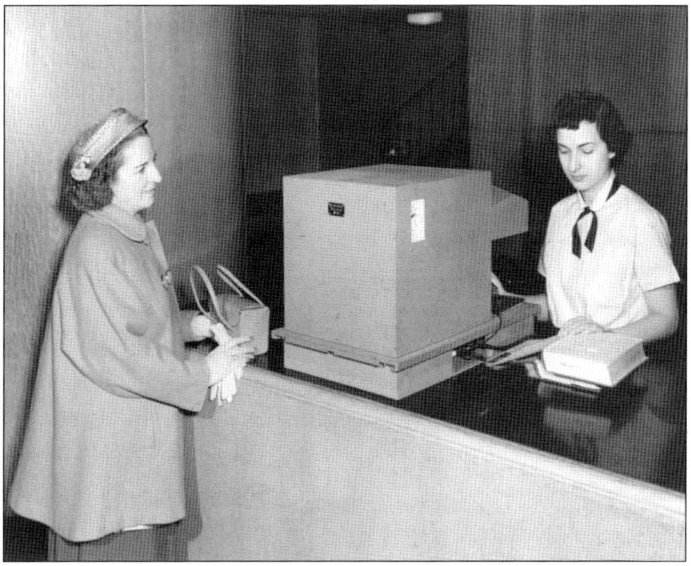

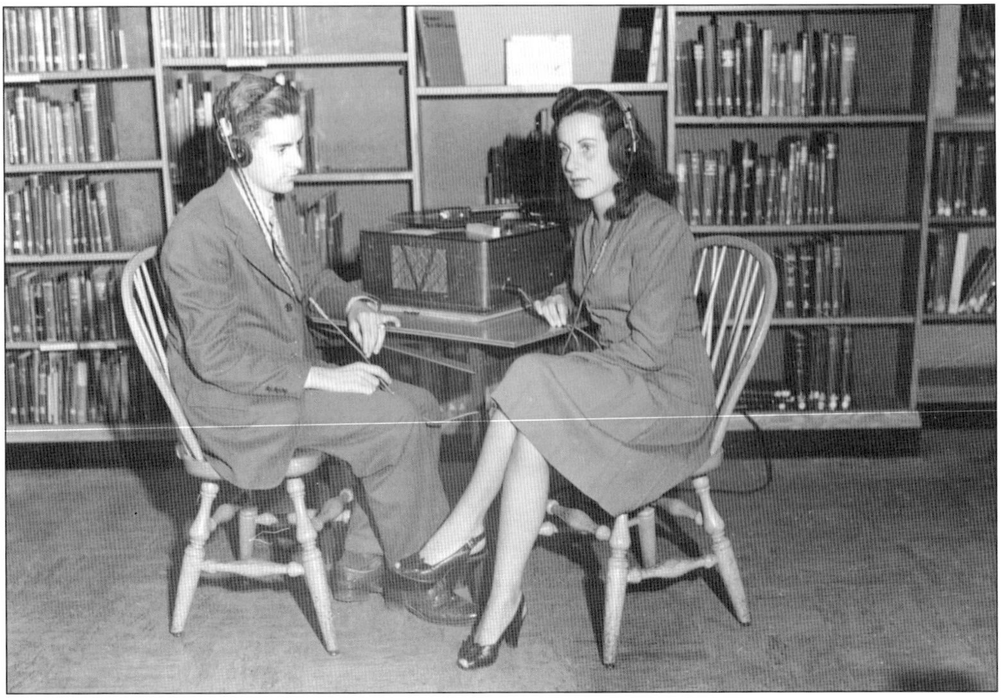

The audiovisual department was created in 1952, allowing patrons to borrow recordings and films for home listening and viewing. According to the library's 1952 annual report, the 11,000 vinyl records available for loan ran the gamut "from jazz band to symphony orchestra, night club singer to Metropolitan star." These undated photographs were likely taken shortly after the vinyl record collection was introduced.

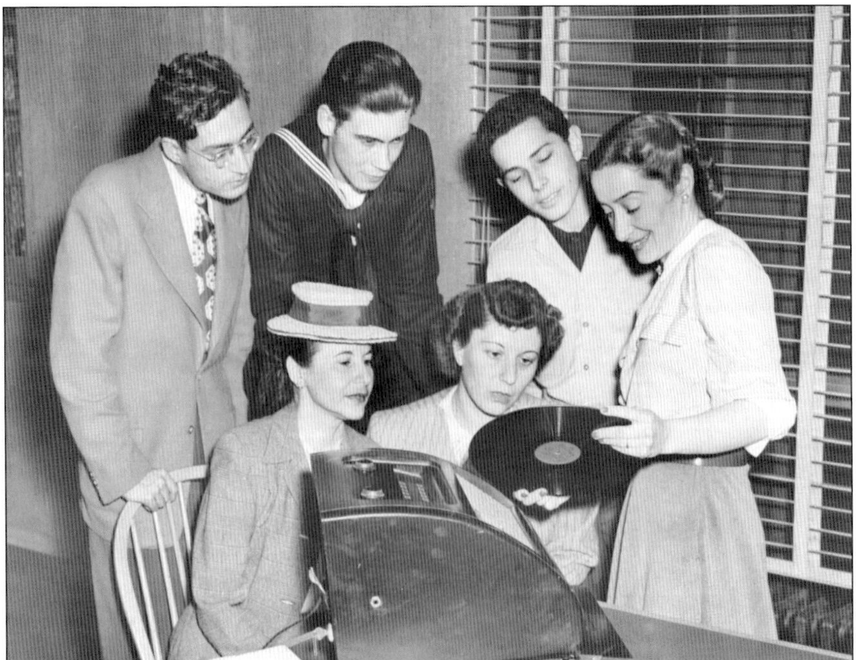

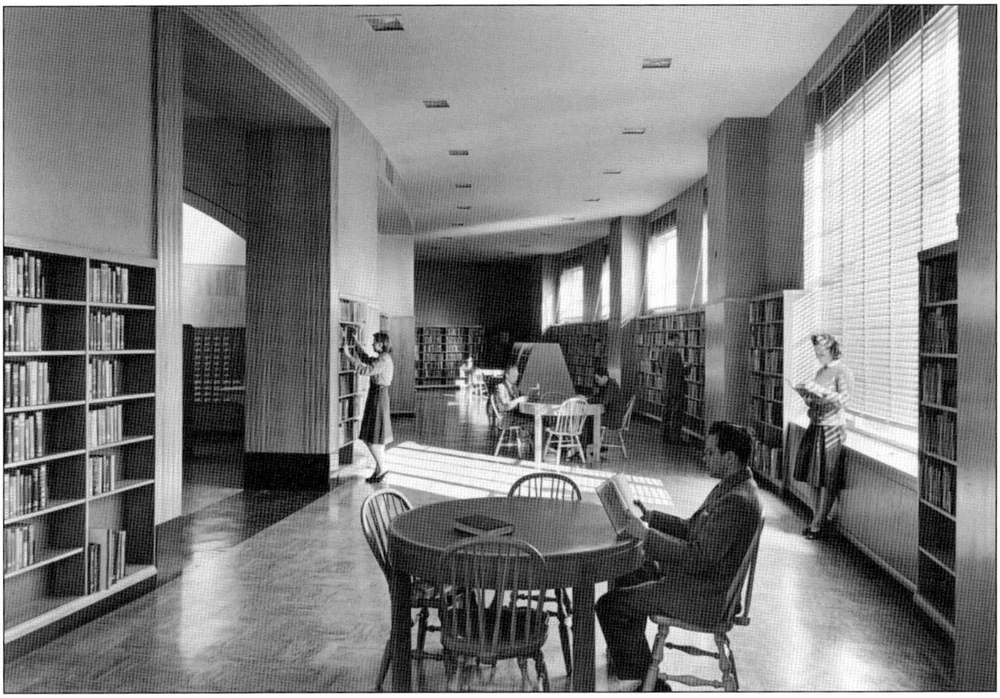

This reading room, which followed the curve of the building behind the Grand Lobby, once housed popular books and periodicals. Renovations extended the back of the building in 1969; the windows were removed as garages were added to the rear of the building. The room continued to house periodicals, as well as several microfilm readers and audiovisual materials like audiobooks, VHS cassettes, and eventually DVDs. In 2013, the space was remodeled and reopened as the Shelby White and Leon Levy Information Commons, offering public meeting rooms, work spaces, and a training lab for larger groups.

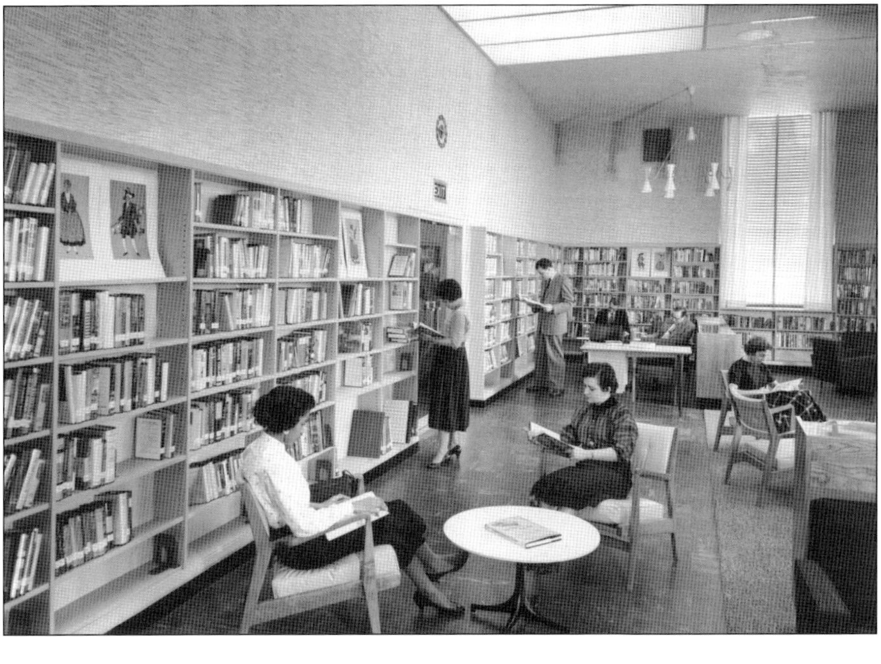

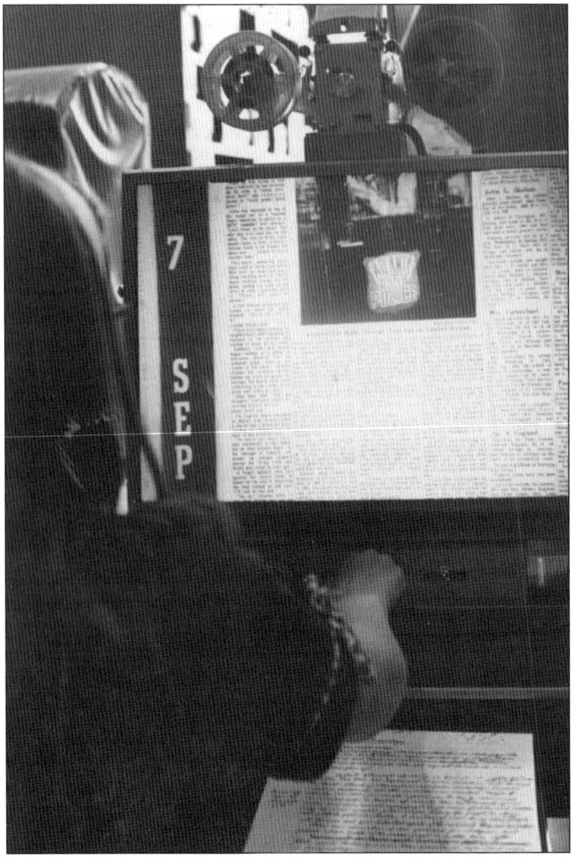

Microformatting of library materials like periodicals and historic records has long provided a way to consolidate space on crowded library shelves. An entire year of a newspaper can be condensed into a single reel of 35-millimeter film. The renovations of 1952 brought new microfilm readers to Central Library. Both of these photographs show patrons accessing information on the blow-up screens of the readers, which are still used today in the Popular Library and Brooklyn Collection divisions. Many of the periodicals that patrons once accessed via microfilm are now available on digital databases, and long banks of bulky microfilm reader machines have been replaced by computer terminals or laptop work spaces.

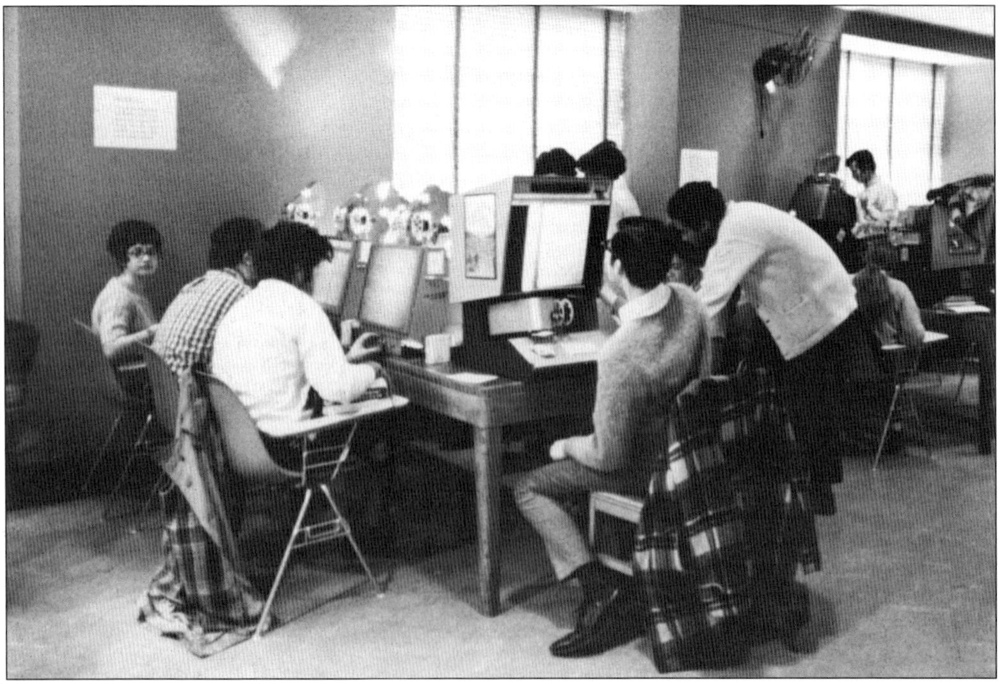

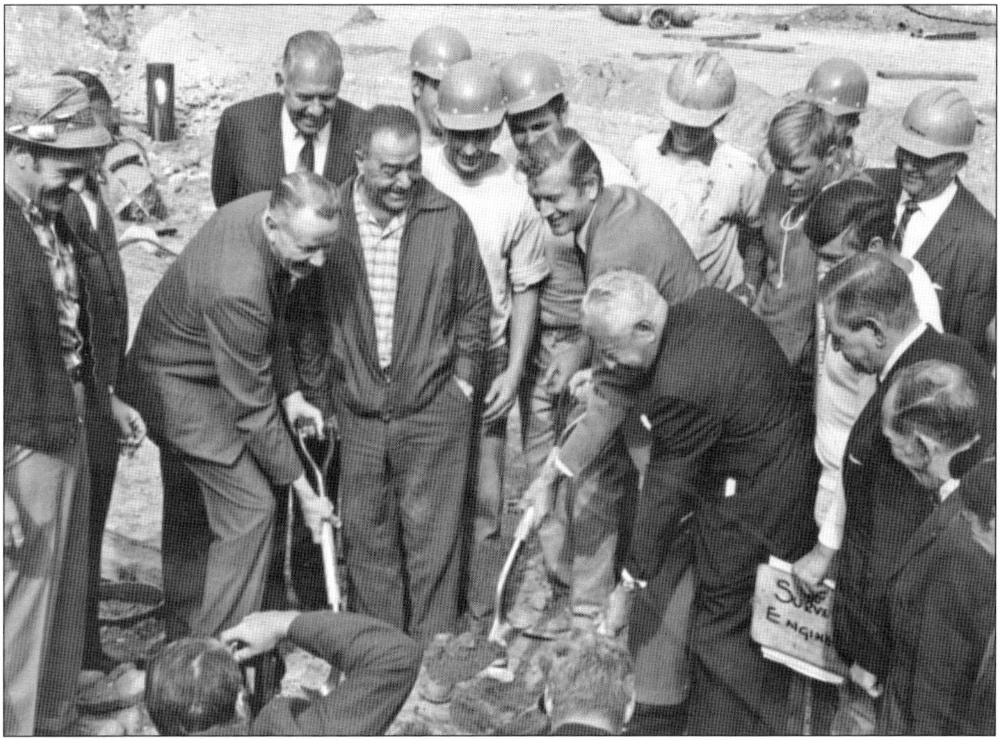

The library had begun to show its age by the late 1960s. From 1969 to 1972, the building's interiors received a much-needed face-lift, along with long-postponed renovations. This photograph from 1969 shows Mayor John Lindsay (holding shovel at right) and Brooklyn borough president Abe Stark (right of Lindsay) at the ground-breaking ceremony.

This photograph, taken in July 1970, shows the renovation work being done on the plaza in front of the library. Original library plans by Almirall had envisioned this area as a grand staircase leading up to a first floor well above street level. With Githens and Keally's redesign, the plaza became a relatively flat space, allowing the area to be used for music and dance programming.

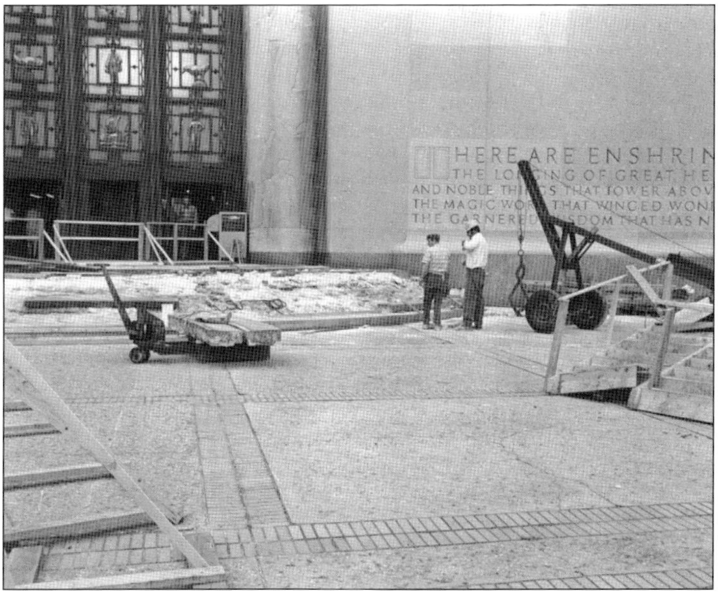

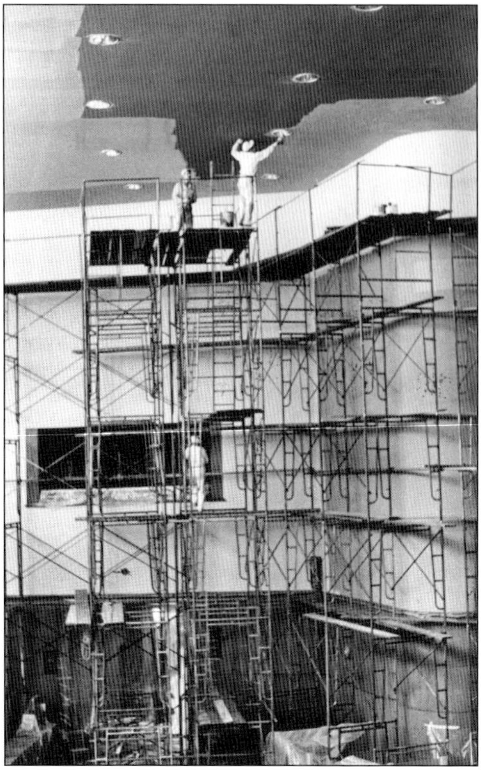

These photographs were taken during the renovations of the late 1960s and early 1970s. At left, an intricate web of scaffolding gives painters access to the ceiling of the Grand Lobby, three stories up from ground level. Below, patrons approach the information desk in front of the lobby, which is temporarily closed off due to the renovations. As part of the renovation, the art and music division was moved to the third floor of the Flatbush Avenue wing, displacing the cataloging functions to another location and opening that space to public use for the first time.

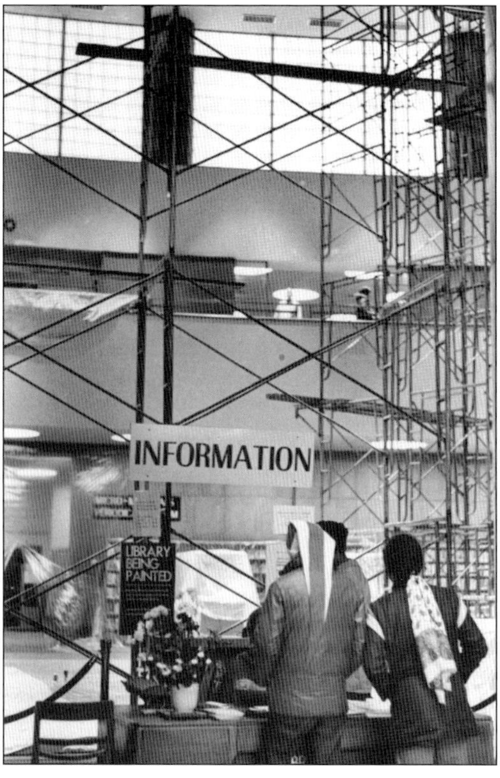

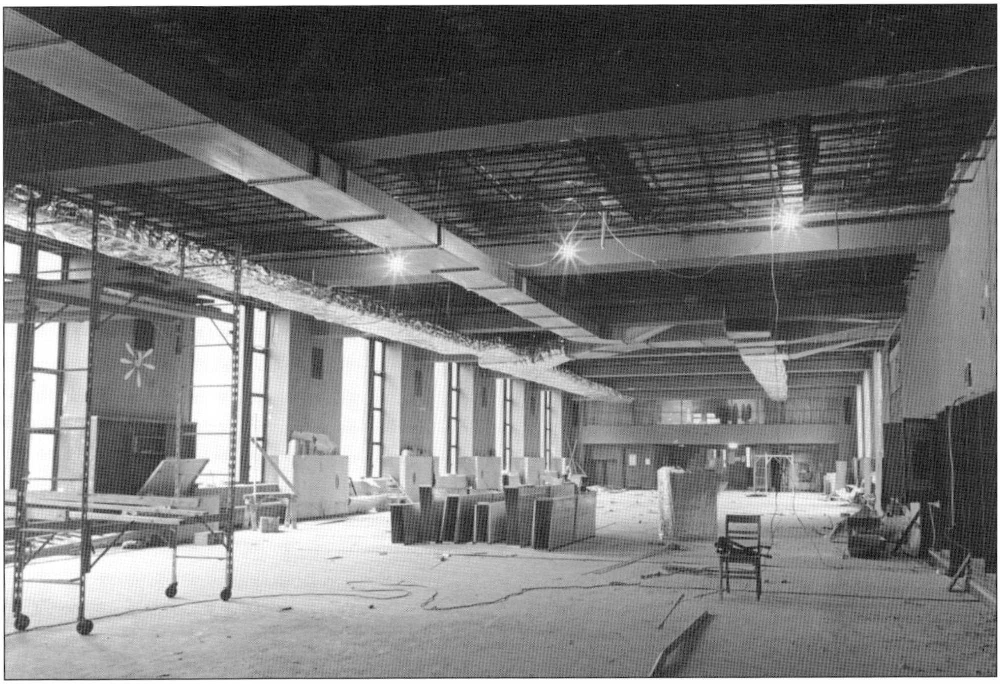

These photographs show a complete gutting of the children's and young adult rooms in 1972. Although this wing had originally been segregated from the rest of Central Library by a wall, the barriers were brought down over the years. By 1959, junior high students were allowed access to adult book collections throughout the system. According to the library's annual reports, the renovations were very disruptive to public service; the building stayed open throughout the work, requiring that collections and staff be shuffled around the building as renovations progressed.

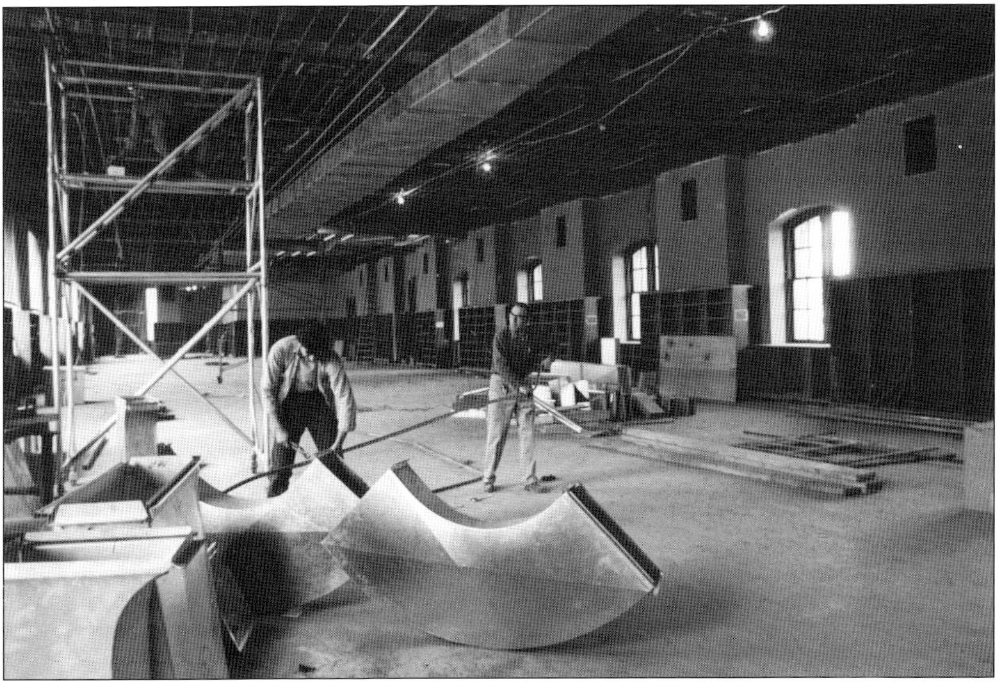

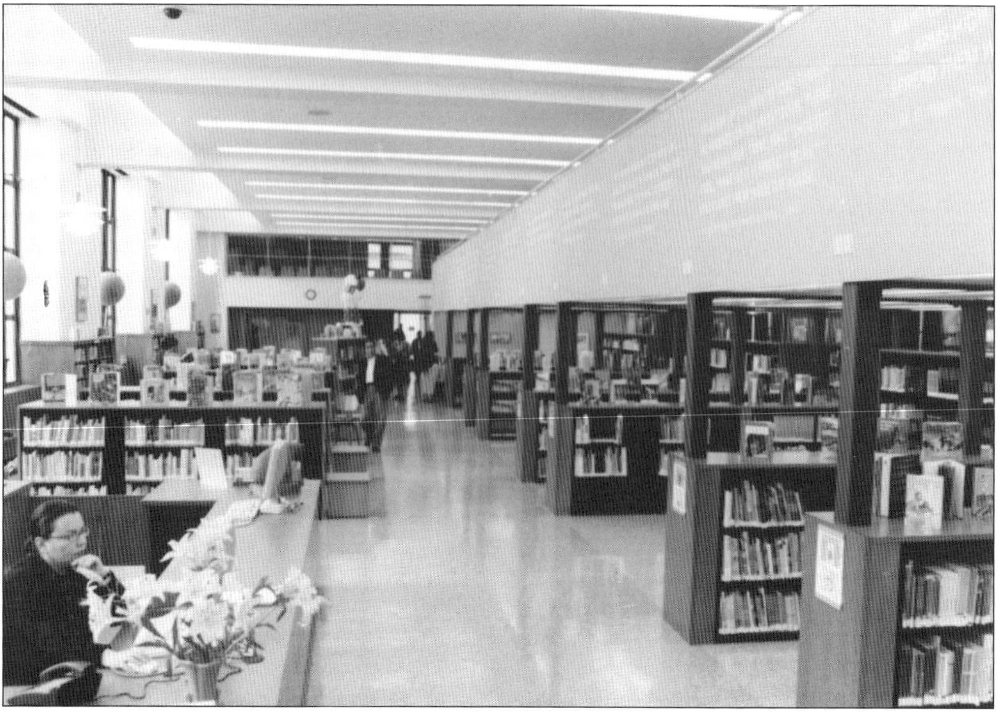

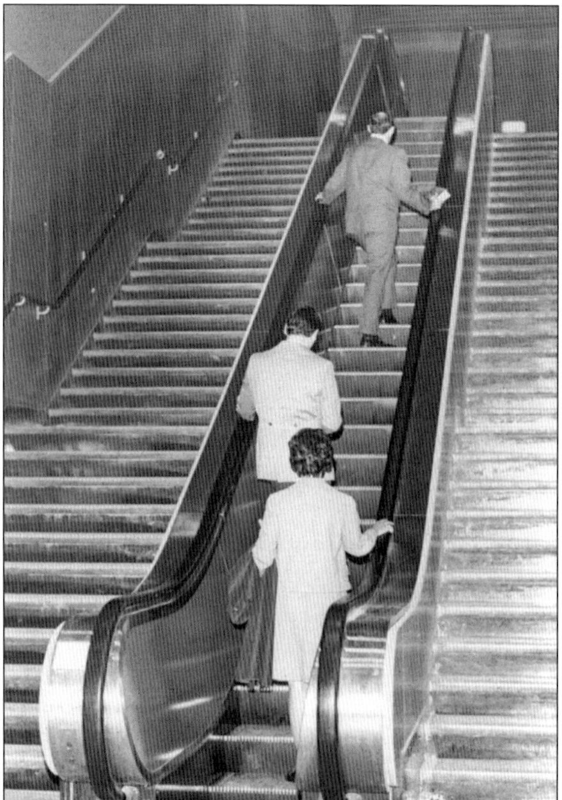

The Youth Wing was dramatically altered again in 2000 when a large lofted area was built in the middle of the room to create space for a computer lab. Additional shelving was created under the loft so that no book space was lost with the introduction of new computers. The walls of the "tech loft," as it is now called, are decorated with quotes from children's literature.

Despite the difficulty and discomfort, the renovations brought one much-needed amenity—escalators, which had been part of Githens and Keally's redesign of the building in 1937. At that time, funds were not available to complete the second floor, rendering escalators irrelevant. Even after the second floor opened in the 1950s, it would still be another 20 years before Central Library had its escalators.

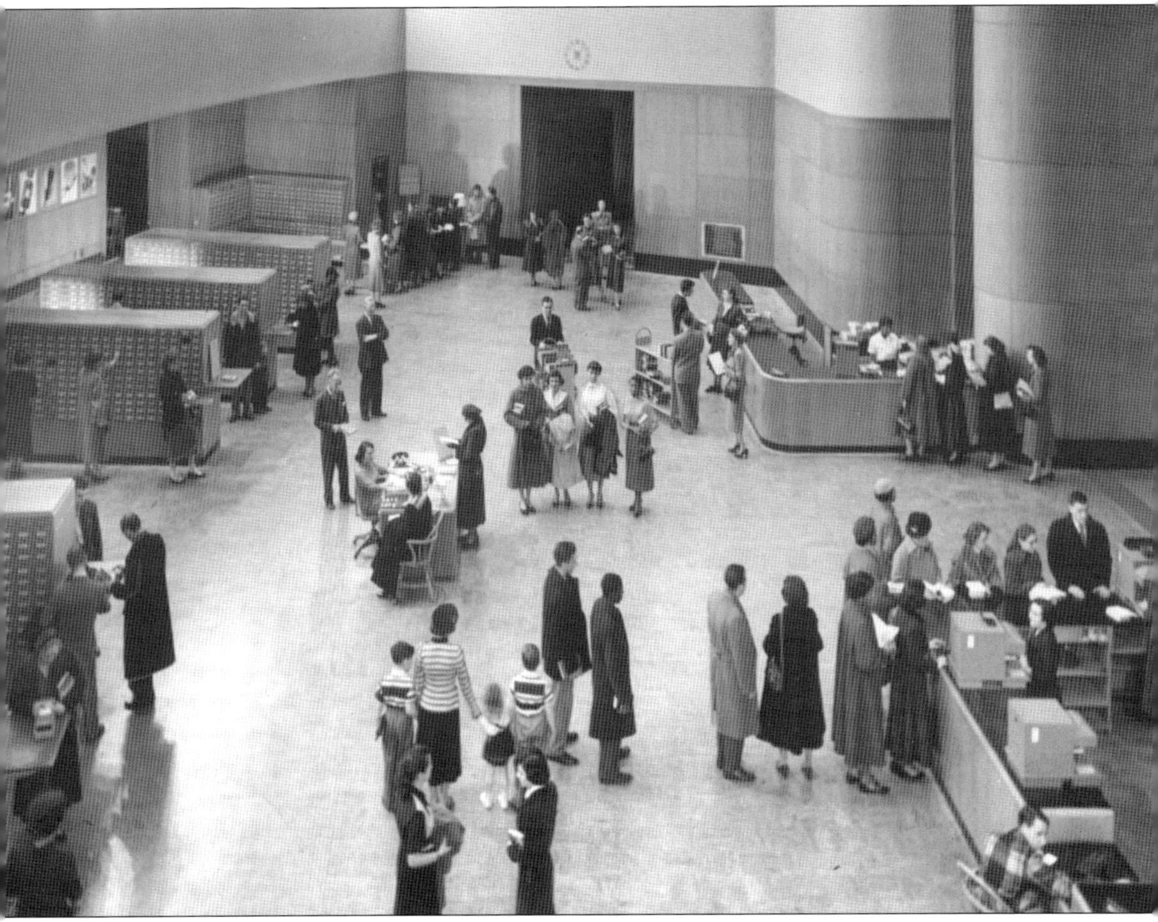

Early photographs of Central Library show a once-indispensable piece of furniture that has since nearly vanished from Brooklyn Public Library and most libraries around the world—card catalogs. Though they may look quaintly old fashioned now, card catalogs were critical to organizing and finding information in the library. Details like author, subject, and title were printed on small paper cards, which were arranged alphabetically within long drawers. One set of card catalogs would list items by author, one by subject, and one by title so that any one item was cross-referenced in at least three places. Each card catalog also indicated an item's Dewey decimal number, which could be used to find the desired book on the shelf anywhere in the building. Keeping card catalogs up to date was very labor intensive, and libraries began phasing them out once machine-readable library records paved the way for computerization of the catalogs in the 1970s.

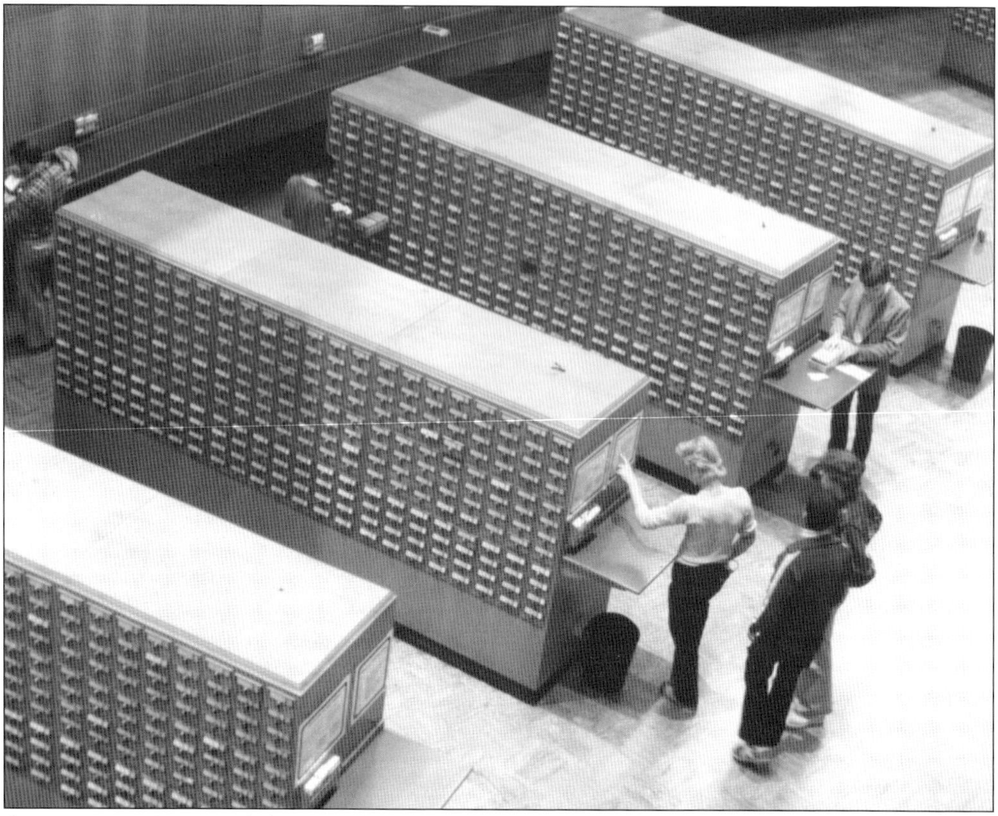

Once a main feature of the Grand Lobby, the rows of wooden card catalogs became obsolete with the advent of computerized catalog systems. The library's 1982 annual report mentions switching over to a computerized system, stating that the change was hardly noticed by patrons. The photograph below shows the dismantling of the old card catalogs in 1996. Because they were so large, they were destroyed in situ rather than moved out intact. Note the computer terminals on raised wooden tables throughout the lobby; these compact machines revolutionized the way patrons find materials in the library.

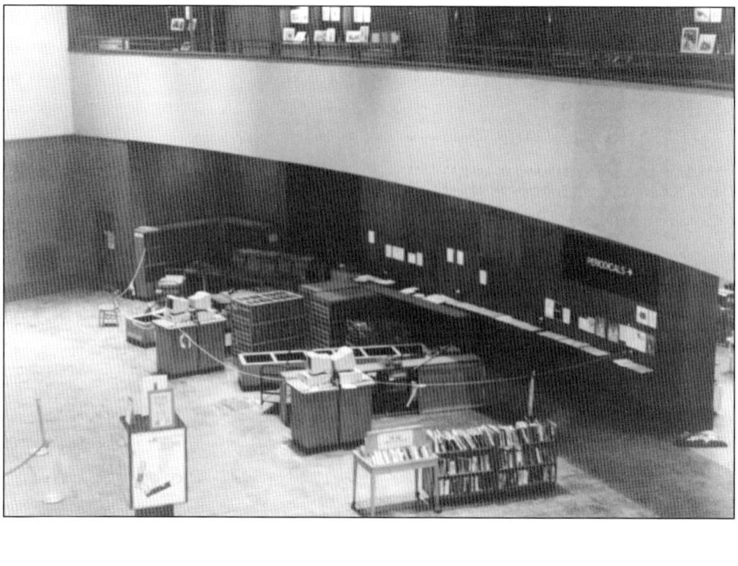

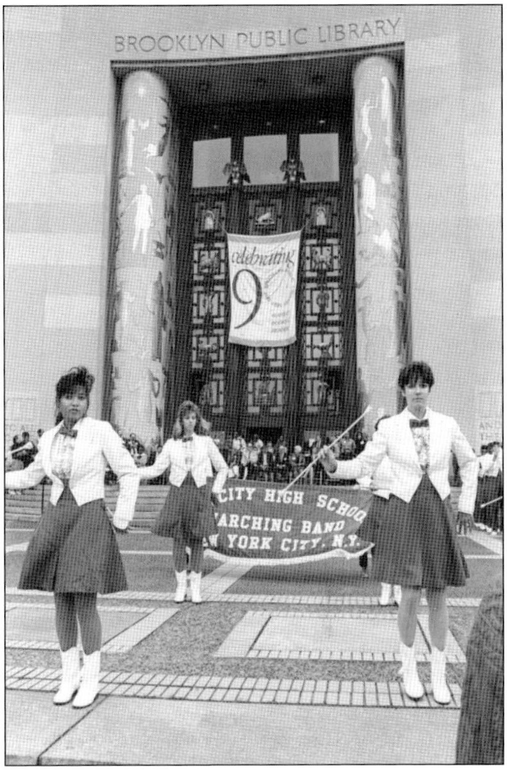

The Brooklyn Public Library system celebrated 90 years of service in 1987 with a grand event at Central Library. The All-City High School marching band, pictured at right, performed on the plaza and Congressman Major Owens addressed the crowd. Owens had a special connection to the library system; he had started out as a librarian at Brooklyn Public Library before pursuing a career in politics. Starting with the Bedford branch in Public School No. 3 in 1897, the library system had grown to 60 branches throughout Brooklyn in its 90-year history.

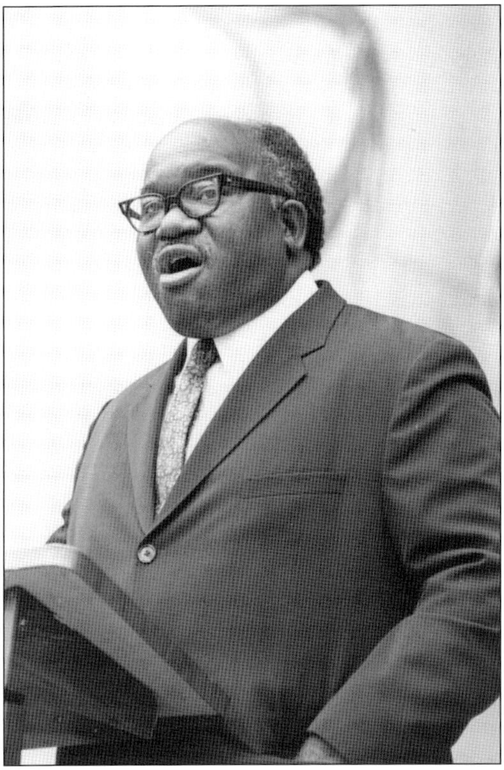

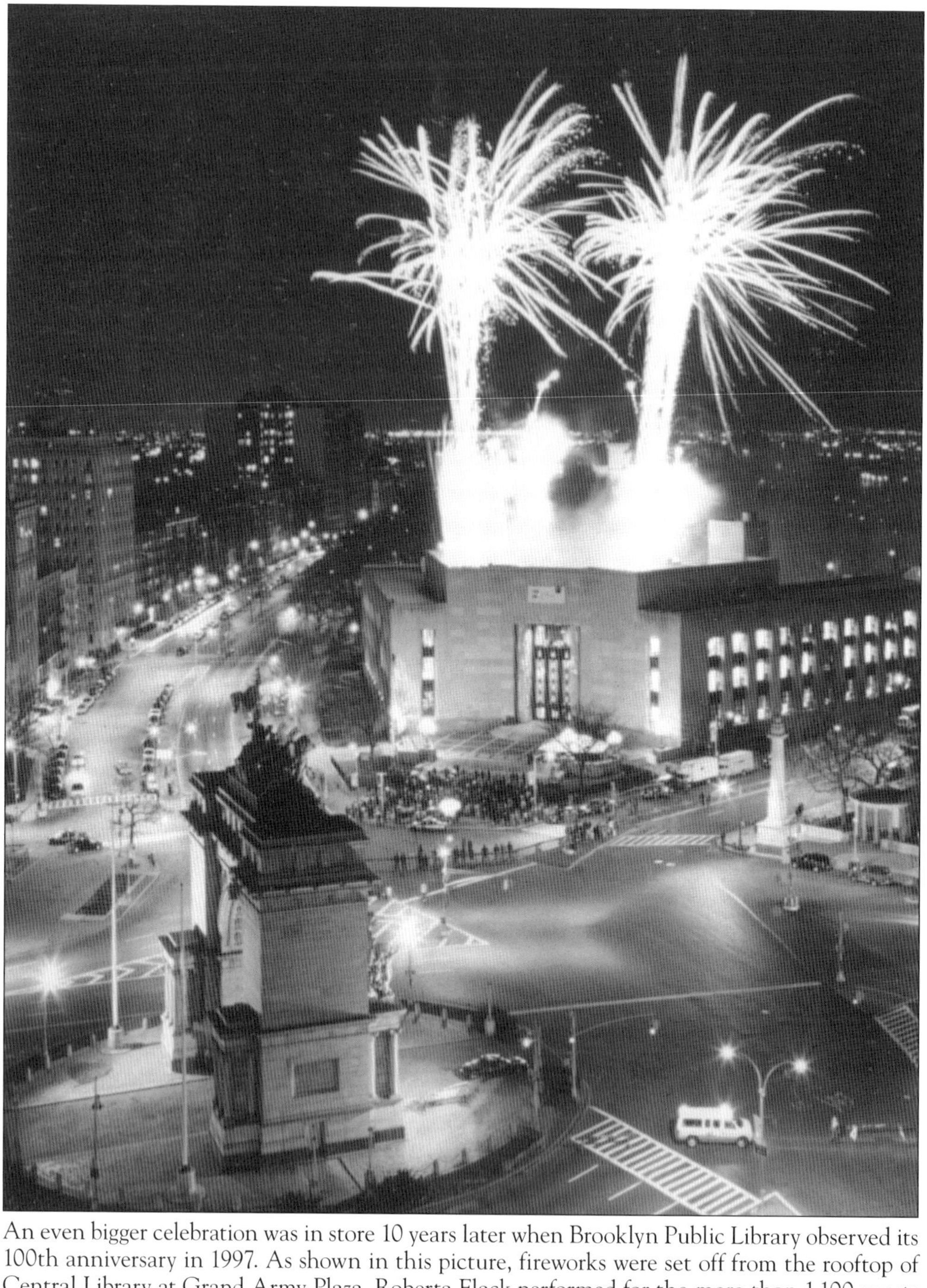

An even bigger celebration was in store 10 years later when Brooklyn Public Library observed its 100th anniversary in 1997. As shown in this picture, fireworks were set off from the rooftop of Central Library at Grand Army Plaza. Roberta Flack performed for the more than 1,100 guests who gathered for the celebration on April 14, 1997. That same year, the library was given landmark designation by New York City's Landmarks Preservation Commission. In its report, the commission found that Central Library "has a special character and a special historical and aesthetic interest and value as part of the development, heritage, and cultural characteristics of New York City" and "is one of the borough's best known and most heavily used public buildings."

Six

The Cast of Characters

When people think of libraries, they envision long rows of wooden shelves lined with books and the quietude necessary for study. What they may not picture is the small army of trained librarians, catalogers, and clerical staffers who keep those library shelves fully stocked and logically organized. Even less heralded are the maintenance workers who build the shelves and the custodians who take care of them. It is the hundreds of staffers working in Central Library at any given time who keep the building humming along and keep the books, magazines, films, and other library materials circulating in and out.

As the hub of the entire Brooklyn Public Library system, Central Library has always served more than its immediate area. The many thousands of books that circulated at neighborhood branches throughout the borough every year were once purchased and processed by staff of Central Library. In 1953, the library reported that just 15 cataloging staffers processed 1,000 items on a daily basis. Some of that work was very physical—carting books, stamping records, adding dust jackets, gluing labels—and required equipment that is obsolete today. As formats and technologies of library materials have changed, so too has the work of processing those materials. Digital tools have replaced most of the hand tools pictured in these pages. But the staffers remain, and through their work, they not only bring books, programs, special events, and information to the public, but they also bring life and vivacity to the library institution.

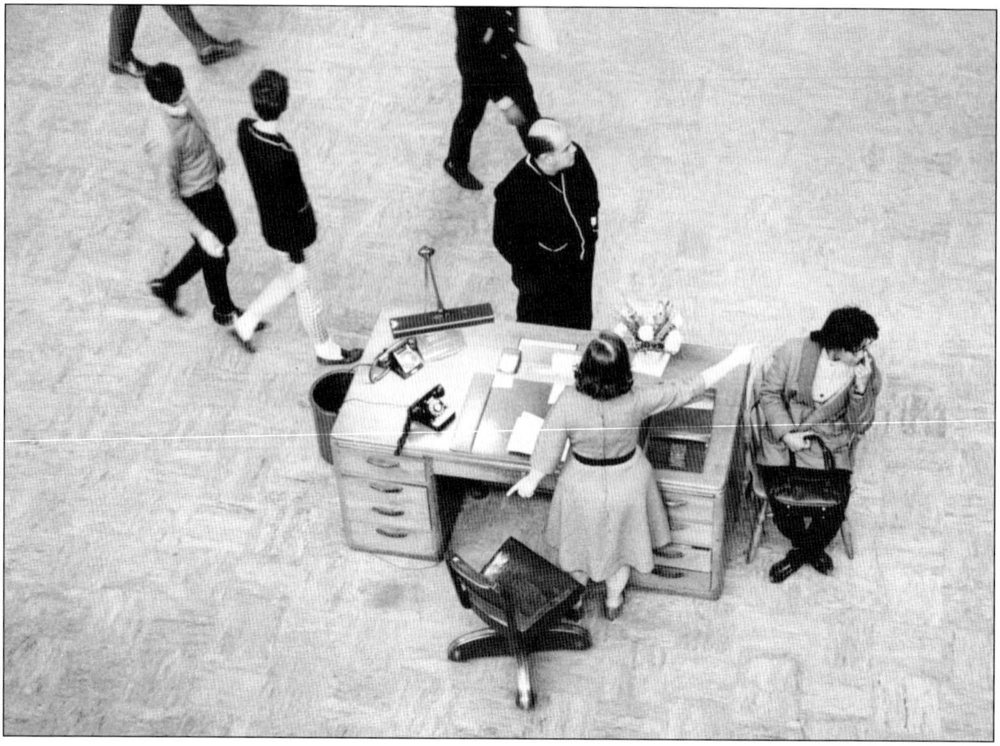

Patrons' first point of contact in Central Library, or any library, is often with a librarian. The photograph above, taken in 1965, shows a librarian providing direction from the main information desk in the middle of Central's Grand Lobby. The undated image below, most likely from the 1960s as well, shows the first floor of the Flatbush Avenue wing. The sign to the left of the librarian shows some of the categories of the Dewey decimal system, which is used to organize all the nonfiction books in the library into subjects. Although useful, the numerical system is not intuitive, and one of the librarians' roles is to help patrons find a book on the shelf after retrieving its Dewey decimal number from the card catalog.

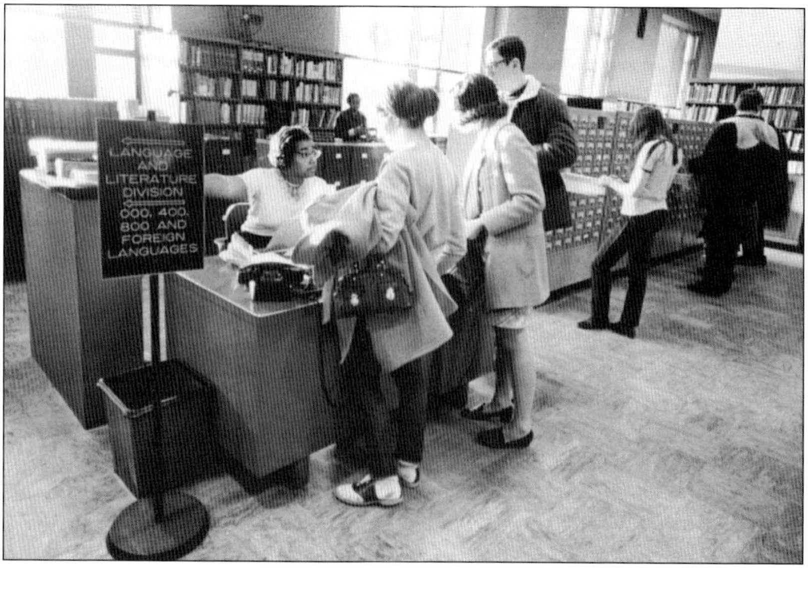

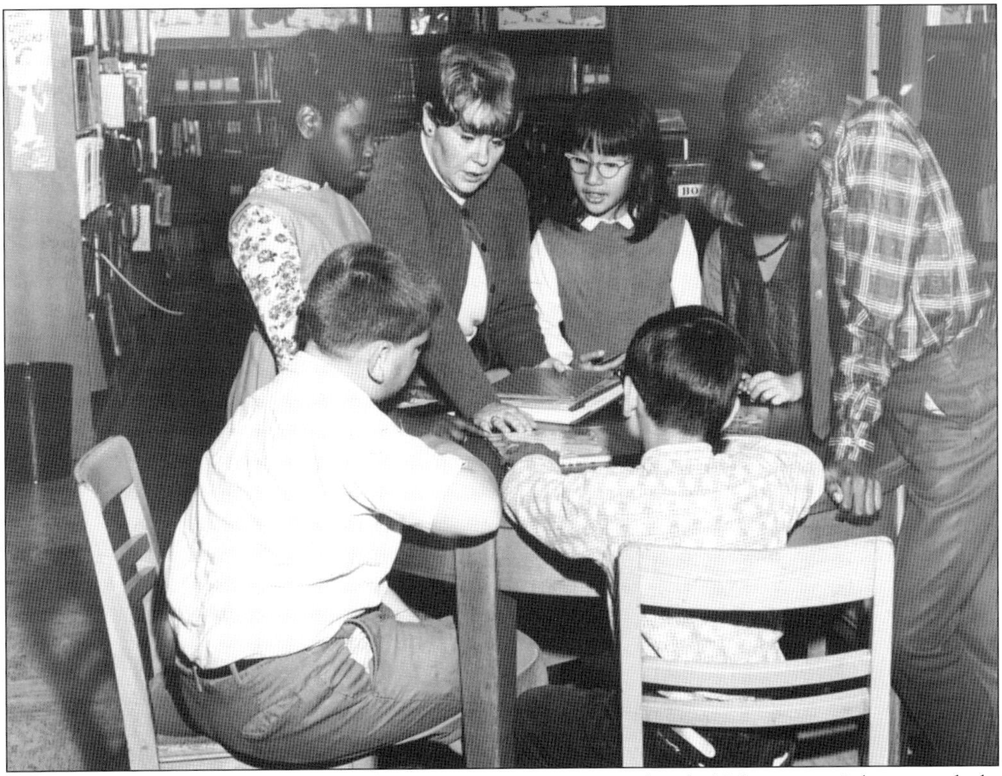

Librarians do more than just direct the public to items on the shelf, however. Librarians help patrons get to deeply buried information, such as articles in journals or photographs in special collections that are hard to unearth through simple catalog searching. They also instruct students on research methods, lead programs in special interest topics, provide book recommendations to avid readers, and conduct outreach in schools and community centers. Above, librarian Ellen Loughran assists students looking for books in the Children's Room in the 1970s. Below, librarian Sylvia Mechanic (center) examines a book display with colleagues. Librarians create such displays to highlight new titles and niche topics from the collection.

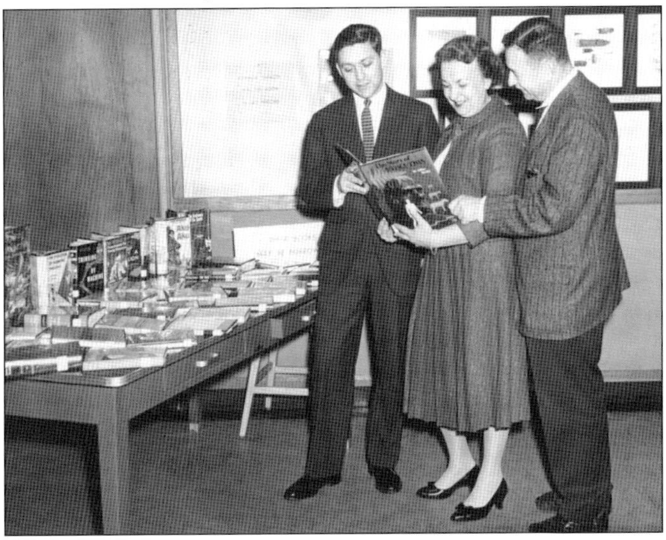

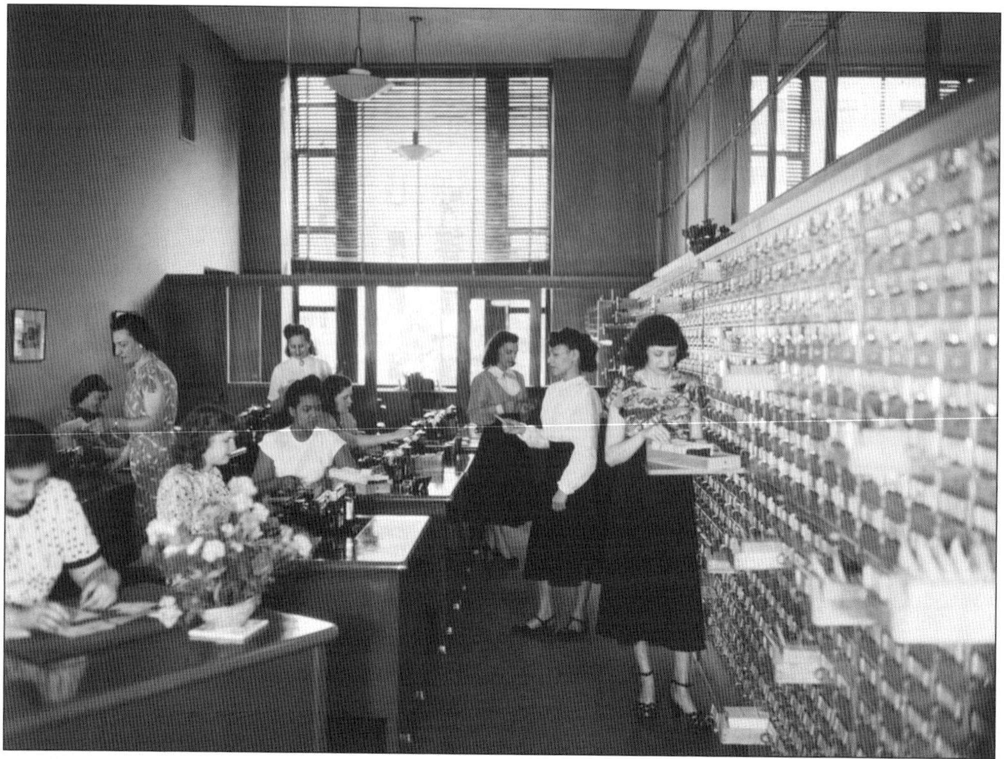

Card catalogs like the ones lining the walls in these photographs were a common sight in libraries until the late 20th century. Used by members of the reading public to look up books and subjects, the card catalogs were also used by staff members to organize the circulation records of thousands of Brooklynites who joined the library. The photograph above dates to the 1950s. By the time the photograph below was taken in the 1980s, the Brooklyn Public Library system boasted more than 600,000 registered borrowers. All patron records are now stored digitally, rendering this system obsolete.

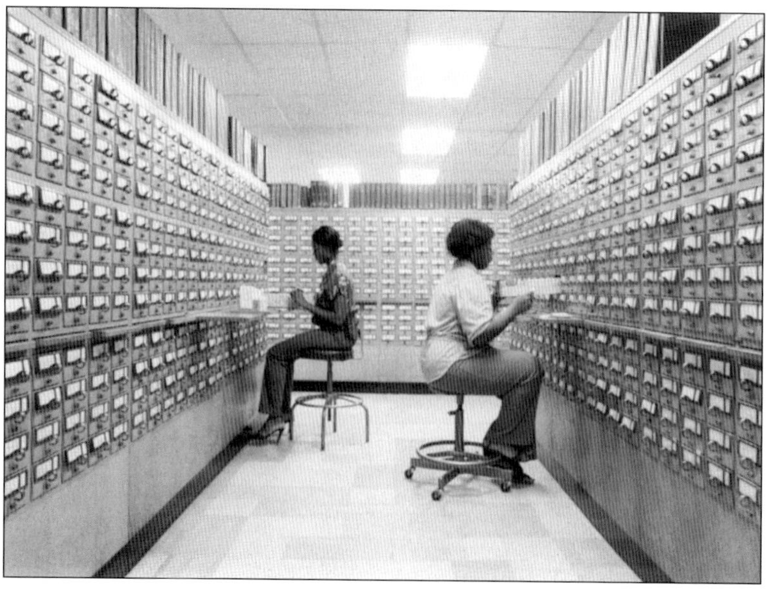

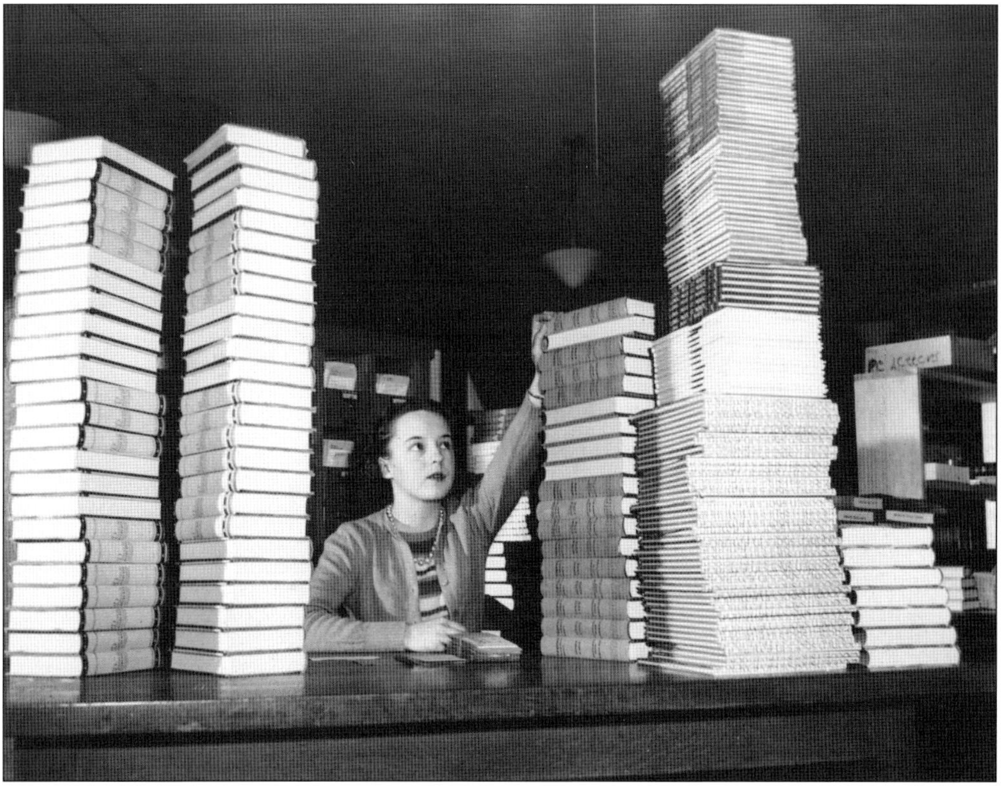

Much of the behind-the-scenes work of running a library was once centralized at the Grand Army Plaza building. In 1953, when this picture was taken, the Brooklyn Public Library system consisted of 43 branches located throughout the borough. Staff at Central Library handled the selection, ordering, processing, and distribution of books for the entire network of neighborhood branches.

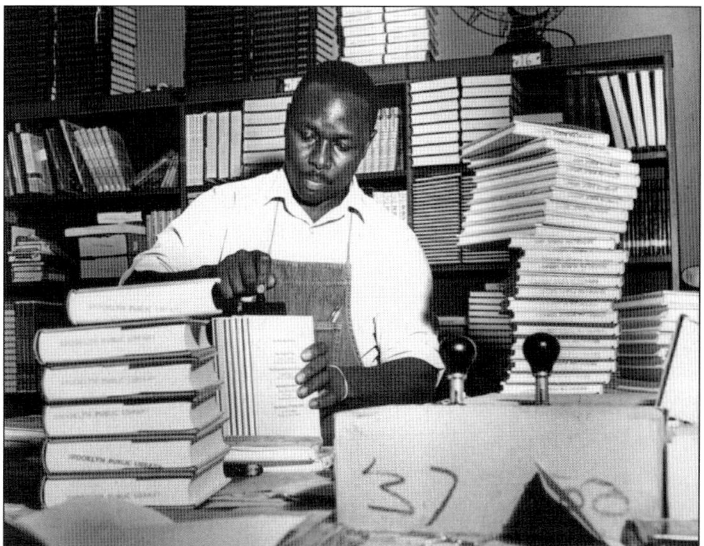

Because Brooklyn Public Library is just one of three systems independently operating in New York City, it is not uncommon for books checked out in Brooklyn to find their way to Queens, Manhattan, the Bronx, or Staten Island. To combat the loss of these materials, all books were (and are) stamped with "Brooklyn Public Library" and clearly labeled to indicate their home branch, as seen in this 1967 image.

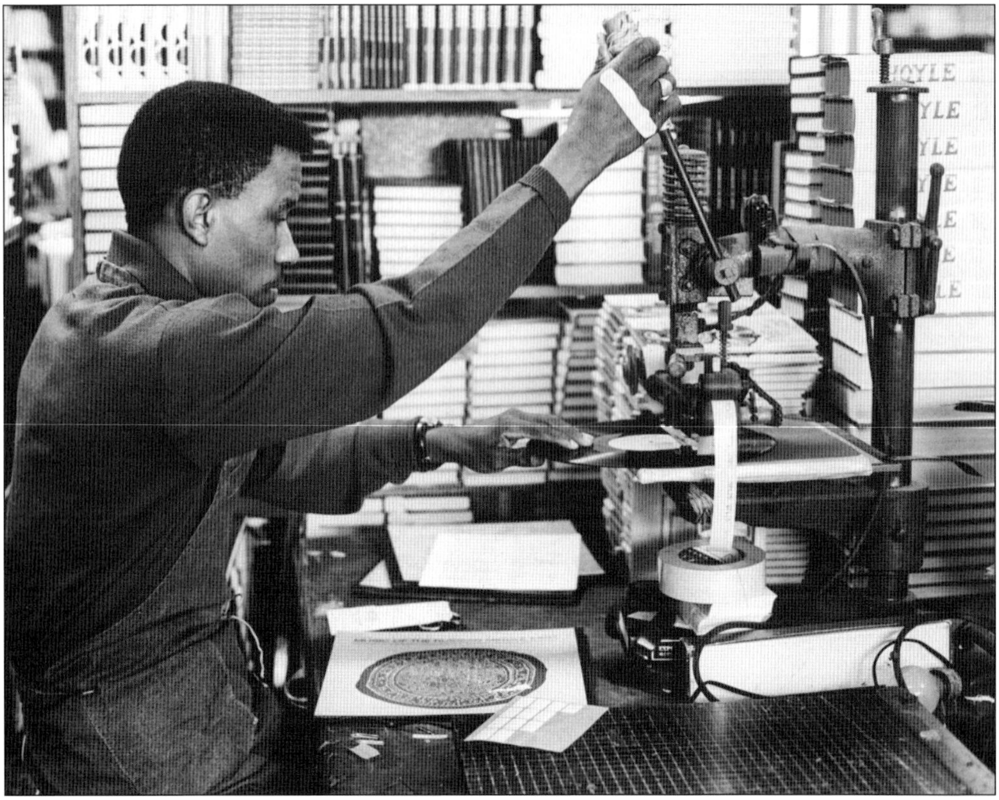

Central Library's cataloging staff processed more than just books, as the library loaned out materials in many formats. Above, a worker uses a hand-operated press to label a vinyl record in 1968. In 1971, the library circulated items from its record collection more than 40,000 times. The photograph below is undated, but likely from the 1980s. In it, two librarians work in the multimedia division, examining a reel of 16-millimeter film. The library once loaned out 16-millimeter films for home viewing. Although these collections were de-accessioned, the library archives have copies of the catalog of films the library once held.

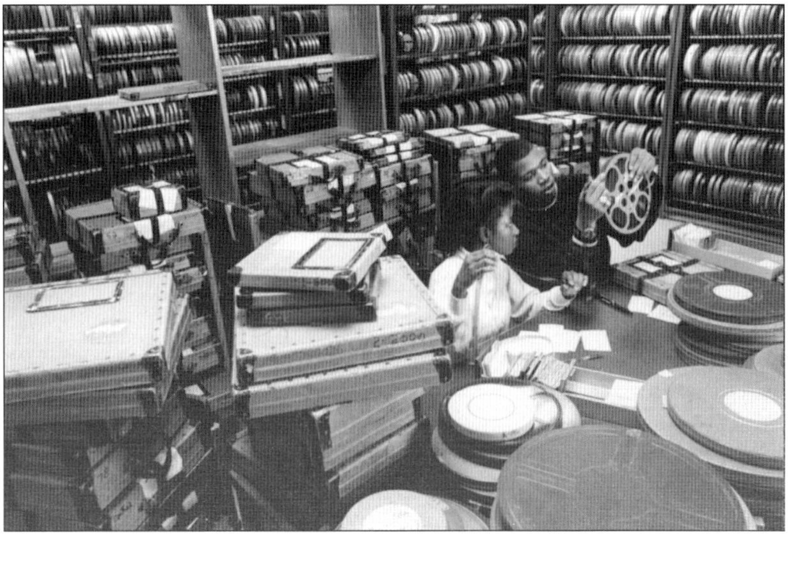

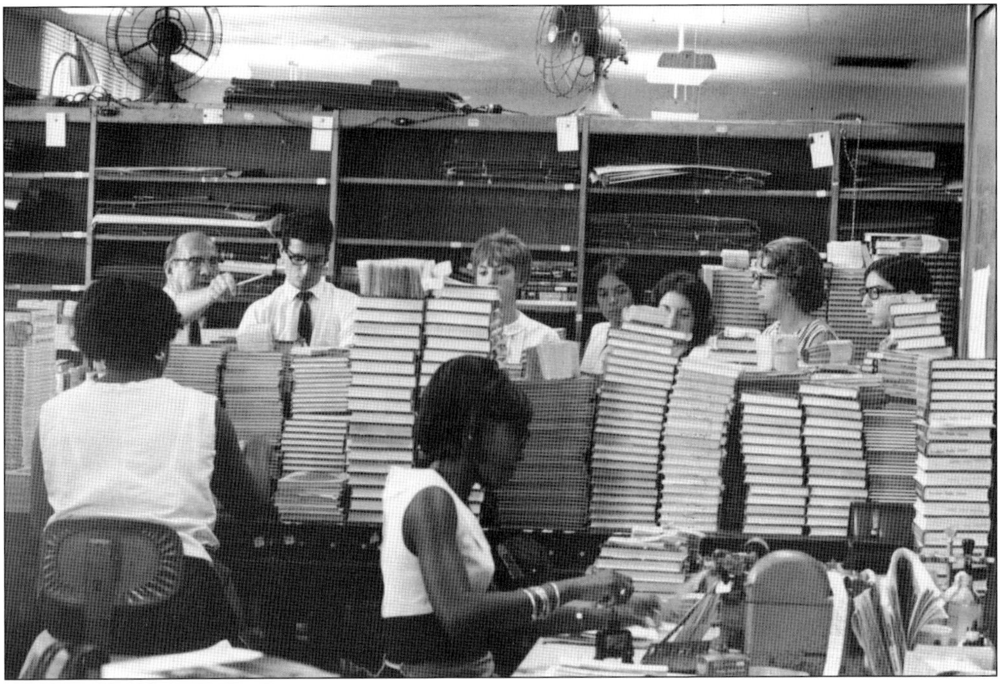

These images, showing technical services center staff at work in 1971, give some sense of the scale of the operation at Central Library. That year, more than 7.5 million books circulated through the branches of the Brooklyn Public Library system, and most of them came through this department at some point in their journey from warehouse to library shelf to patron. Technical services staff also rebound and repaired older books that became damaged through overuse. Repairs could range from mending a ripped page to giving a book a completely new cover and binding.

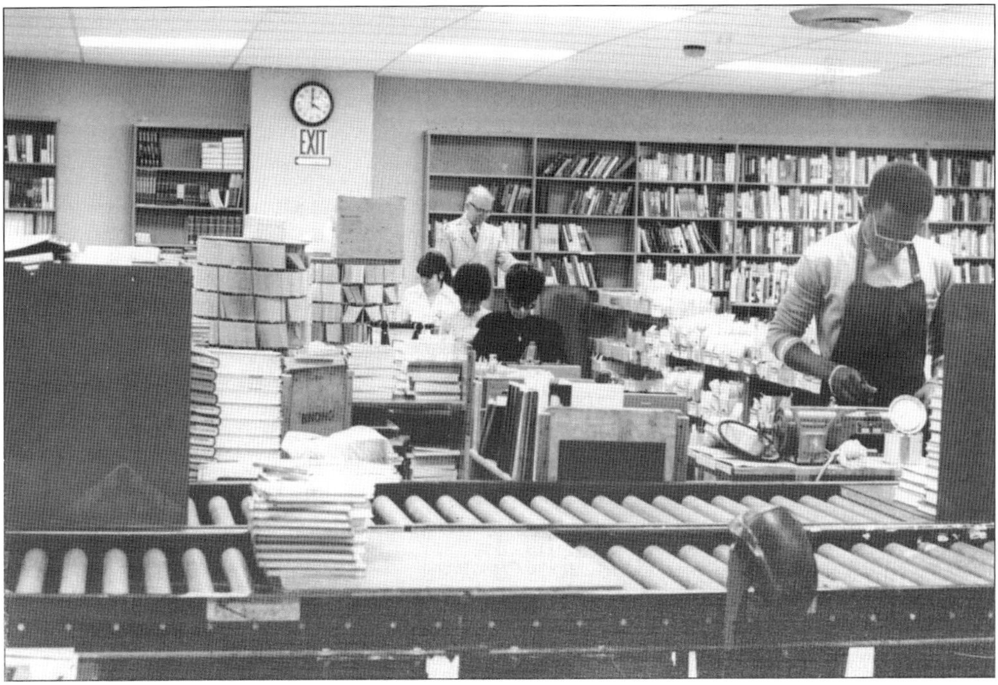

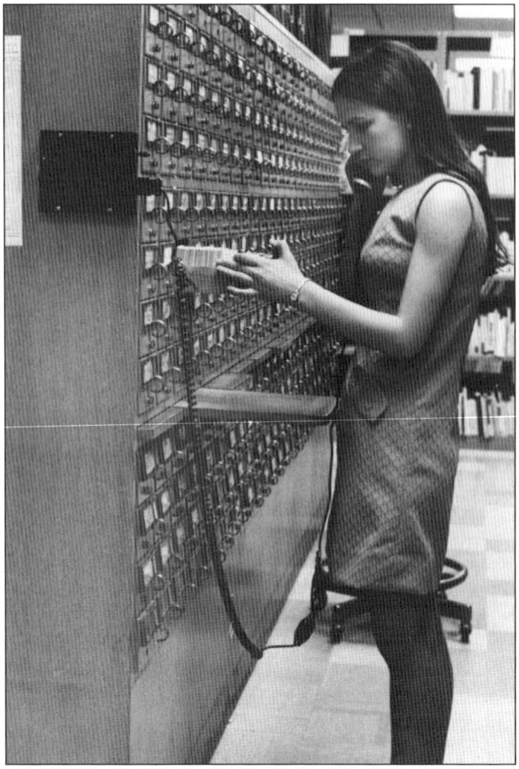

These photographs from 1971 illustrate the book call system that operated in Central Library from its opening. Maintaining the open, airy floor plan of the Grand Lobby and upper floors meant that many of the volumes held by the library had to be stored in subbasements below the building. These "decks," as library staff call them, extend four stories underground and house thousands of books. Librarians would call the book location staff to request specific volumes for patrons; book call staff then found the book in its storage area and ferried it upstairs for the waiting patron. This system is still used today, although book calls are now sent via e-mail directly from the online catalog.

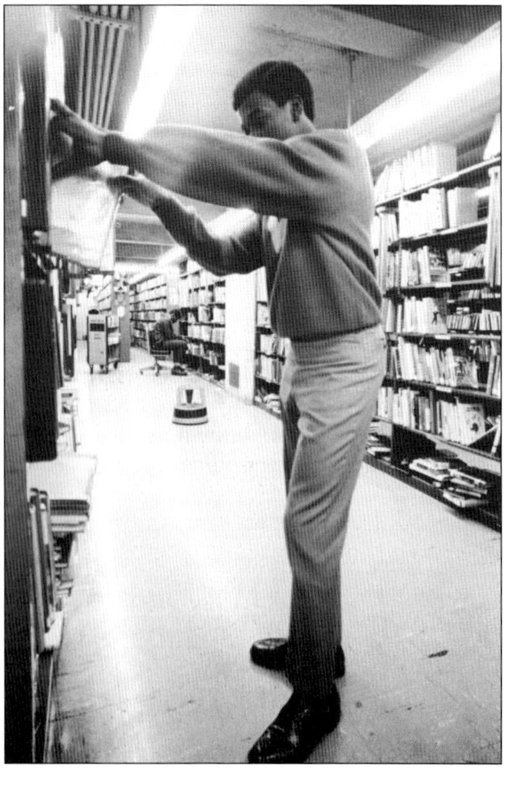

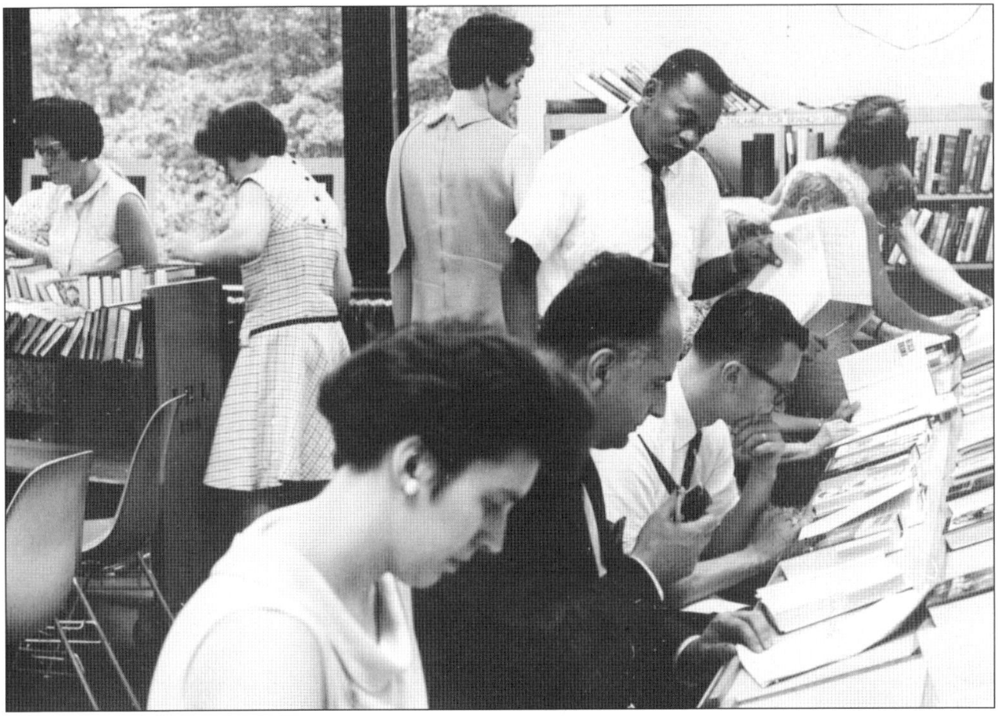

Even though library branches are spread out all over the borough, the selection of new books for these branches was consolidated at Central Library. This photograph from 1967 shows staff working in the third-floor cataloging area, reviewing books for possible inclusion in the library's collections. If a new book was selected as an addition to the library catalog, multiple copies were ordered to meet the demand throughout the borough.

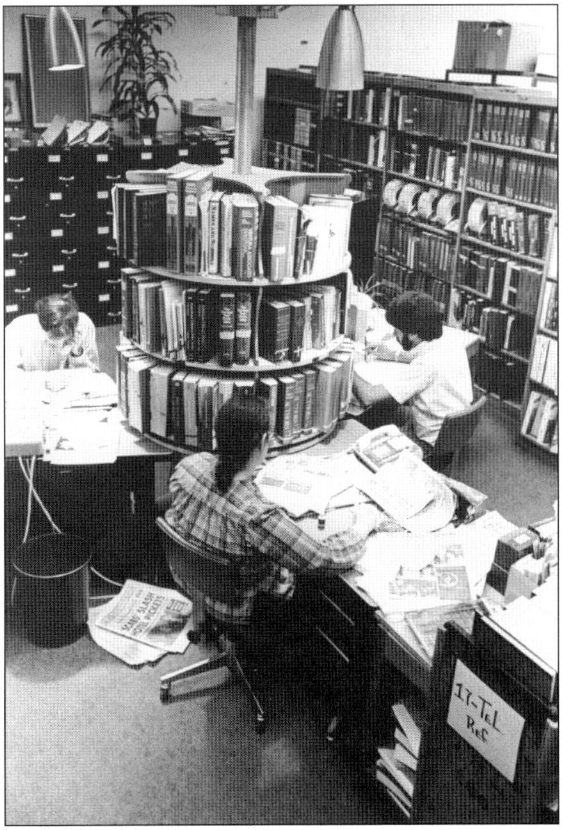

The library's telephone reference staff offered service by phone to those who could not visit a library branch in person. Pictured in their offices on the third floor in 1967, telephone reference staff needed to have a wide array of sources on hand to answer whatever questions came over the phone. Books were kept on a rotating shelf that could be accessed from any desk, making it easier to grab items while staying on the phone line. The library continues to offer telephone reference, along with chat and email reference.

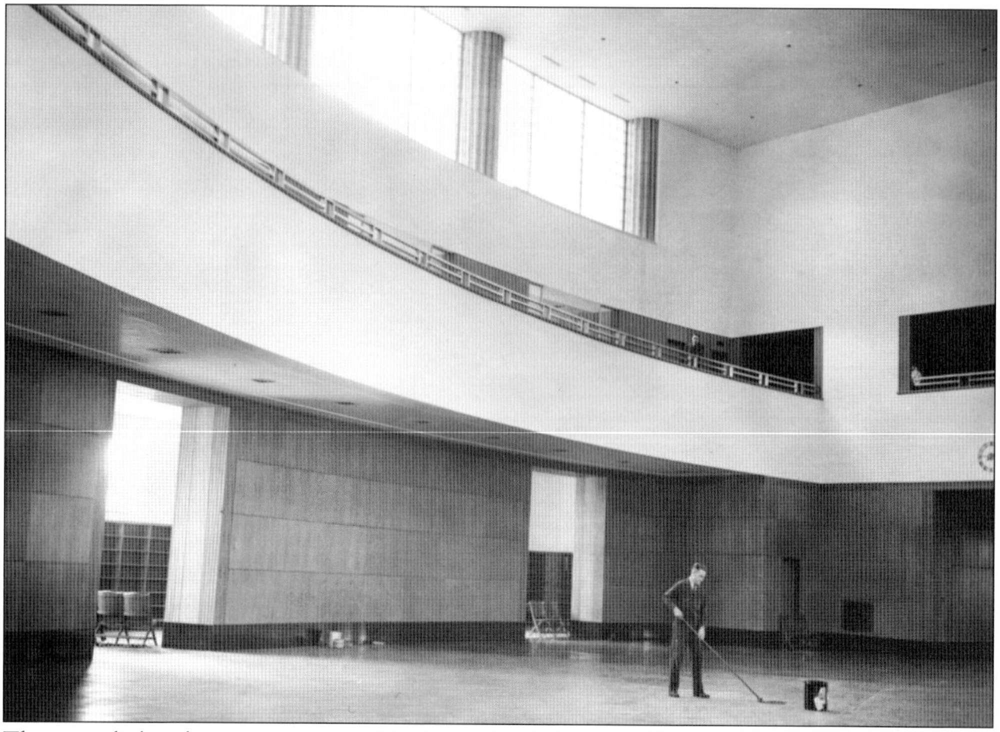

The custodial and maintenance staff is charged with keeping Central Library functioning year-round. In the photograph above, taken shortly before the building opened in 1941, a lone custodian mops the expansive floors of the Grand Lobby. Maintenance crews work in the boiler room in the image below, taken in the 1950s. When the library opened, much was made of its temperature controls; in the 1940s, air-conditioning was still a relatively new luxury in public buildings.

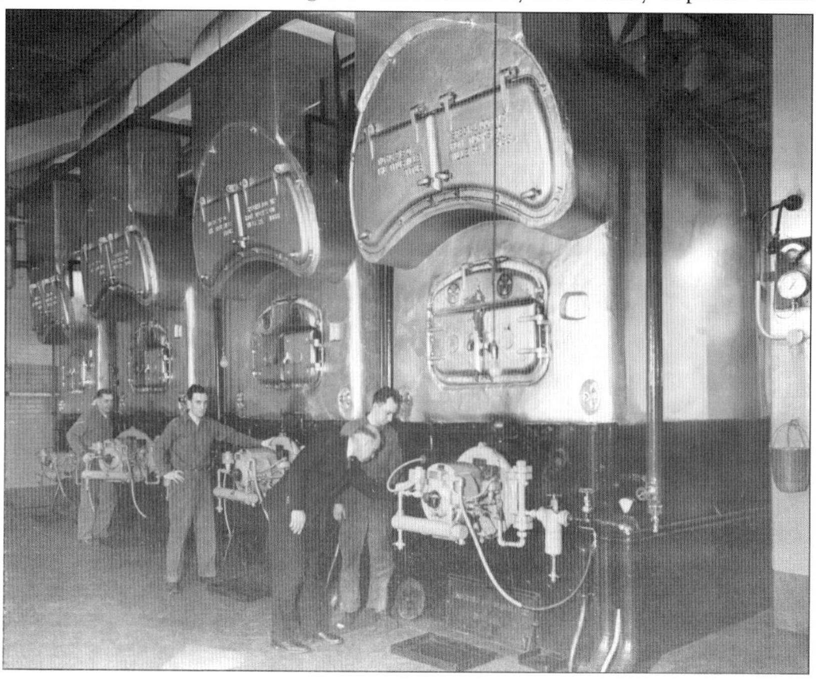

Seven

A World of Readers

Central Library teems with life from the moment it opens to the second it closes because of its huge and active customer base—the people of Brooklyn. Central Library belongs to the 2.5 million residents of the borough, existing to serve their informational and cultural needs. On any given day, thousands enter under its marvelous gilded entryway to access books, databases, technology, cultural programs, films, classes, job resources, and government services.

As the centerpiece of the Brooklyn Public Library system, Central Library has always offered something for every Brooklynite. Toddlers (and their parents) flock to story hours in the Youth Wing, while senior citizens gather for computer classes upstairs. Recent immigrants attend English language workshops, while budding writers present their work at open mic sessions. The large plaza in front has seen a vast array of events through the decades, from dance performances to book fairs to bike rallies. Because all these resources are offered completely free of charge, everyone is welcome at the library regardless of class. For 75 years, Central Library has served as an inspiration and a refuge for anyone who wants to learn.

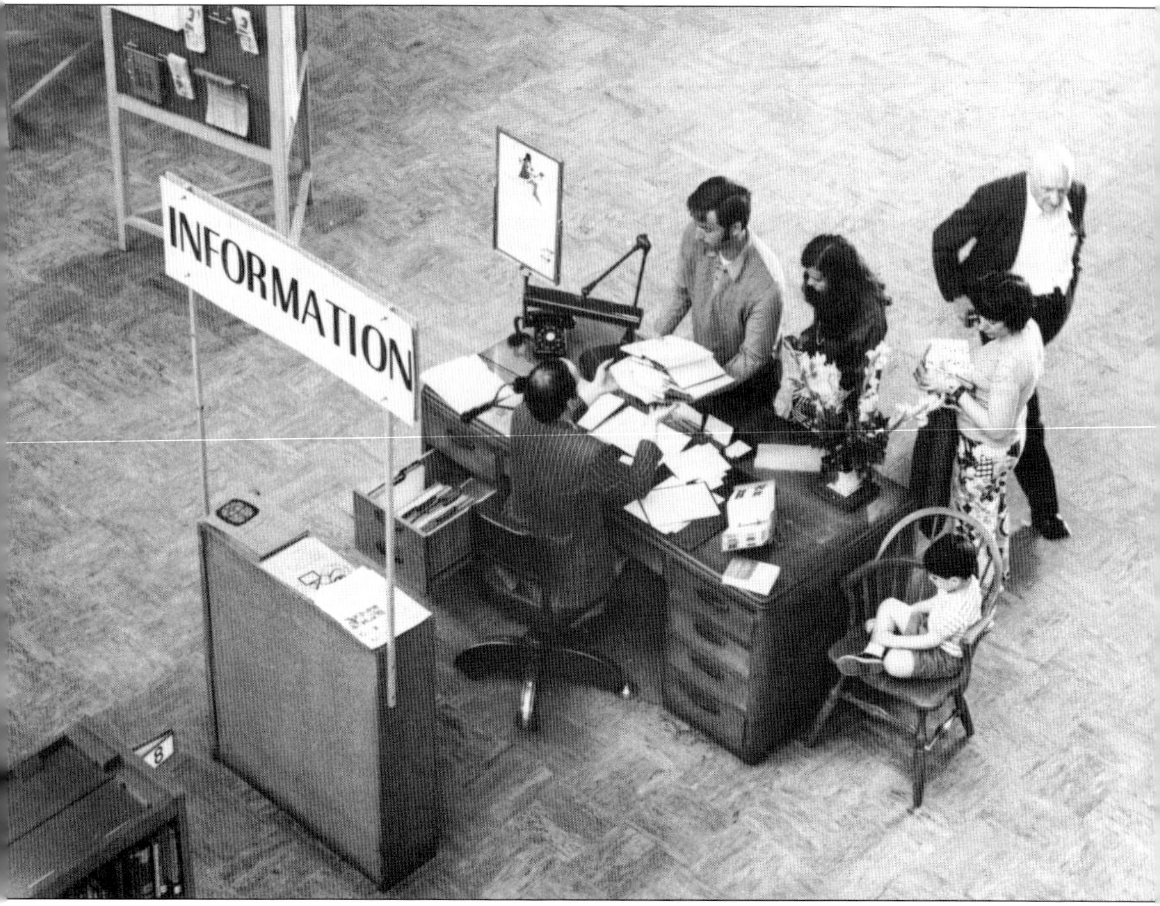

Although the library of today is increasingly accessible online, human interaction has always been a major part of a patron's experience at the library. This image from the 1960s shows patrons in the Grand Lobby at their first point of contact in their search for knowledge—the librarian seated at the information desk.

The library has long been a haven for the autodidact, as patrons are able to seek and find materials on their own in pursuit of their unique interests. The card catalogs that once filled the lobby of Central Library allowed self-motivated patrons to look up books themselves before heading to the shelves to pull materials, as seen in this photograph from 1978.

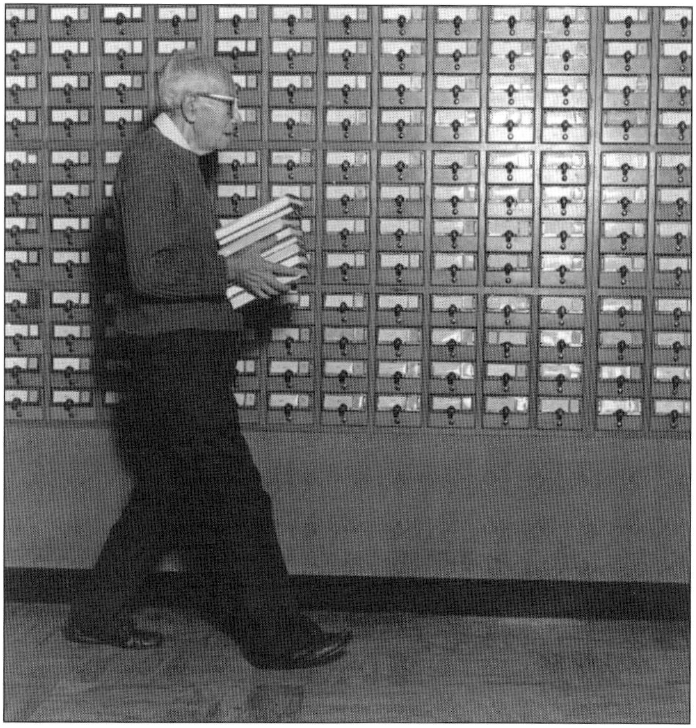

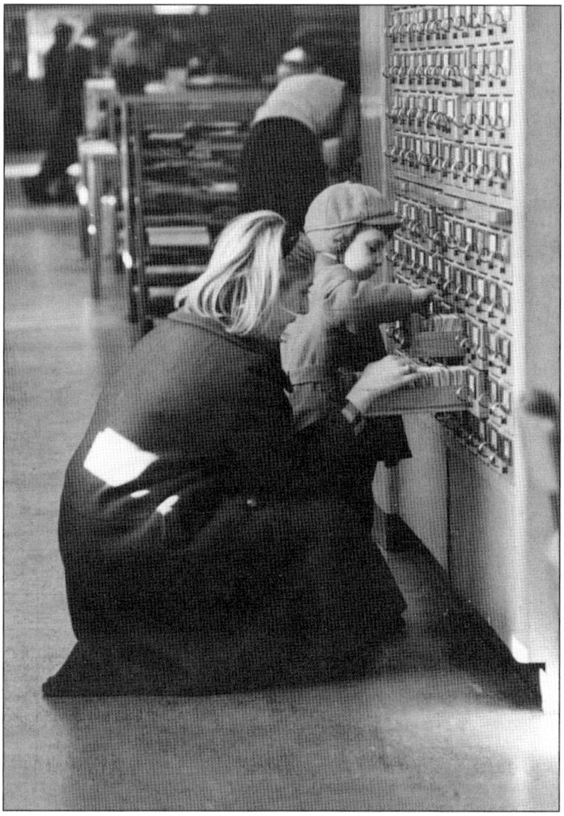

Learning how to use a card catalog and the Dewey decimal system was an essential part of accessing resources in the library. In this 1967 photograph, a toddler picks up some of the fundamentals of cross-indexing in one of Central Library's card catalogs. Today, more user-friendly digital catalogs allow searching by keyword to assist in discovery of resources.

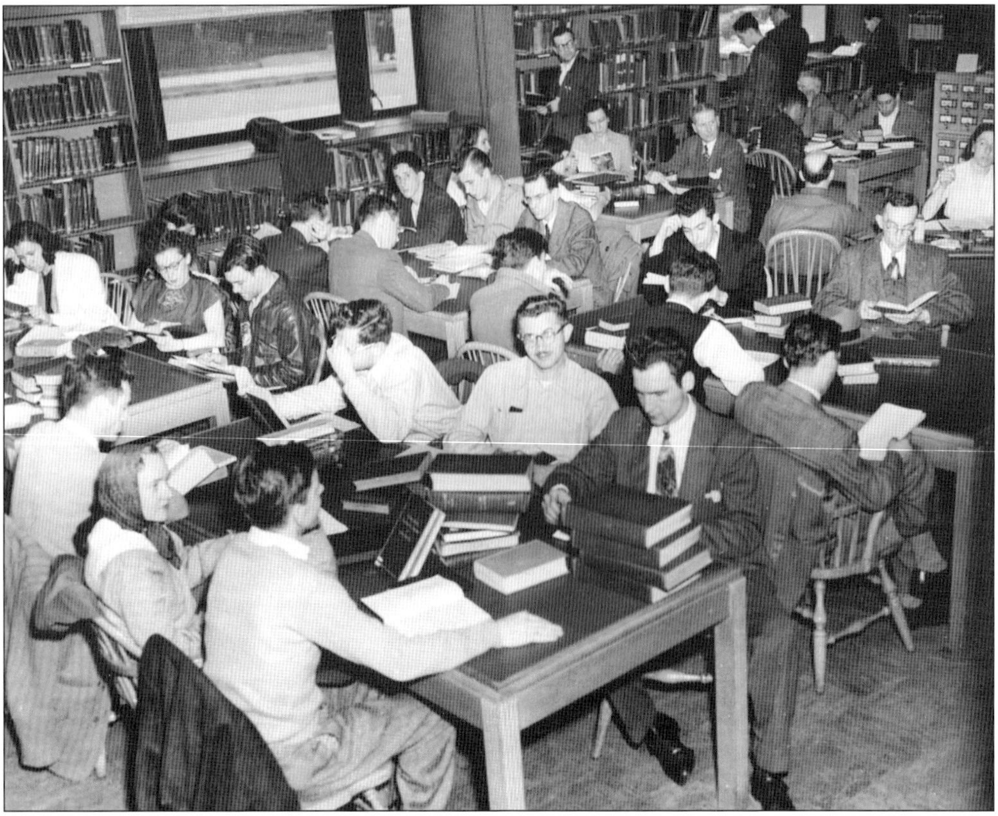

Patrons thronged the library's reading rooms, carving out private space for study amid crowds of like-minded readers. The image above, likely from the 1950s, shows college students making use of the Languages and Literature Division on the ground floor of the Flatbush Avenue wing. A note written by a library staffer on the back reads, "Question: does the public use our services?" The image below, taken roughly 25 years later, shows a mostly unchanged scene with crowded library tables of studious patrons poring over books and periodicals.

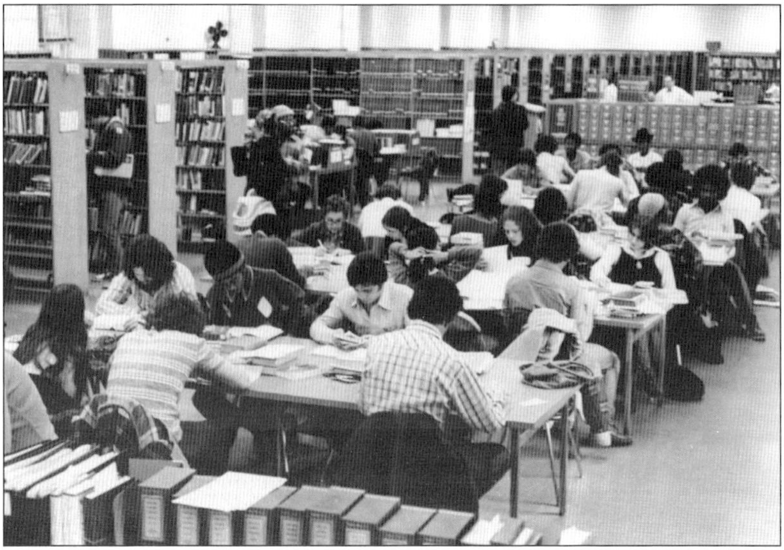

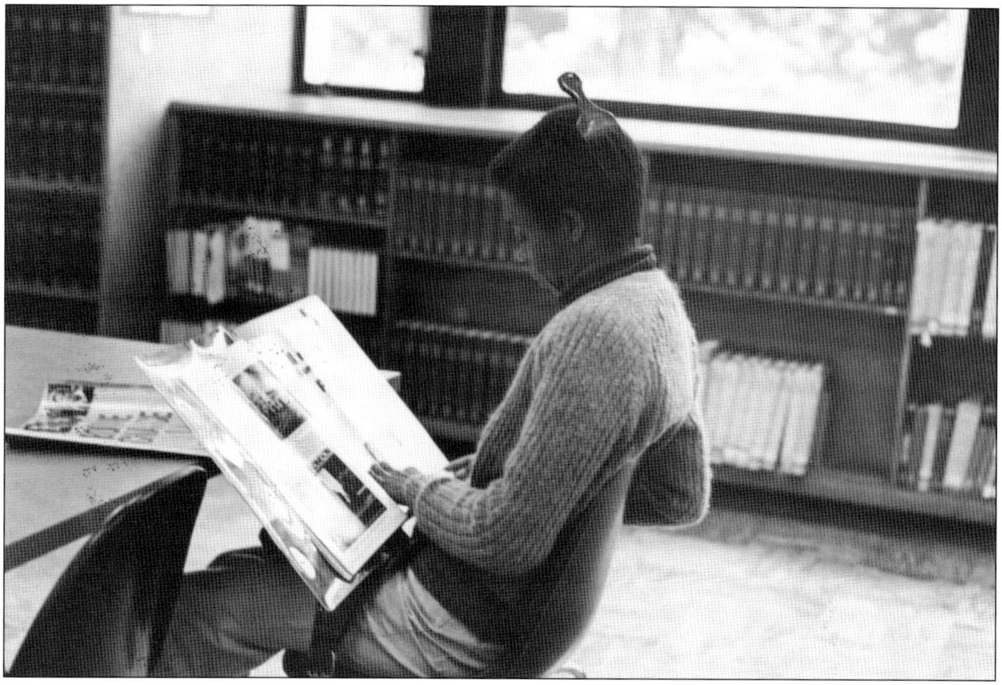

For many, the library is simply a quiet space where one can sit and read without distraction. Central Library continues to collect daily newspapers as well as weekly and monthly magazines in its Popular Library for casual readers.

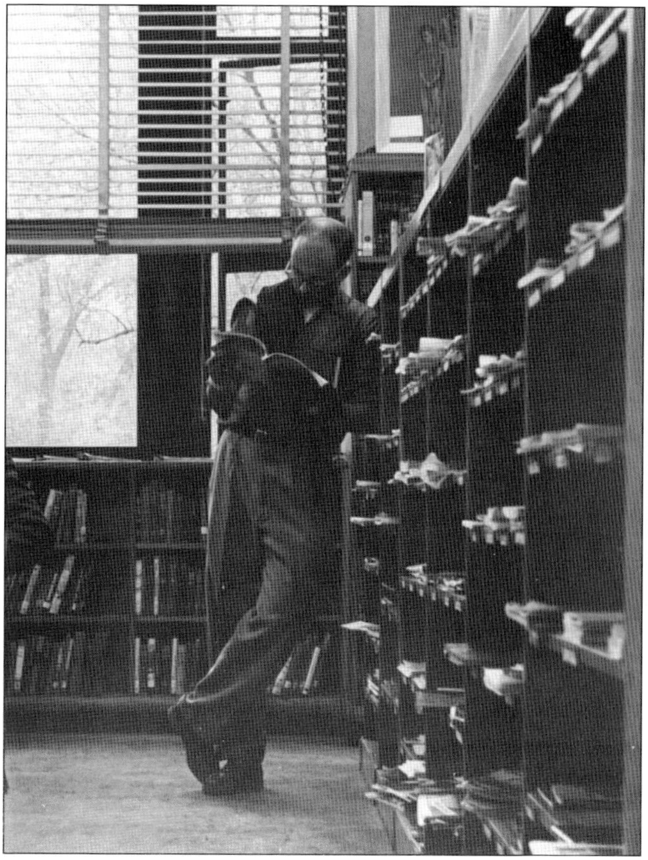

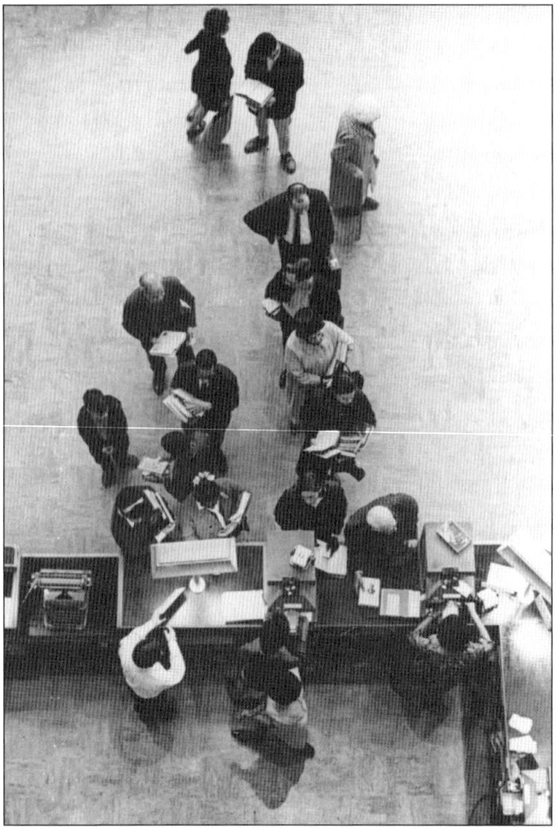

Even though the layout inside Central Library has changed dramatically over the years, with subject divisions closing in one wing and reopening in another, the circulation desks have been a stalwart of the Grand Lobby. This is where patrons present their library cards to borrow items to take home. The undated photograph on the left gives an aerial view of this transaction. The photograph below shows a particularly long checkout line during the holiday rush in 1969. The photocharge machines used in both images have since become obsolete.

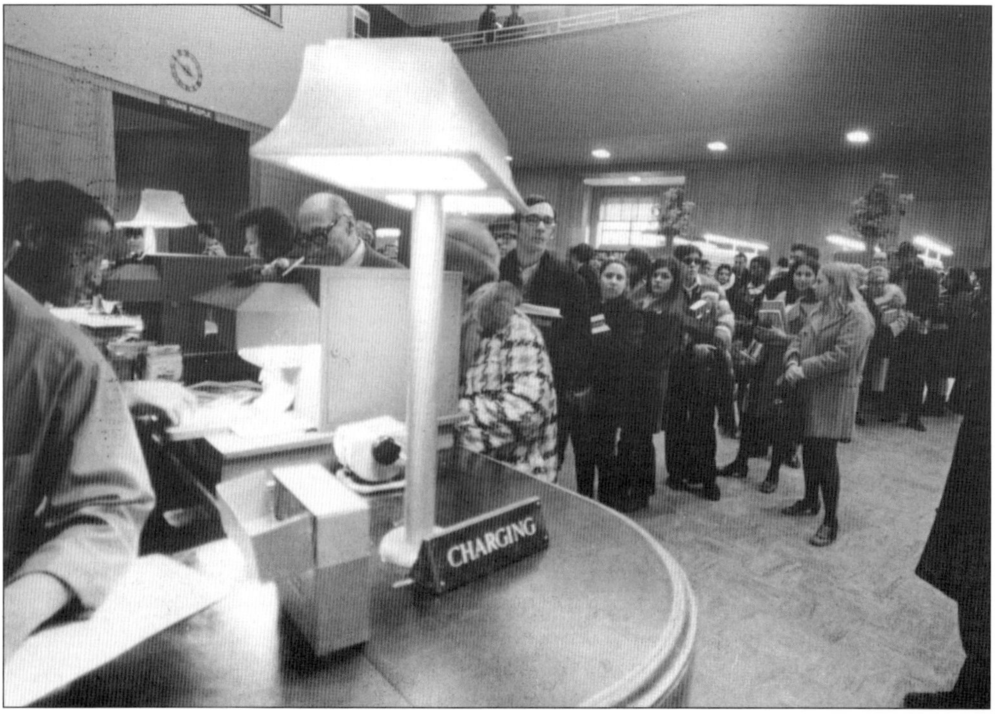

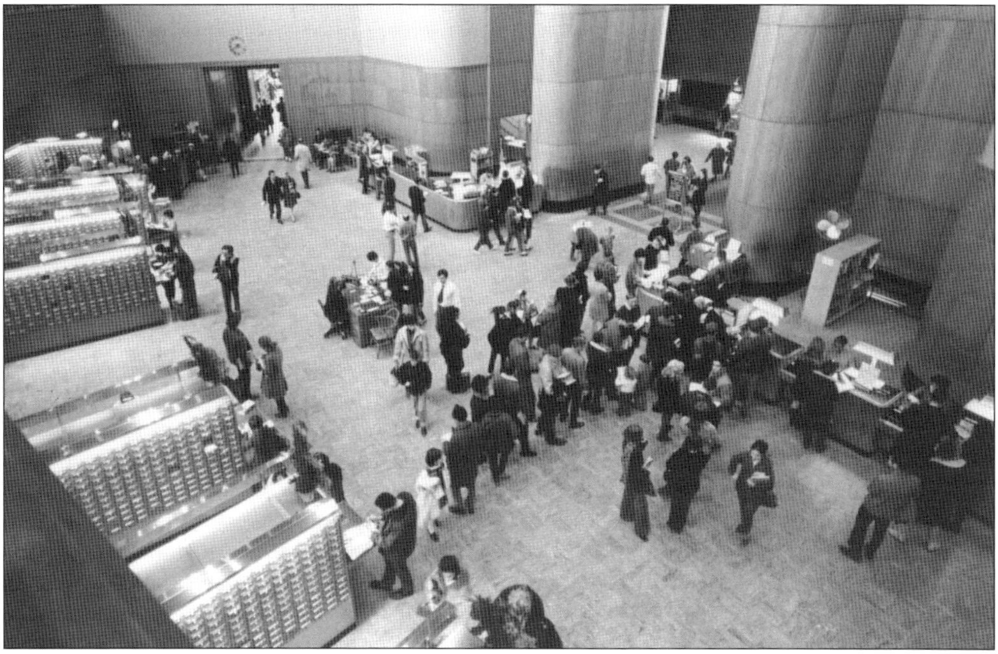

During rush times, Central Library's lobby can look more like a bustling train station than a sedate temple of knowledge. These images from the 1960s show long lines snaking through the lobby area as patrons wait to check out materials. The lines are understandable; in 1960, more than one million items were checked out at this library alone. Self-checkout kiosks have since helped to alleviate these waits. The card catalogs no longer fill the library; in their place are photography and artwork exhibits, as well as café seating.

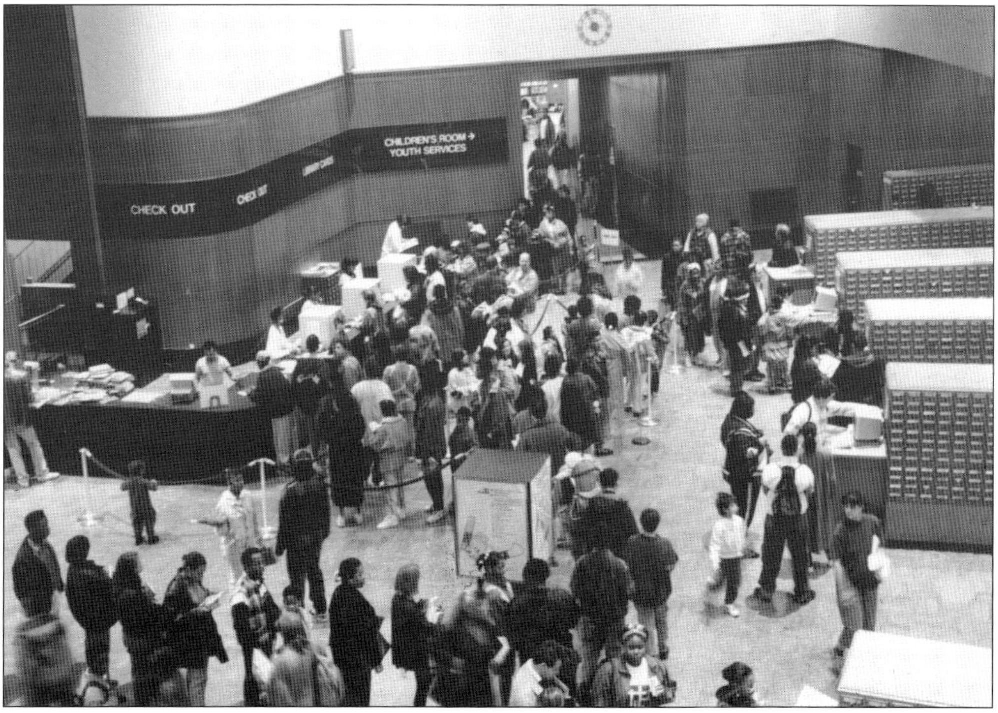

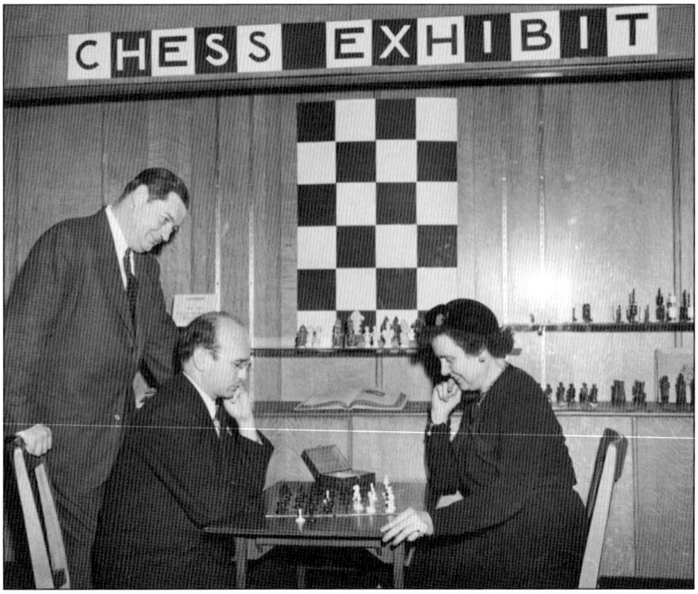

Central Library is not just a place for books, however. Patrons also visit the library to take in arts and culture exhibits. For an exhibit on the history of chess in 1954, the library hosted Samuel Reshevsky (left), pictured here playing chess, with chief librarian Francis St. John looking over his shoulder. By the time this photograph was taken, Reshevsky had won the US Chess Championship six times and had come in second at the World Chess Championships in 1948.

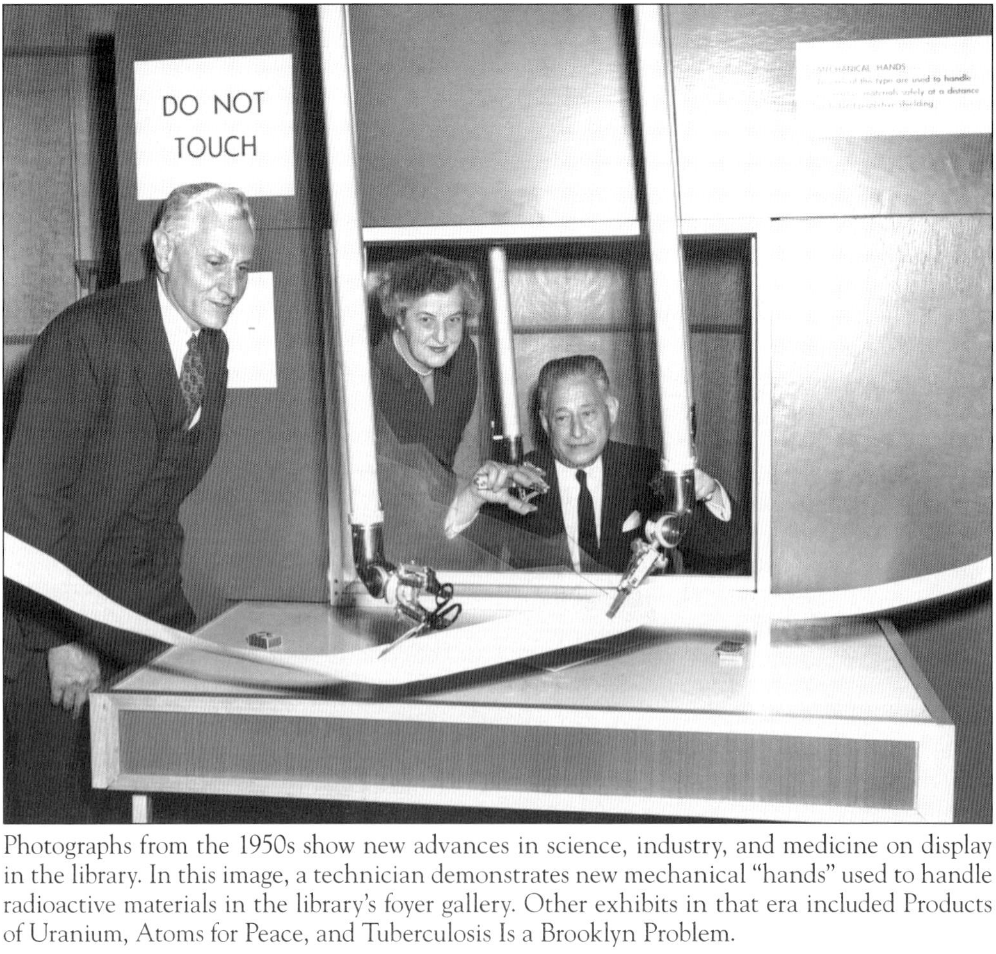

Photographs from the 1950s show new advances in science, industry, and medicine on display in the library. In this image, a technician demonstrates new mechanical "hands" used to handle radioactive materials in the library's foyer gallery. Other exhibits in that era included Products of Uranium, Atoms for Peace, and Tuberculosis Is a Brooklyn Problem.

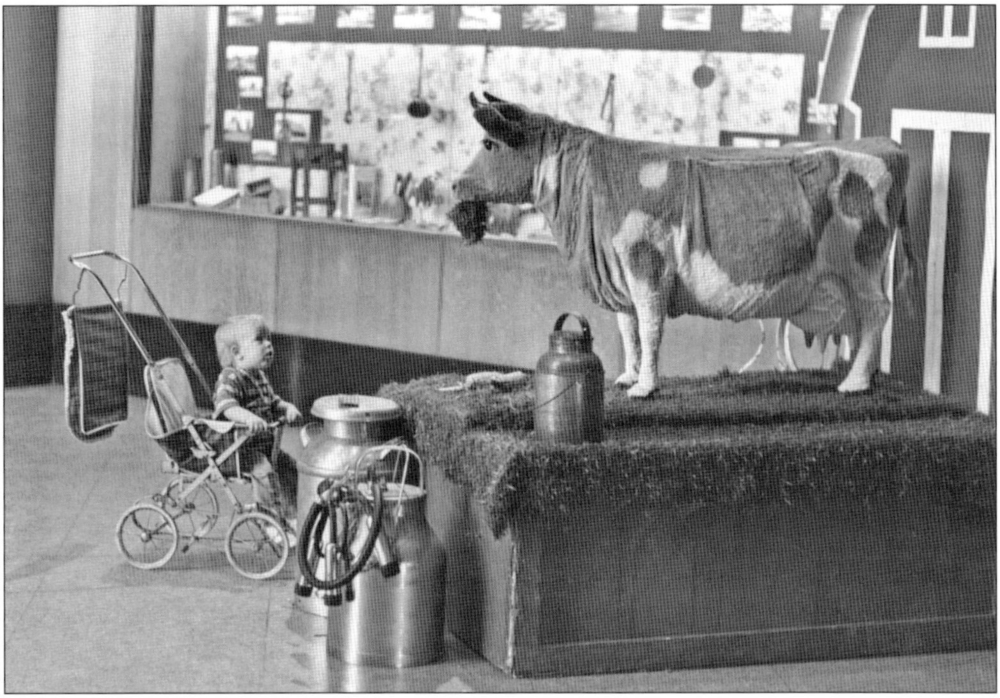

This image shows a toddler transfixed by a Dairy Month exhibit in 1968. Although old photographs show the library's spaces hosting dioramas or promotional exhibits, these cases are now dedicated to displaying work from local artists as well as pieces from the library's archives.

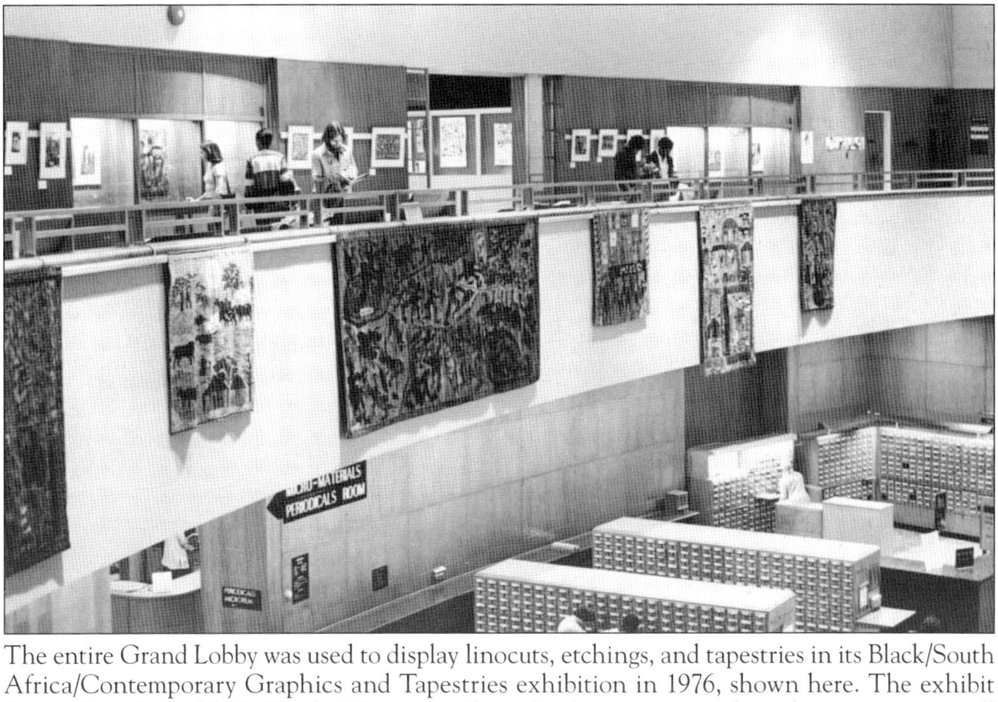

The entire Grand Lobby was used to display linocuts, etchings, and tapestries in its Black/South Africa/Contemporary Graphics and Tapestries exhibition in 1976, shown here. The exhibit featured works by black South Africans exclusively, during a time when that nation was still segregated under apartheid.

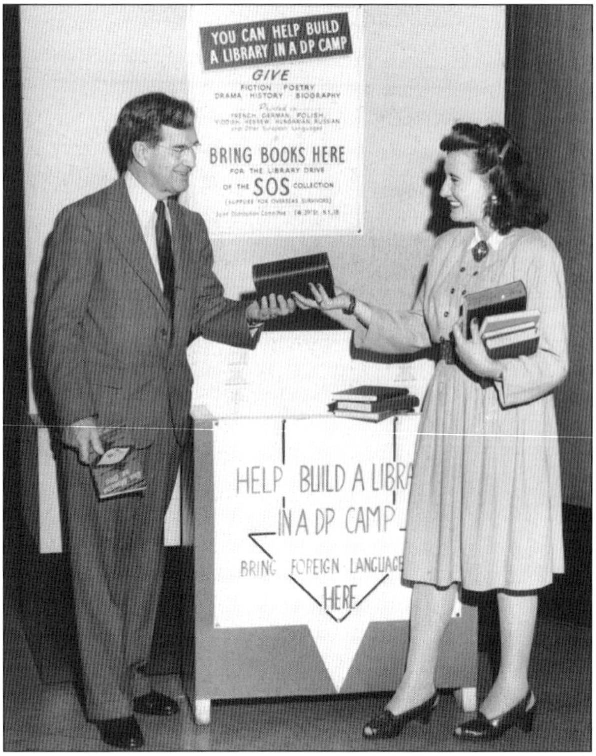

Central Library has long been a participatory space for patrons, a place where users can give something back to their community. During the Korean War, the library served as a drop-off location for those who wanted to donate books to displaced persons (DPs) living in camps overseas. This image shows chief librarian Milton Ferguson accepting a donation from a patron under a sign that reads, "You can help build a library in a DP camp."

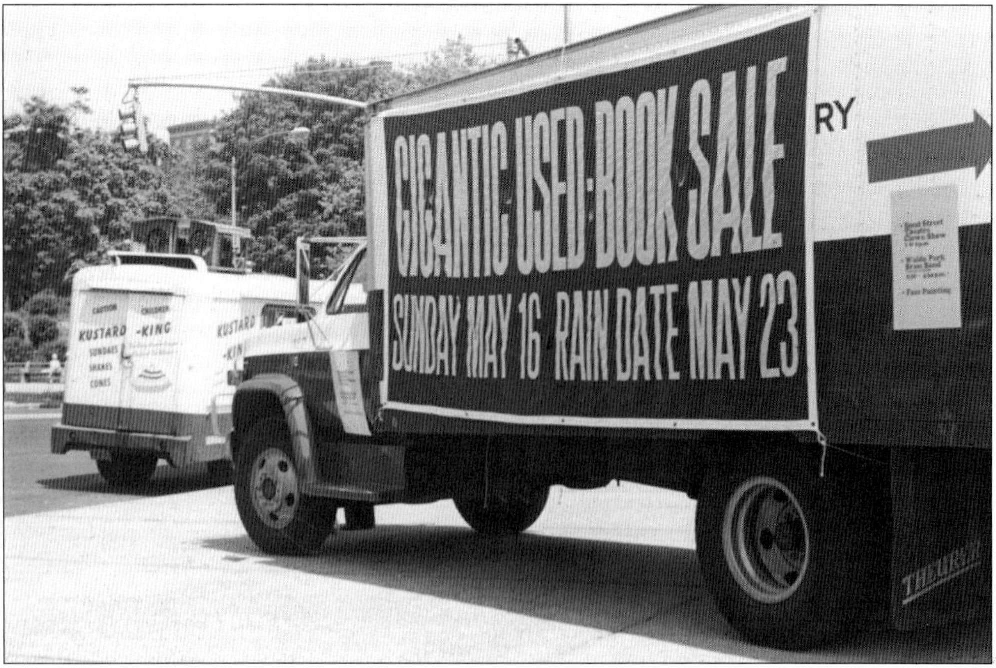

Book drives have since become an annual event at the library. In 1982, when this photograph was taken, the library held two "Books-by-the-Pound" sales, offering donated and discarded books for sale to the public. With its budget diminishing from the 1970s into the 1980s, the library used these events to raise funds to purchase new books.

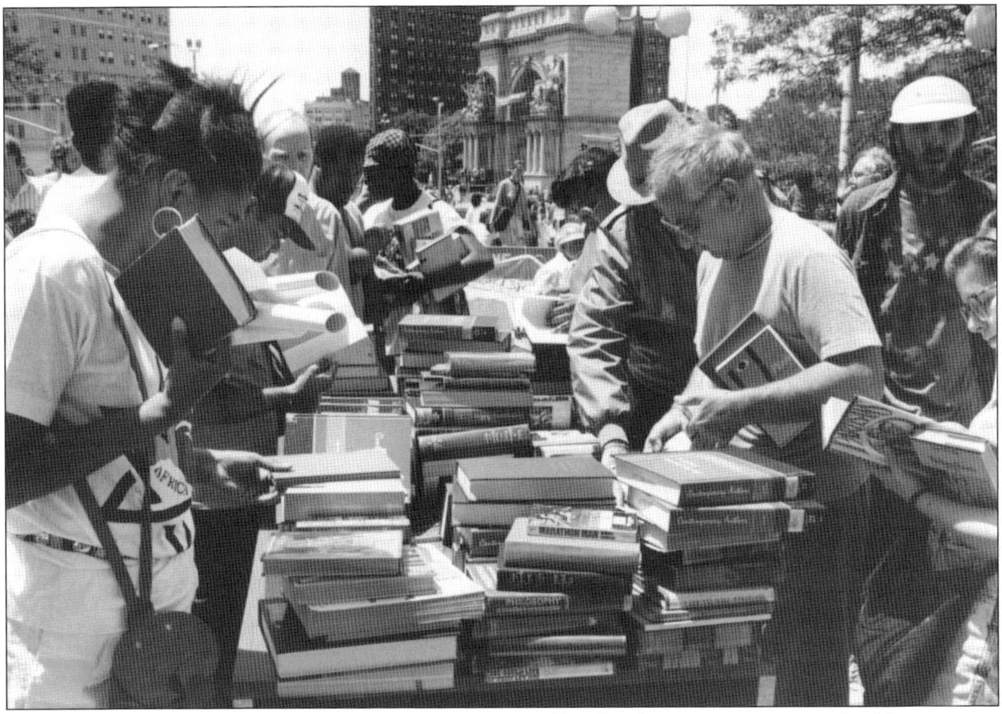

In addition to raising much-needed funds, the biannual book sales were community-building events. People from all over Brooklyn (and of all ages) came out to browse titles and commiserate in the open-air market on Central Library's plaza. These public events also helped the library develop advocates for its cause among the people of Brooklyn, who could petition their representatives in local government for more library funding. Notables from the literary world also lent aid; in 1982, Arthur Miller, Isaac B. Singer, and Norman Mailer all spoke in support of Brooklyn Public Library.

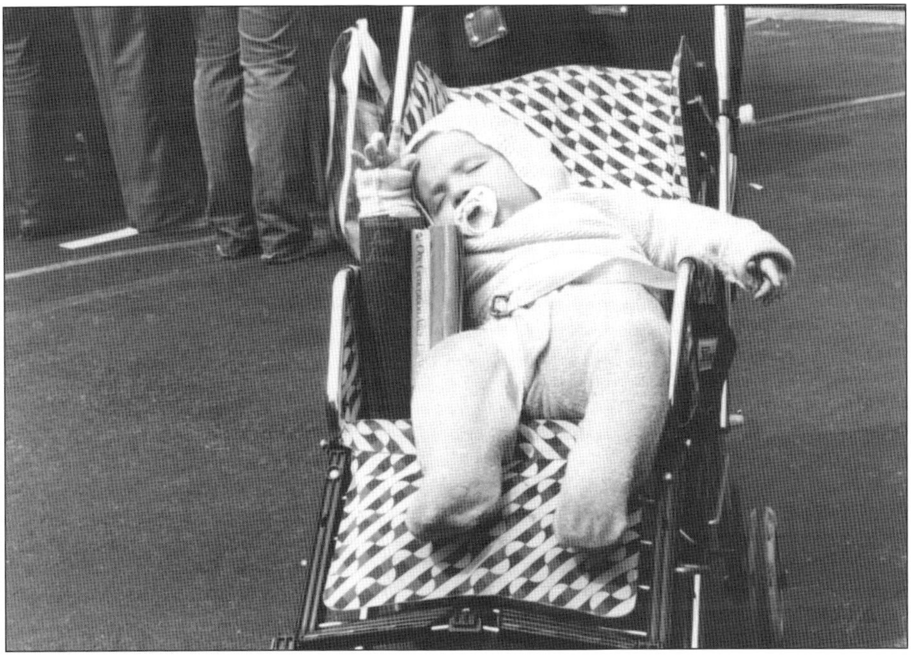

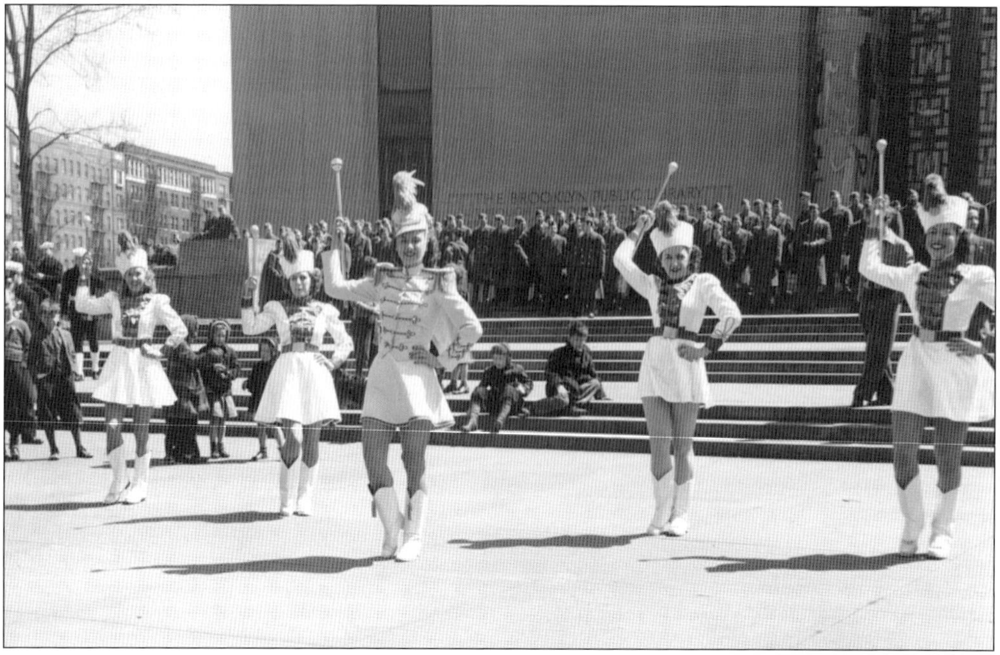

As a hub of Brooklyn's many communities, Central Library is also a place of civic celebration. The image above shows majorettes twirling batons on the steps of the plaza in front of the building's impressive entryway. This scene is likely from a Memorial Day parade, which annually marched down Eastern Parkway to the Soldiers and Sailors Memorial Arch. The image below shows holiday carolers from Public School No. 59 serenading patrons and staff in Central Library's Grand Lobby.

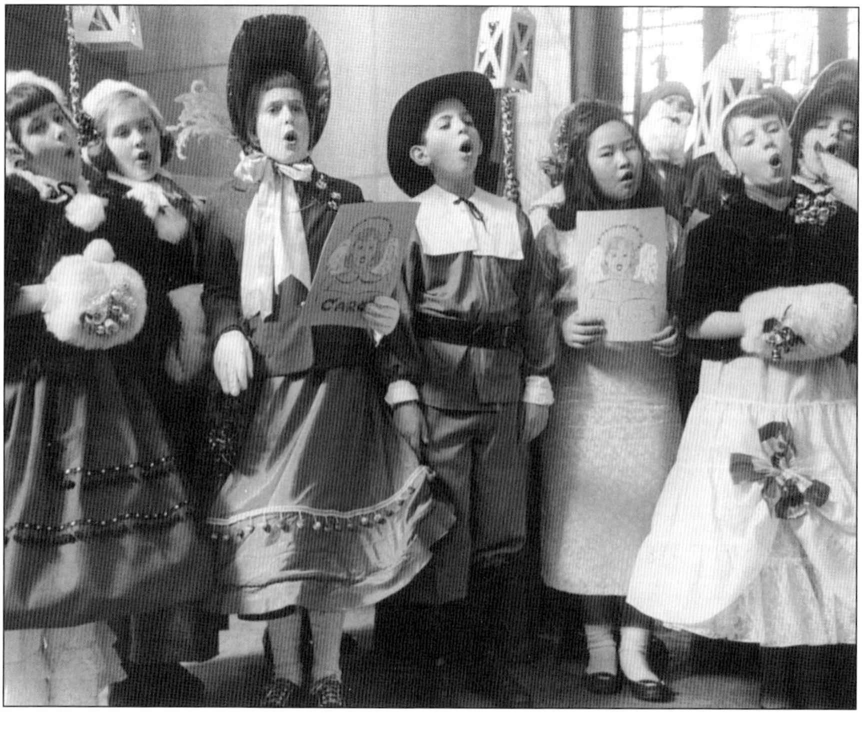

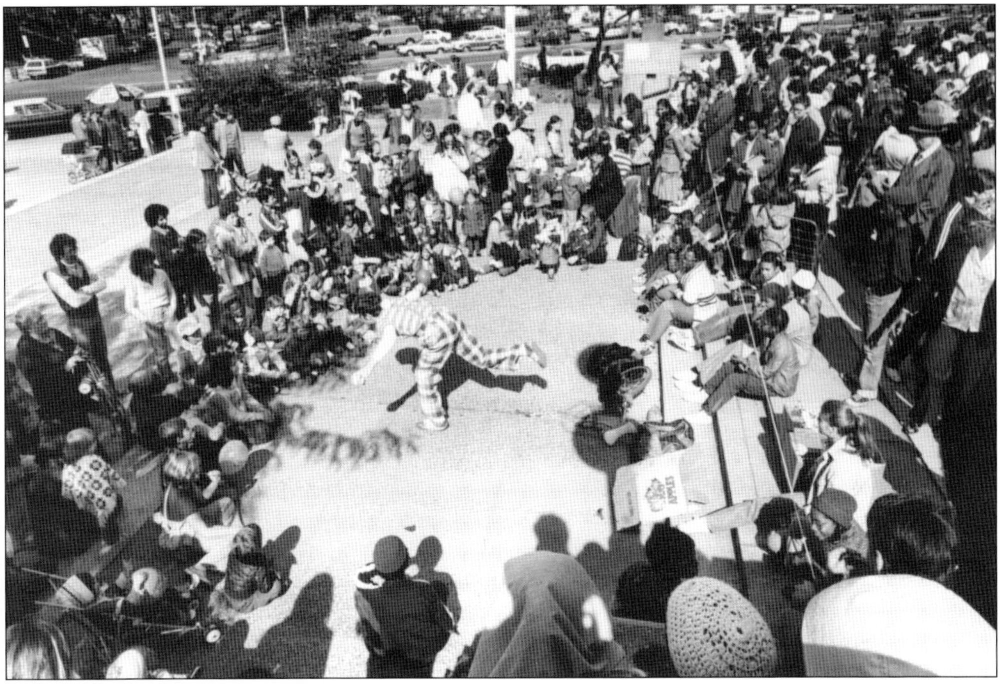

Patrons have long been drawn to the plaza itself as a public gathering space. Wide and flat, it allows for large performances like the 1981 clown act pictured above, as well as annual book sales, music concerts, and dance events. The low steps also make excellent seating after a long day, as seen in the picture from 1971 below. Today, the plaza also offers tables with umbrellas during warm months, as well as 24-hour free Wi-Fi access.

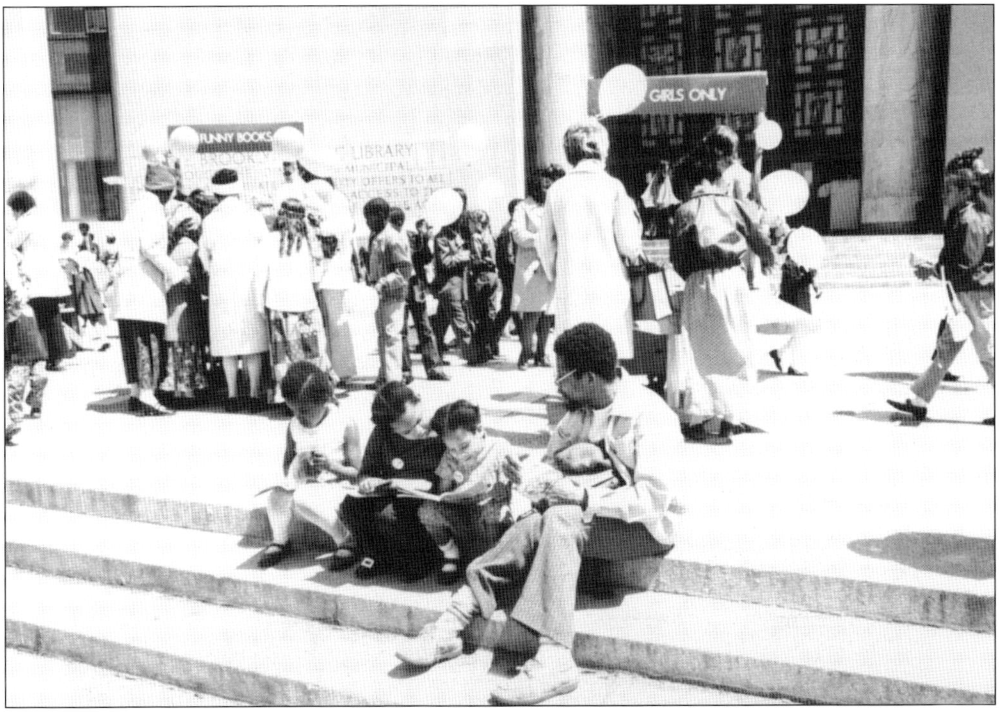

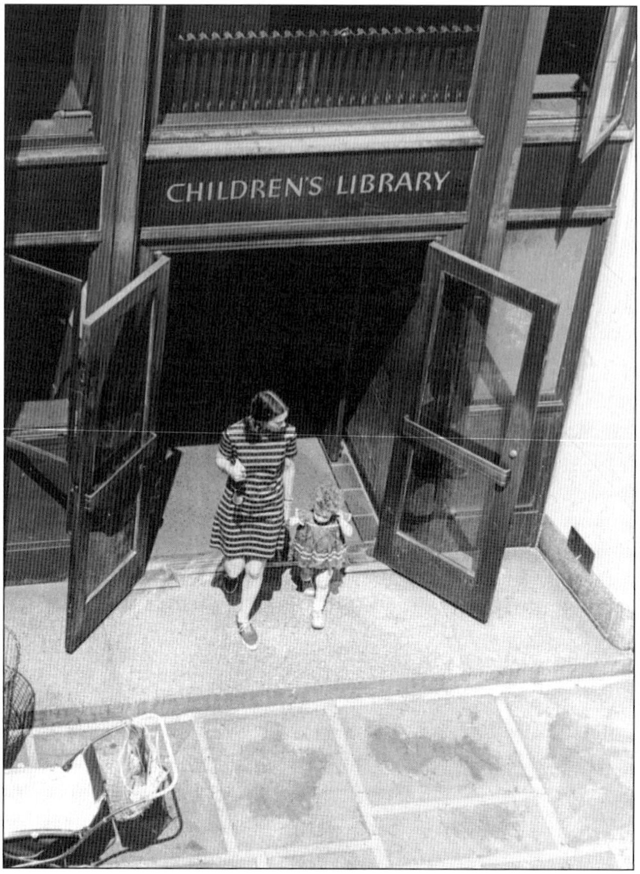

As noted before, in the library's early years, children were not allowed to roam the entirety of Central Library but were restricted to their own wing on Eastern Parkway. Known as the Children's Library, this room had its own entrance onto the parkway. There is no longer a wall between the children's and adult portions of the library, but the entrance, pictured here in 1967, is still heavily used.

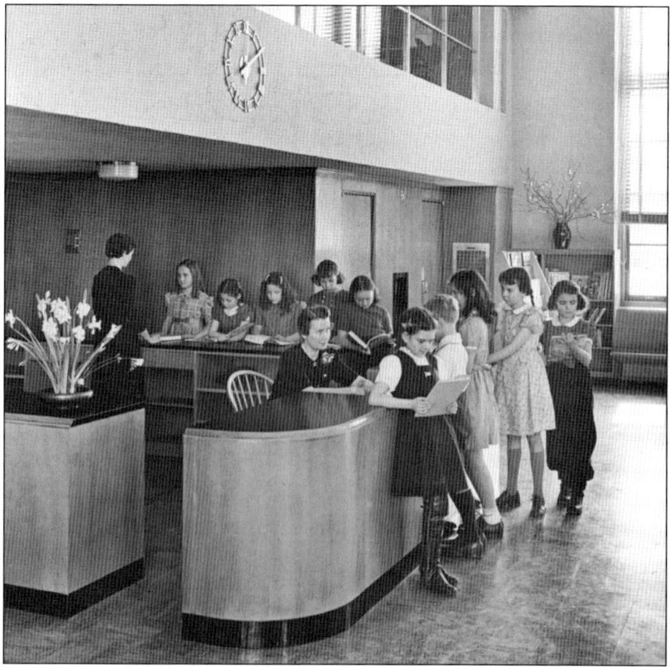

Because it was a separate unit from the rest of the library, the Children's Room of course needed its own librarians, clerical workers, and checkout desk, as pictured here in the 1950s. The room above the desk was and continues to be used for children's and young adult programs.

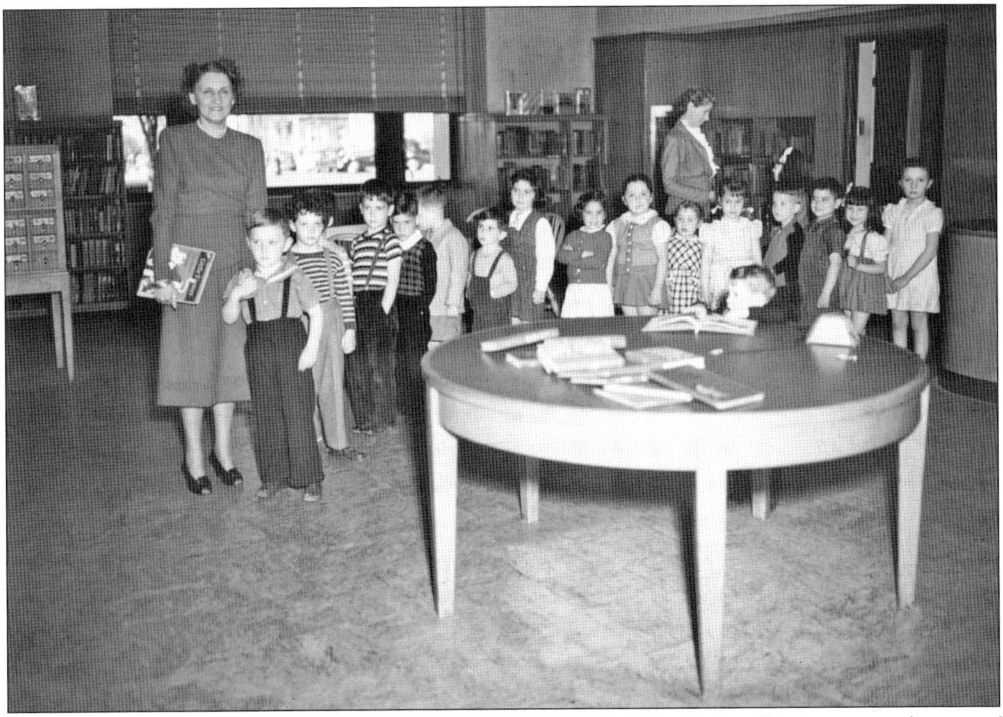

The library has always fostered partnerships with local schools to instill curiosity and a joy of reading in young Brooklynites, and students from all over the borough visit Central Library with their teachers every day. In these photographs, students are introduced to library resources during a class visit. Below, students use special viewers to look at historic stereoscopic images. The 1953 annual report gloated, "Class visits continue to justify themselves; the more children read good books, the less they read comics." Such tours are still conducted today, to show students how they can do research and pursue their interests (even comic books) in the library.

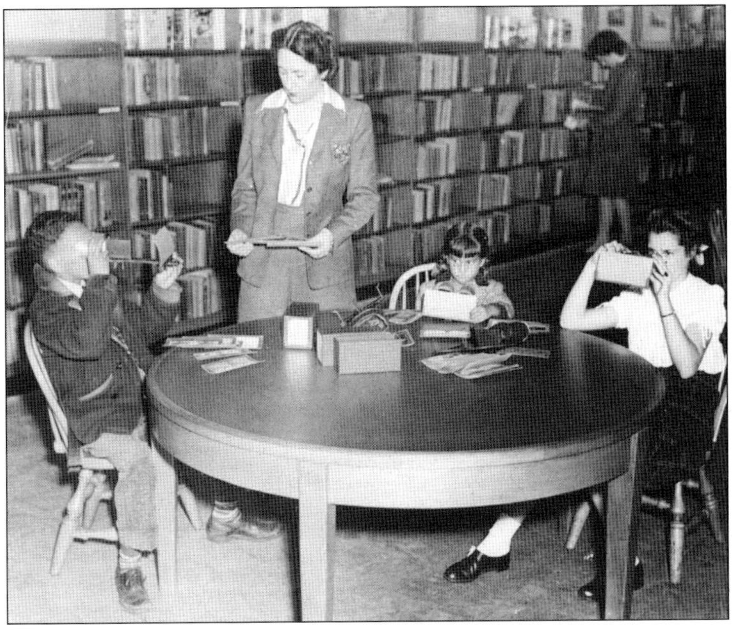

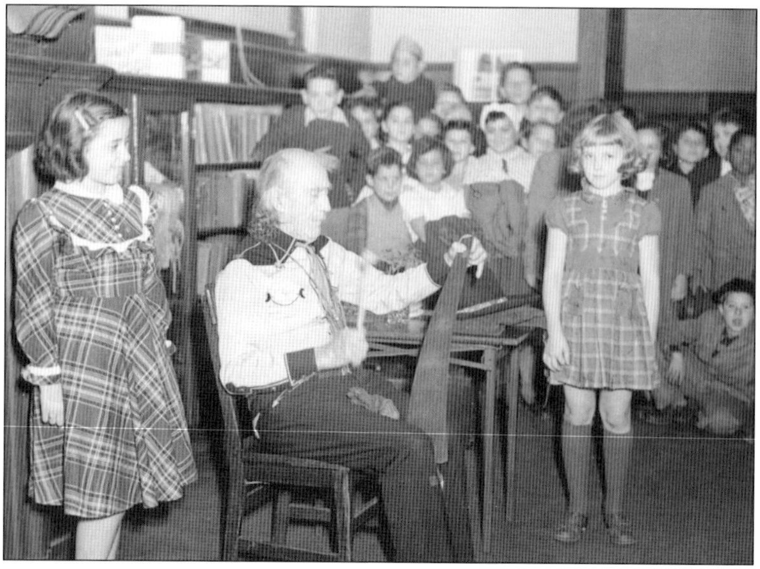

Central Library's Children's Room on Eastern Parkway was, and is, a site for play as well as for study. Magicians, jugglers, puppeteers, storytellers, and musicians have performed for Brooklyn youth in this wing of the building since it first opened in 1941. Here, a musician plays a musical saw, likely in the 1950s.

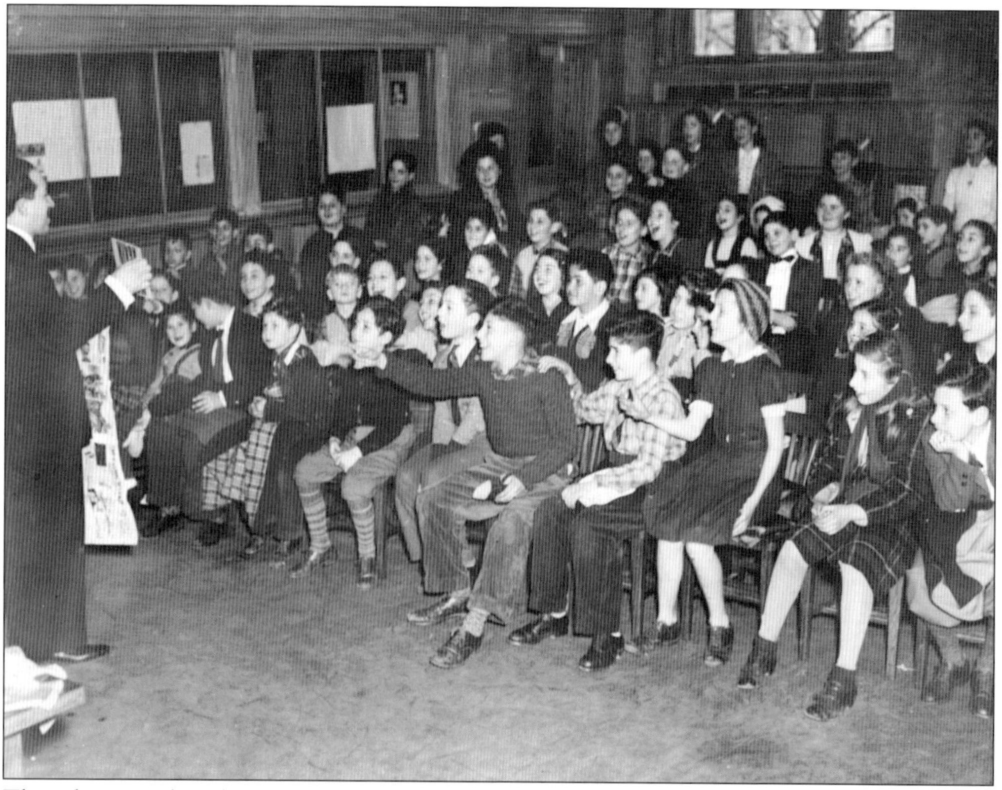

This photograph, taken in the Children's Library and likely from the 1950s, shows a lively performance from the magician Zovell. The caption reads, "Magic show in library teaches children how to use leisure hours to advantage."

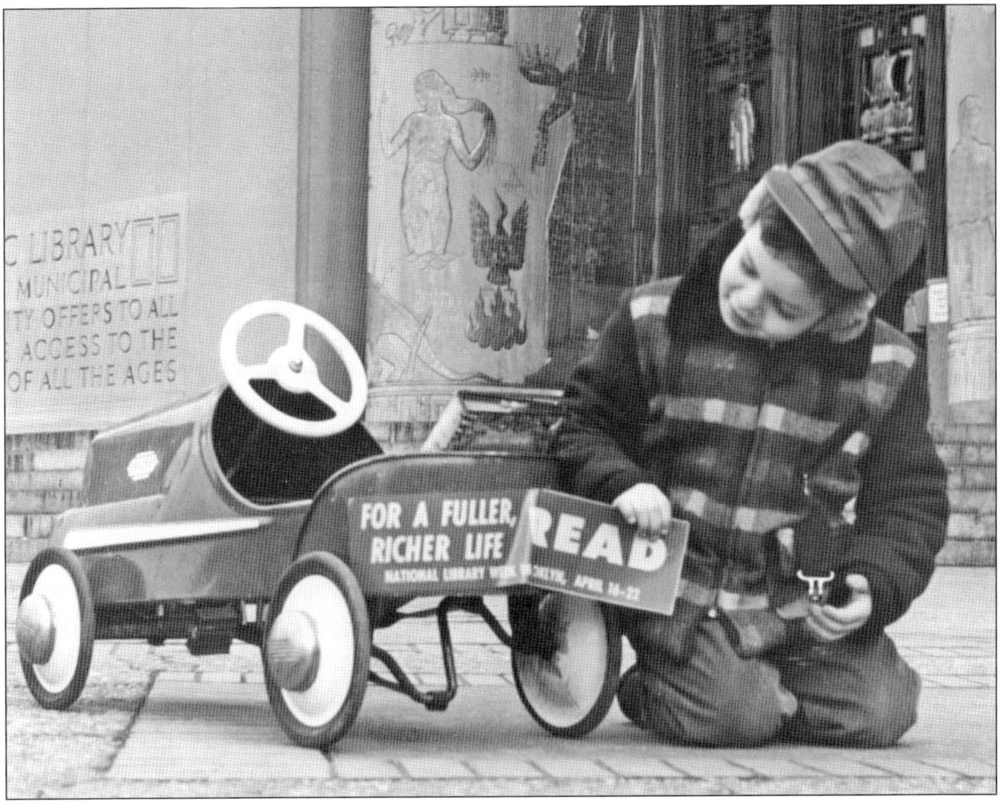

The American Library Association created National Library Week in 1958 to celebrate and promote libraries throughout the country. This photograph, taken in front of Central Library's iconic gate and pylons to promote National Library Week in 1961, shows a boy and his toy car with a bumper sticker reading, "For a fuller, richer life, READ."

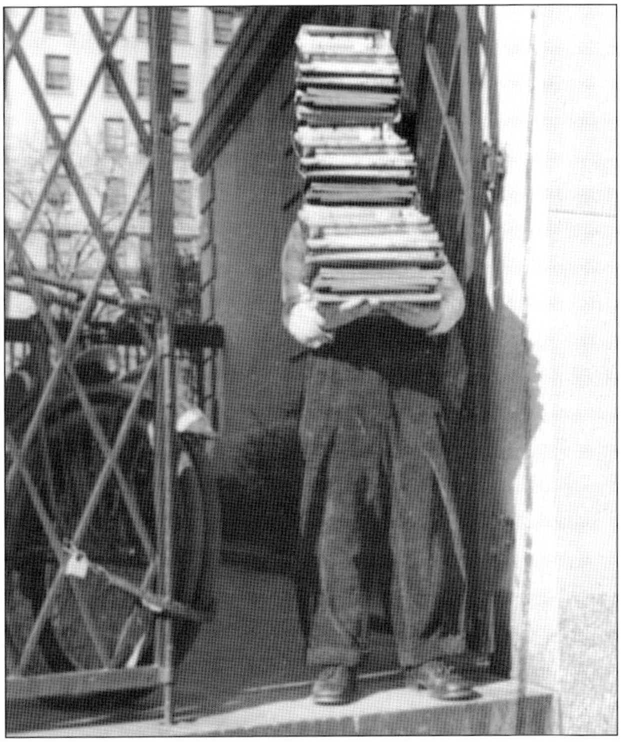

In 1953, roughly when this image was taken, the Children's Room circulated 178,000 books to young readers. A child stands at the gate that once led to a rose garden behind the library, with street access to Flatbush Avenue. Today, that gate is locked, and the area serves as a parking lot and loading dock.

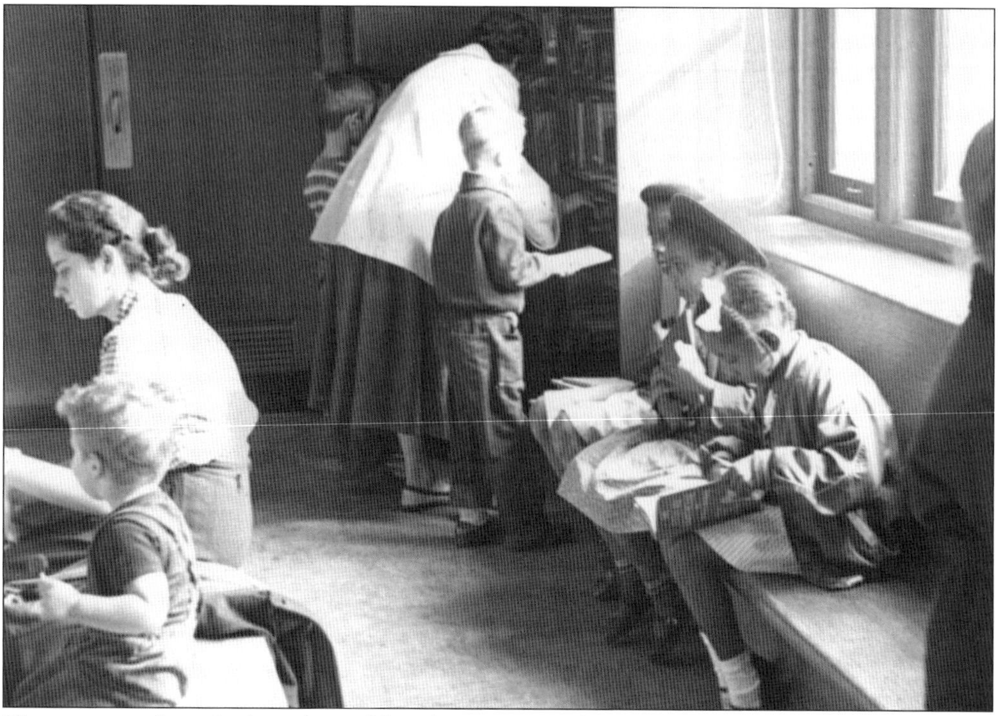

These images show the heavily used benches running along the walls of the Children's Library. Placed low to accommodate short legs, the benches provide a spot to bask in natural light and enjoy a good book. Even though these photographs were taken decades apart (the image above from the 1950s and the image below from 1980), they show that, in many ways, children's use and enjoyment of the library remains unchanged through time.

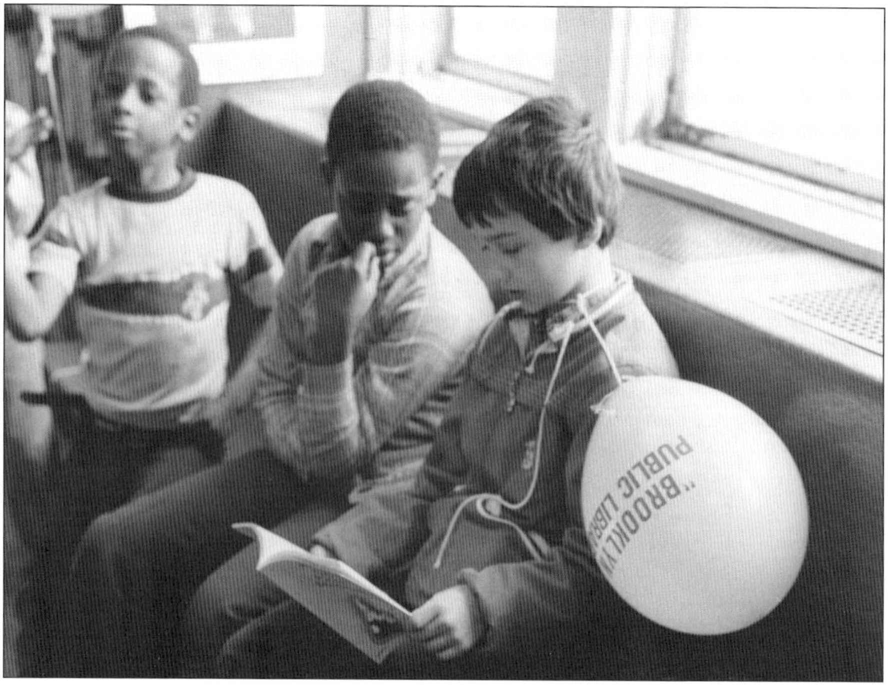

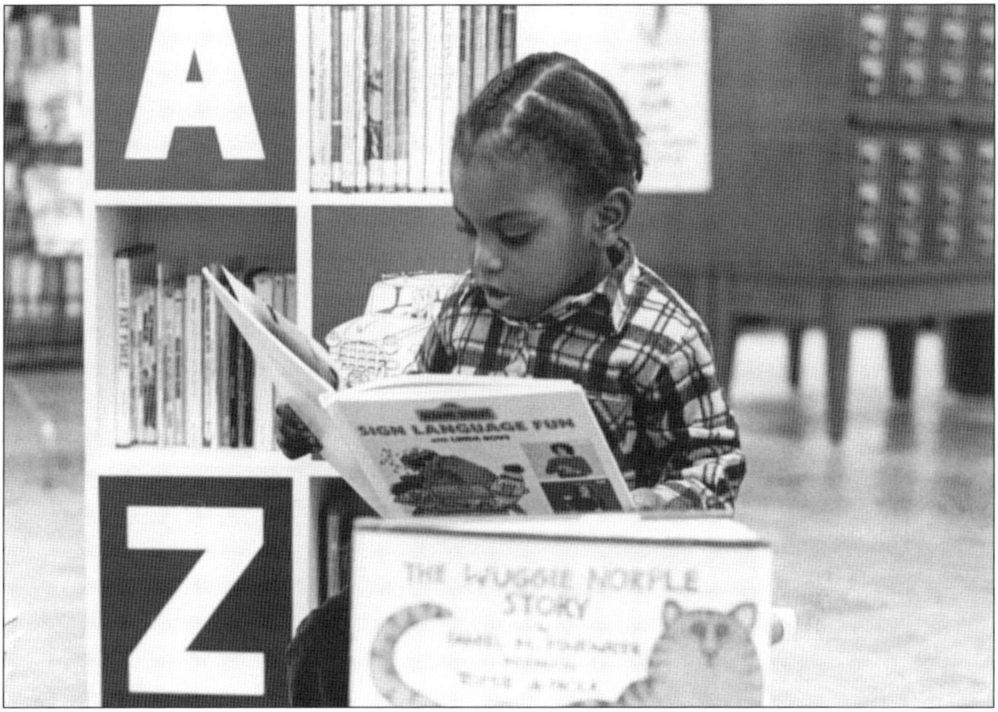

In the 1980s image above, a little boy explores the pictures in a sign language book for children. Below, a librarian leads a story hour for children in the program loft of the Children's Room. The library continues to reach out to young audiences with programs like Babies and Books and Toddler Time. Establishing the habit of reading from a very young age has been the drive behind many of the library's First Five Years and preschool programs.

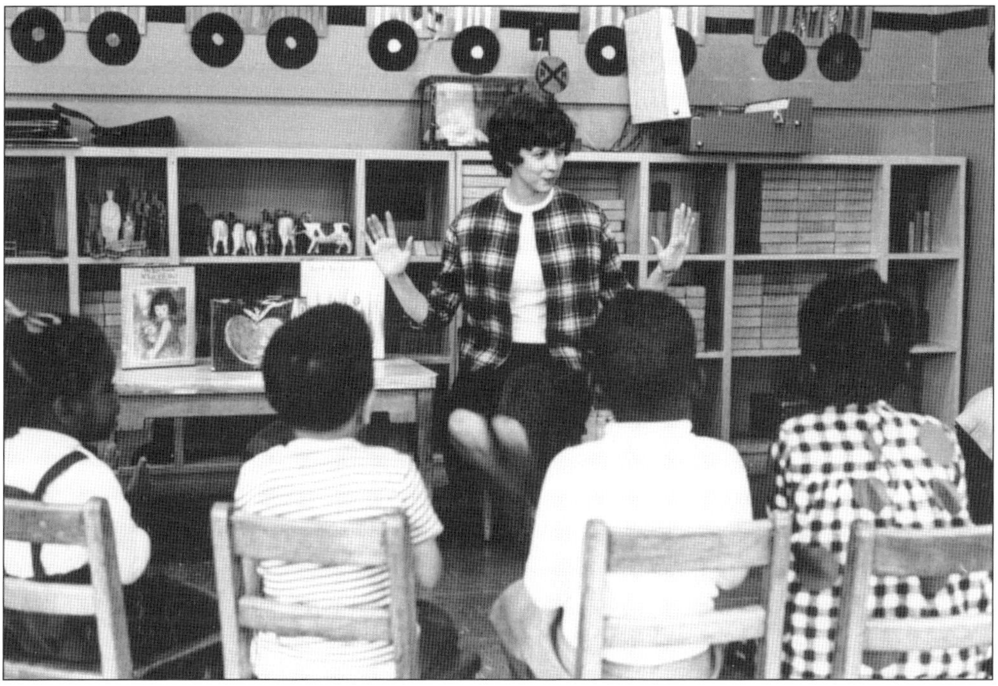

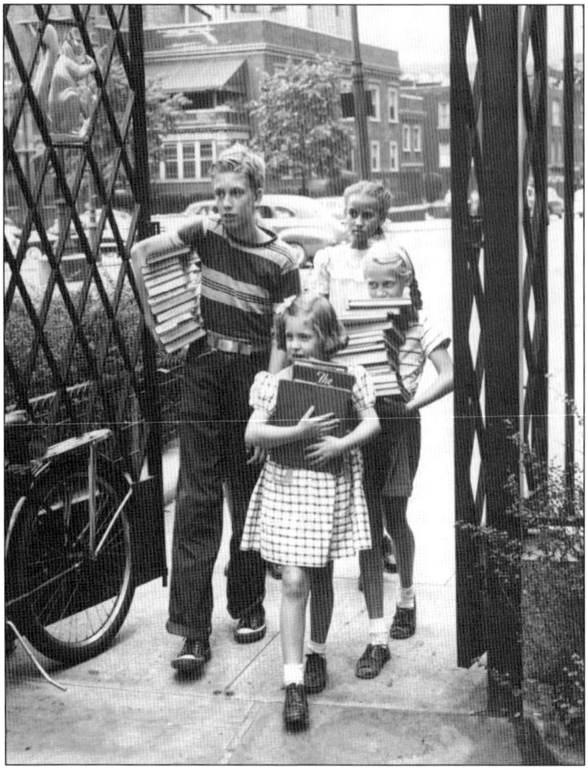

The library also teaches its young patrons important lessons in responsibility by assessing library fines if items are not returned on time. This image shows a crew of conscientious children returning with tottering stacks of books. Although they accumulate slowly, library fines are no small matter. In 1959, about when this photograph was taken, the library collected over $300,000 in fines and book replacement fees from negligent patrons.

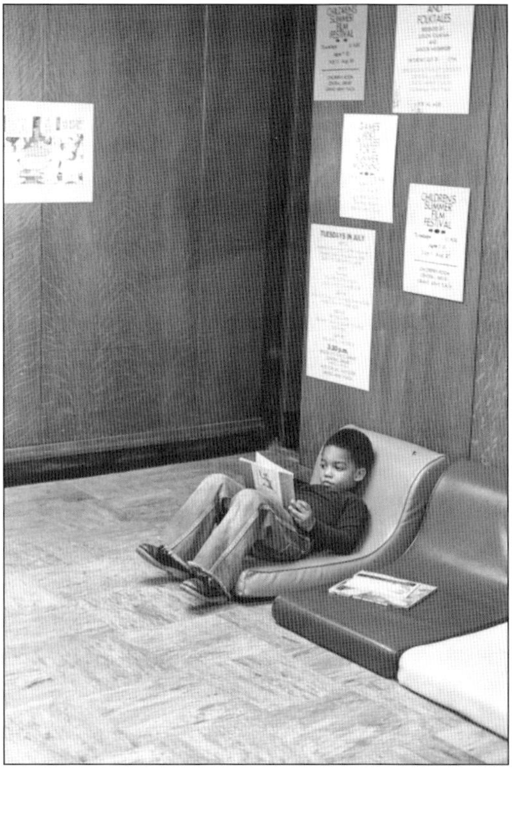

This photograph from June 1974 shows a young reader relaxing on low cushions in the Children's Room. The signs behind him advertise upcoming programs, including a summer film festival for children, a morning games and puzzles program, and a folktale storytelling session. Even though the rest of the city slows down during the summer, the children's area fills up with kids looking for something to do while school is out of session.

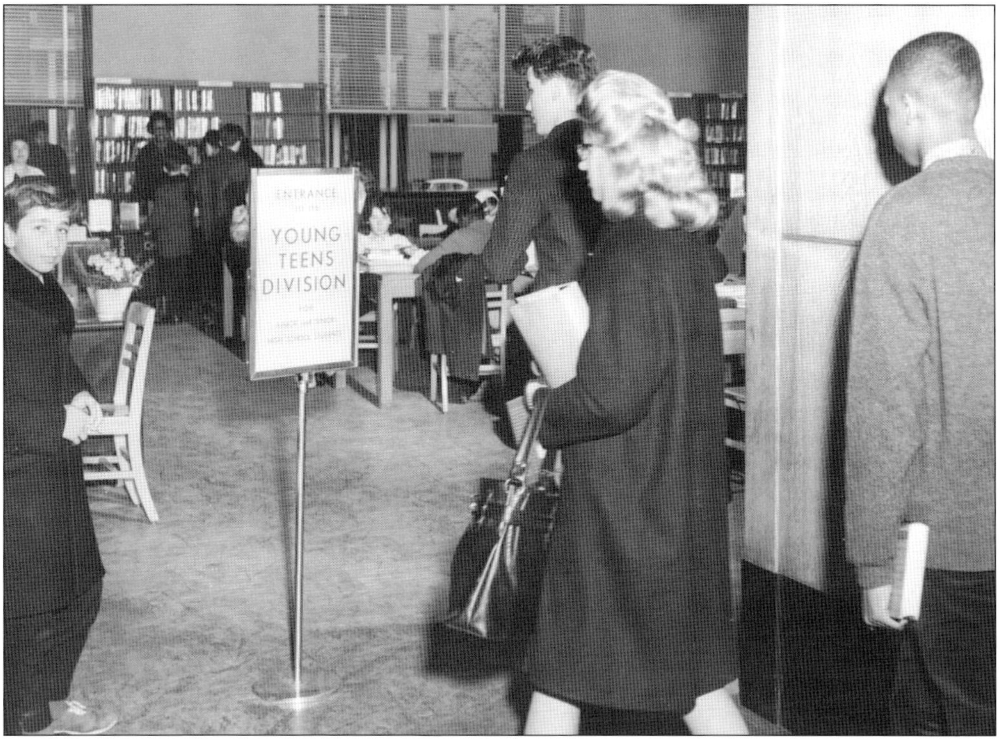

While Central Library catered to children from the moment it first opened its doors, the borough's young adult population would not get equal attention until the late 1950s. In 1959, Central Library started allowing junior high students into the adult collections of the library for the first time. Prior to that, teens had to petition for access and were given a pink slip to identify themselves when they ventured out of the Children's Room. New collections tailored to young adults were also developed, with specialized librarians serving that population. Above, teens are shown entering the young teens division at Central Library in 1962. Below, teens in the young adult section listen to records on benches overlooking Eastern Parkway.

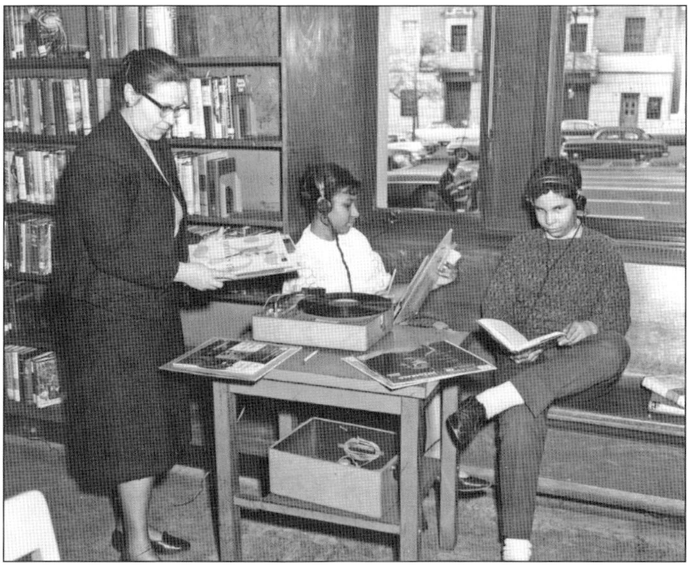

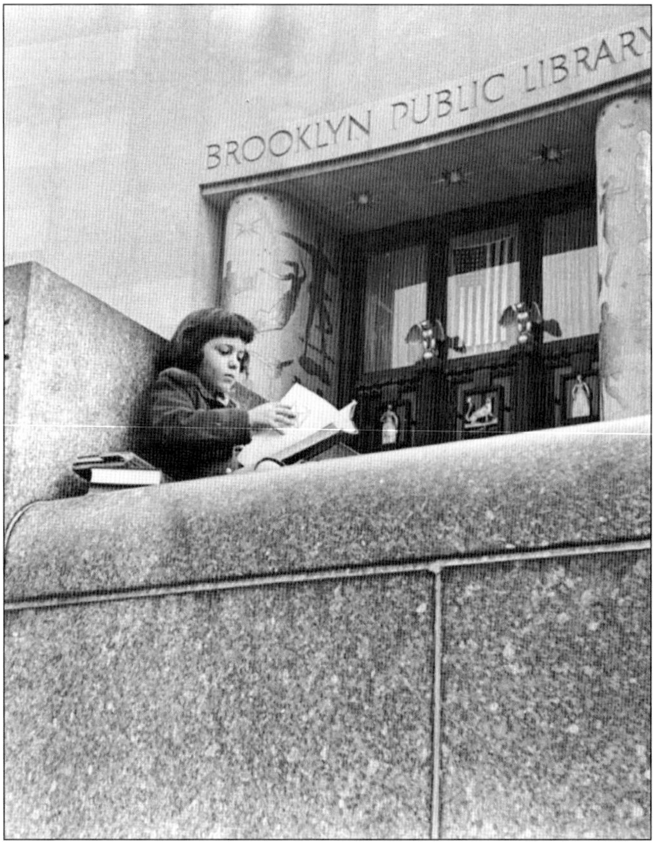

Captured in December 1958, this image shows a child perched on the plaza outside the library's main entrance, deep in a good book. The photograph, titled "Outside Reading," won second prize in an amateur photography contest sponsored by the library.

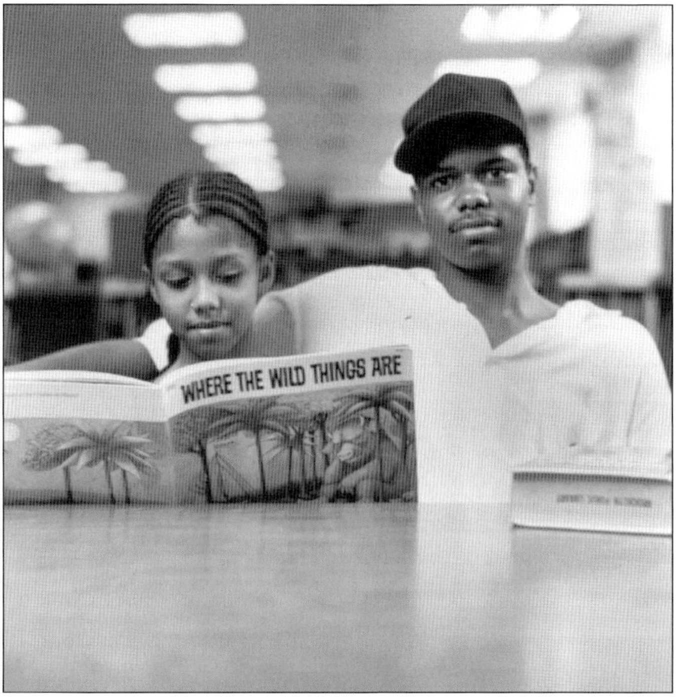

A child reads a book written by one of Brooklyn's most beloved native writers, Maurice Sendak, in this 1992 photograph. Brooklyn has a long history as the birthplace of and adopted home to talented children's authors, including Ezra Jack Keats, Betty Smith, and Jacqueline Woodson, among many others. Central Library regularly hosts local writers to give Brooklynites of all ages a chance to meet and draw inspiration from great storytellers and artists.

Eight

Cover to Cover

As with any book worth reading, there is much more to Central Library than one can imagine just by its austere limestone cover. While much attention is given to the impressive golden figures at the doorway, providing a visual overview of American literature, few notice the historic flagpole standing over the nearby plaza. More surprises lie inside the building, from the giant eagle statue that presides over the front lobby to a more approachable bear figurine that has greeted visiting children in the Youth Wing for decades. Many of these special features have accumulated over the years in this institution dedicated to preserving culture for posterity.

Central Library is an active building, constantly improving to meet modern demands. At the same time, it is a historical icon for Brooklyn, a building instantly recognizable by anyone who has ever visited it. Moreover, it is a landmarked building and is listed in the National Register of Historic Places. The tension between these two forces—the will to change and the need to preserve—defines the spaces of the library. A building born of two distinctly different visions, Central Library's rich history is embedded in its architecture.

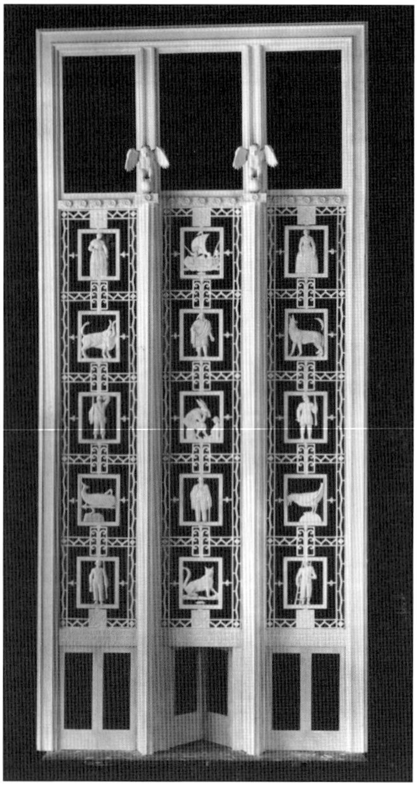

Perhaps the building's most striking feature is its 50-foot-high entry portico, shown in the photograph on the left as a scale model before the grille was constructed. Designed by Thomas Hudson Jones, the dramatic entrance is adorned by 15 bronze sculptures of famous characters and personages from American literature, including Moby Dick, Hester Prynne, and Brooklyn's own poet Walt Whitman. The photograph below shows the grille as it looked in the 1970s and gives some sense of the grand scale of the entrance.

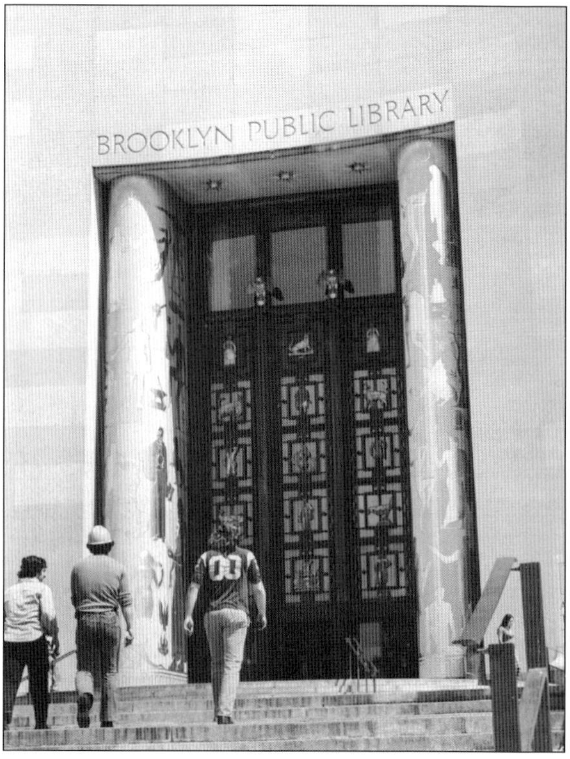

Library staff were invited to contribute to the process of creating the grille. Before sculptor Thomas Hudson Jones began his work, staff throughout the library system were polled for their input on which figures should be included. Among the popular characters were White Fang (right) from the Jack London novel of the same name, and Moby Dick (below) from the novel by Herman Melville. Mickey Mouse also received some votes, but was ultimately left out. With this input from librarians, Jones created these models to be cast in bronze for the grille. Jones was previously known for designing the Tomb of the Unknowns at Arlington National Cemetery in Virginia.

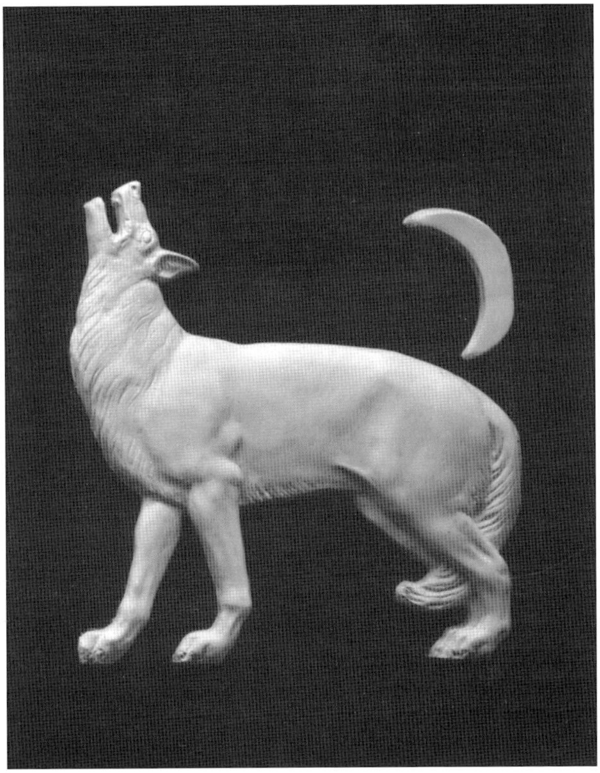

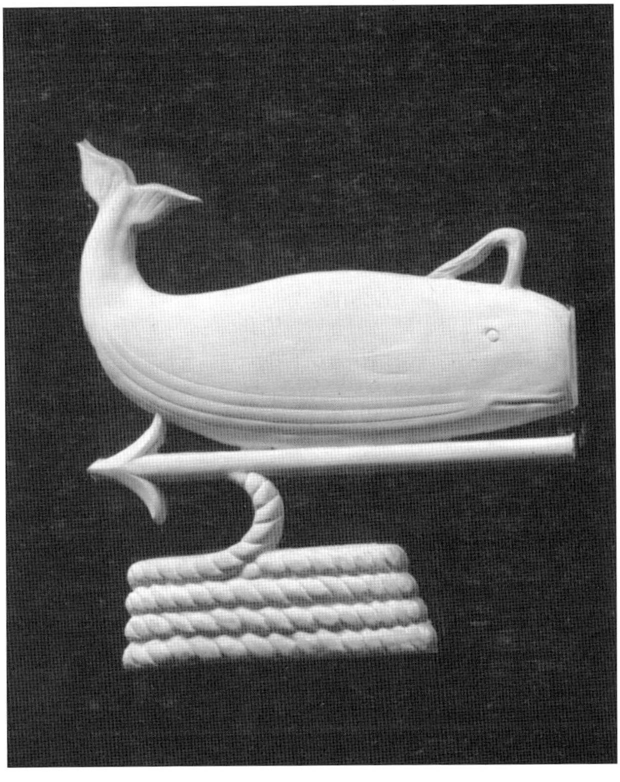

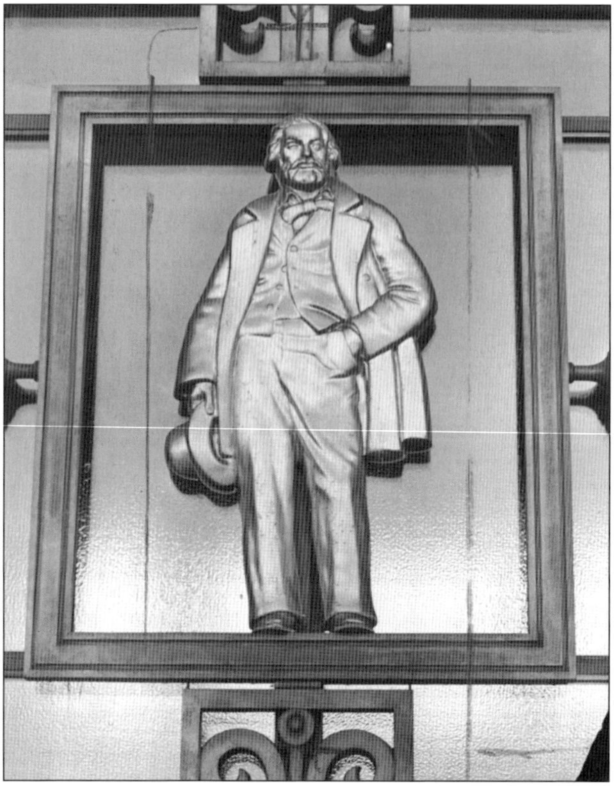

Of the 15 figures in the grille, 14 are fictional characters from American literature. An exception was made for Walt Whitman, whose bronze figure is pictured here. Whitman lived in today's Fort Greene neighborhood of Brooklyn, and his famous poem "Crossing Brooklyn Ferry" captures a ride from Manhattan to his home borough.

This photograph shows sculptor Thomas Hudson Jones putting some finishing touches on the bronze sculpture of Babe the Blue Ox created for the grille. In 1938, the *Brooklyn Daily Eagle* reported that the sculptures at the library's entrance were estimated at $30,000 to produce.

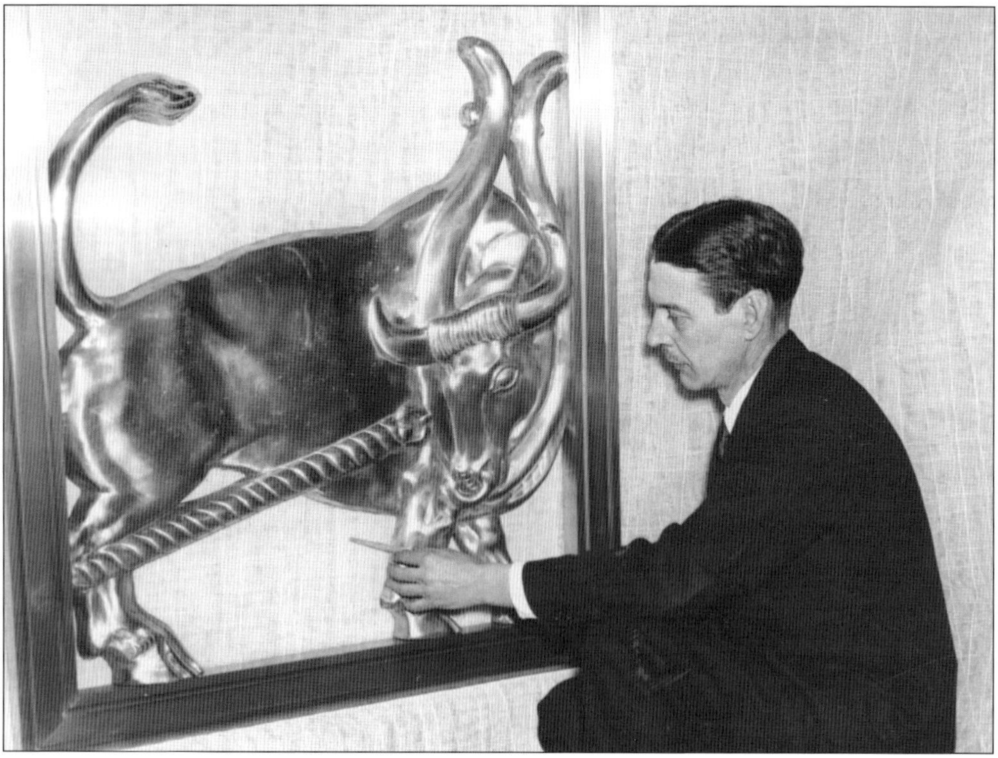

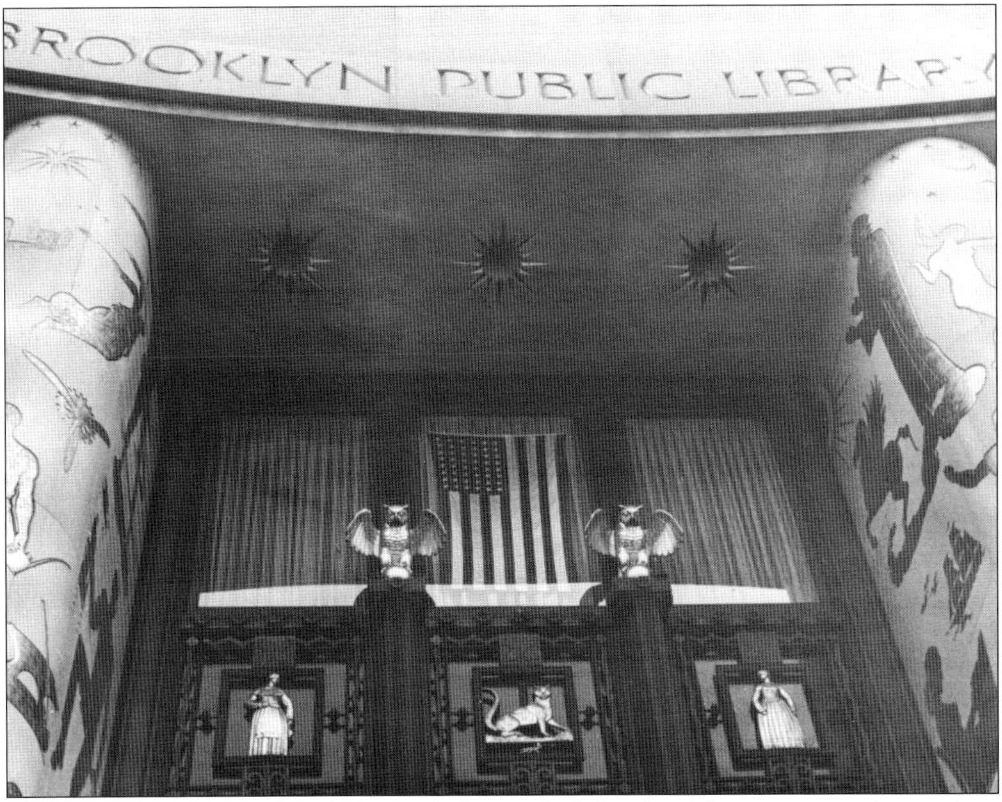

The grille is capped by two large bronze owls that overlook the plaza. These statues can be seen from inside the Trustees' Room, located on the third floor just behind the owls. Below, Jones smooths the surface of one of his sculptures. In October 1940, the *New York Herald Tribune* reported that the owls were used to deter pigeons: "Next to finances, one of the major problems of the library has been the pigeon nuisance. While the new construction provides few roosts for pigeons, they have managed to get inside the building. Two stone owls high above the entrance have been smeared with a gummy substance to keep the pigeons away from the windows of the Trustees' Room."

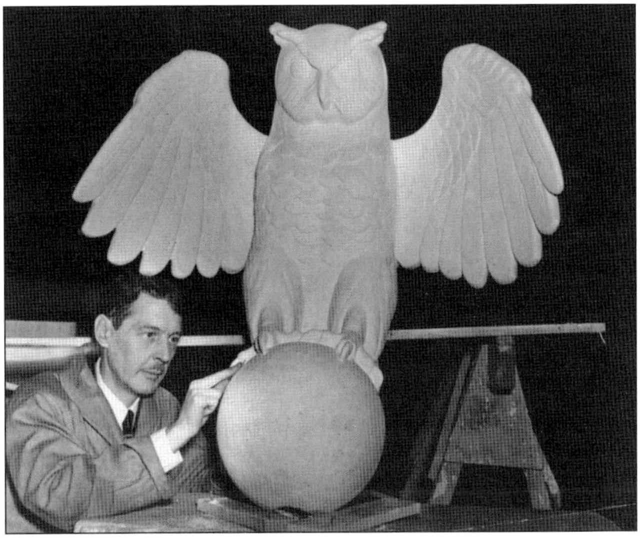

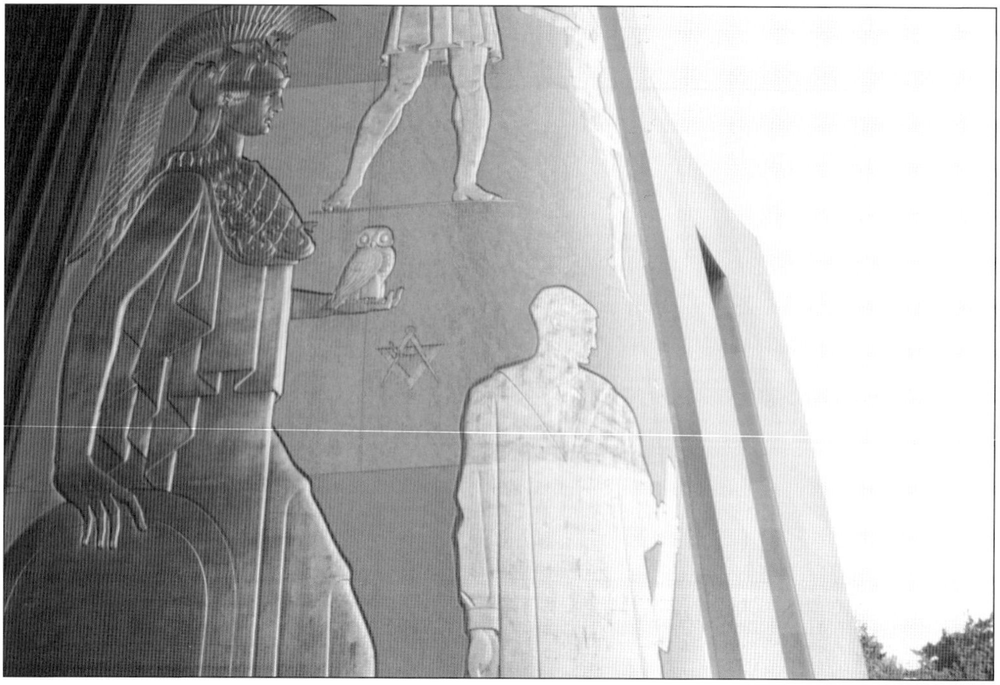

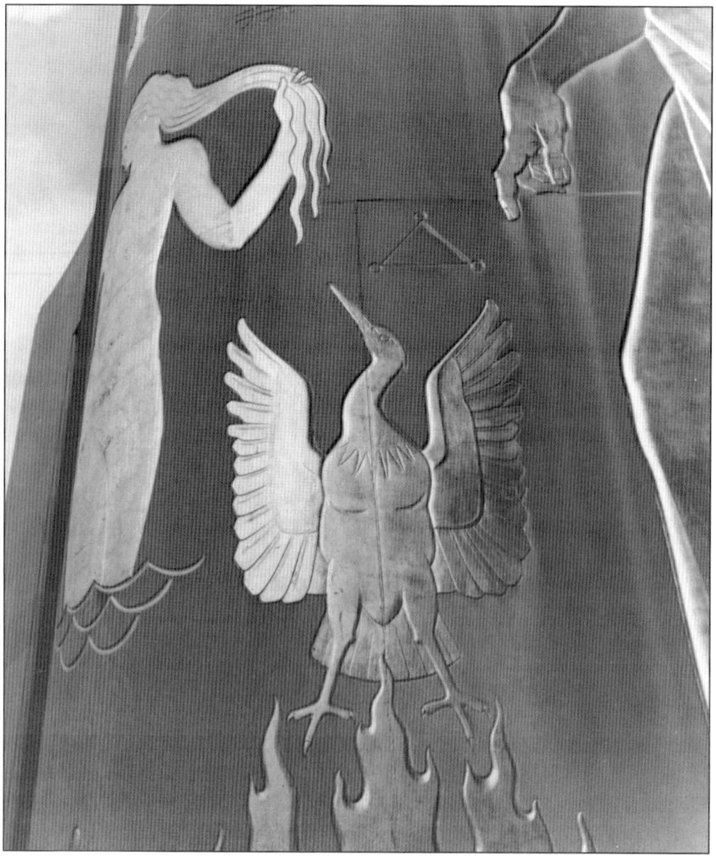

The gold-leaf pylons on either side of the library's main entrance were designed by sculptor C. Paul Jennewein. The bas-relief sculptures depict the evolution of art and science; the figure of the phoenix rising from fire can be seen at left. Jennewein was born in Germany but emigrated to the United States and became a naturalized citizen. His work adorns many public buildings, including the Philadelphia Museum of Art and the Justice Department Building in Washington, DC.

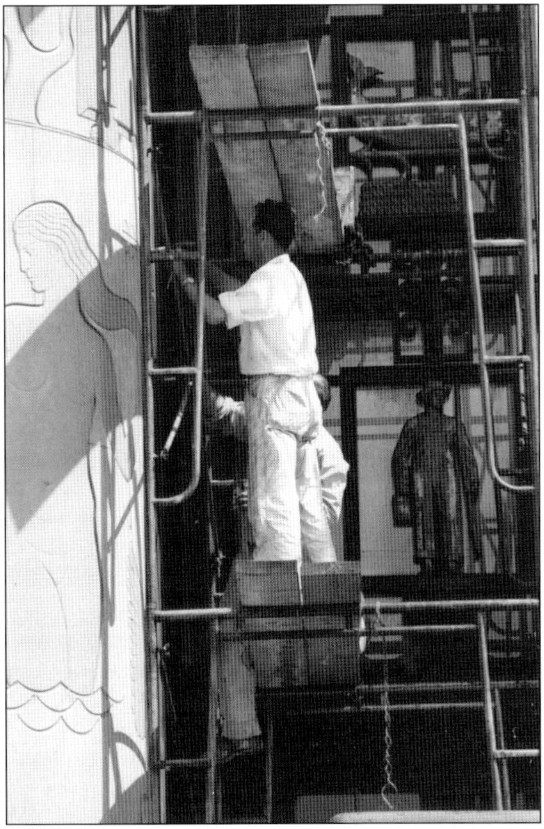

The figures decorating the facade of the library occasionally need rejuvenating. In 1973, scaffolding was put up to allow for the regilding of Jennewein's pylons, pictured at right. The photograph below shows another rehabilitation project in 1995. That year, the entire bronze screen was cleaned and regilded, including the owls standing guard outside the Trustees' Room.

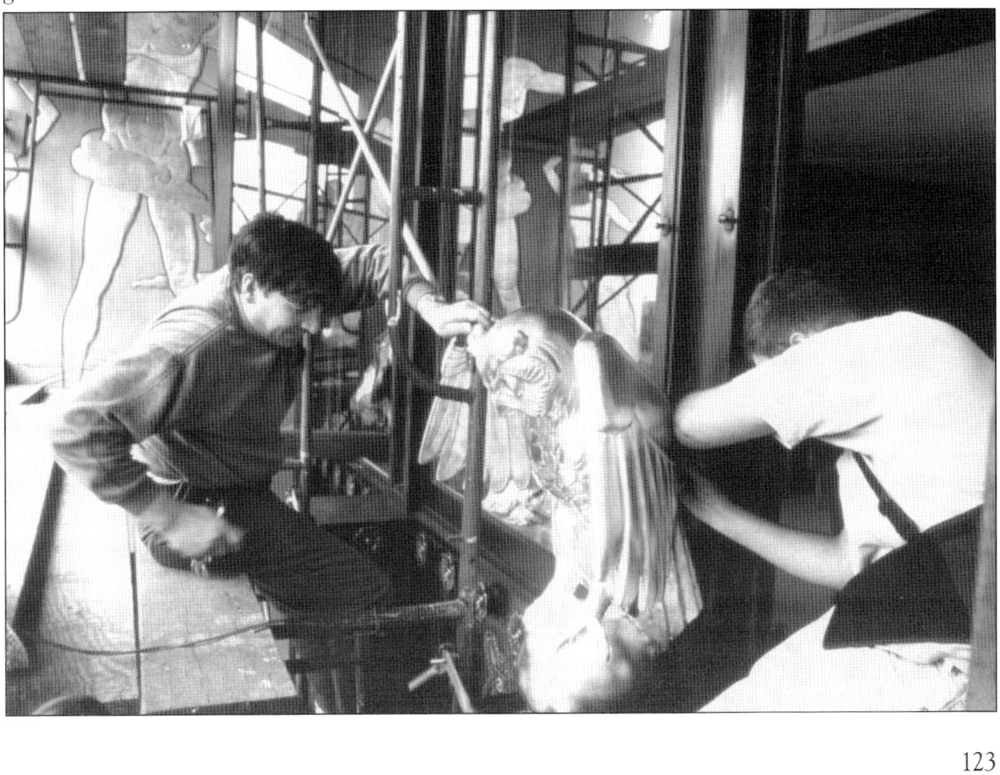

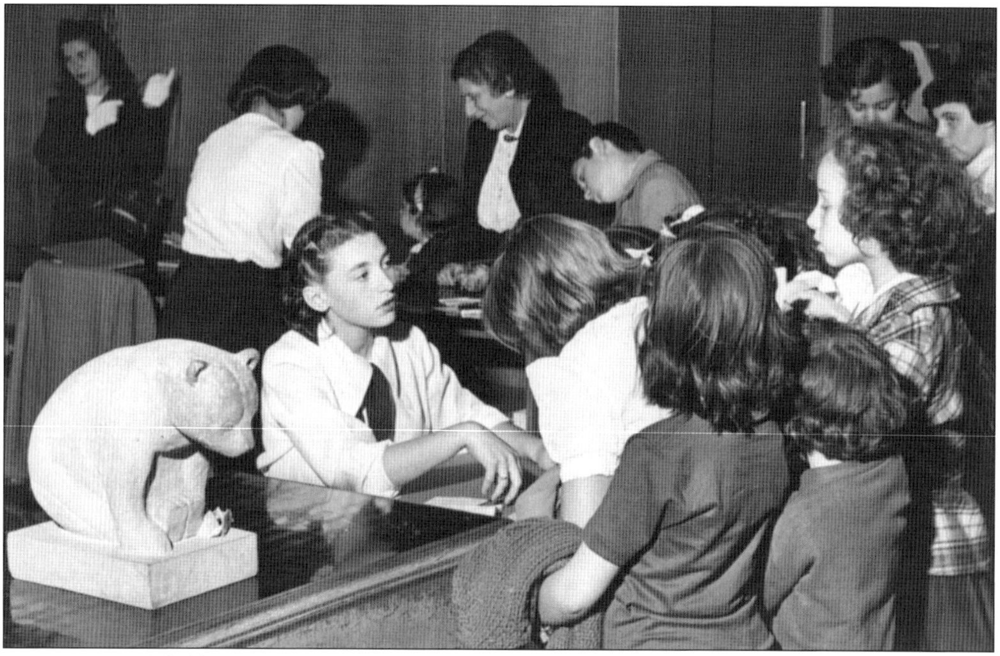

Generations of children have been greeted by the stone bear (pictured here in the 1950s) that has sat perched on the children's reference desk for decades. The sculpture, aptly titled *Bear,* was created by Edna Gluck in 1936 as part of the WPA's efforts to beautify public buildings and employ artists.

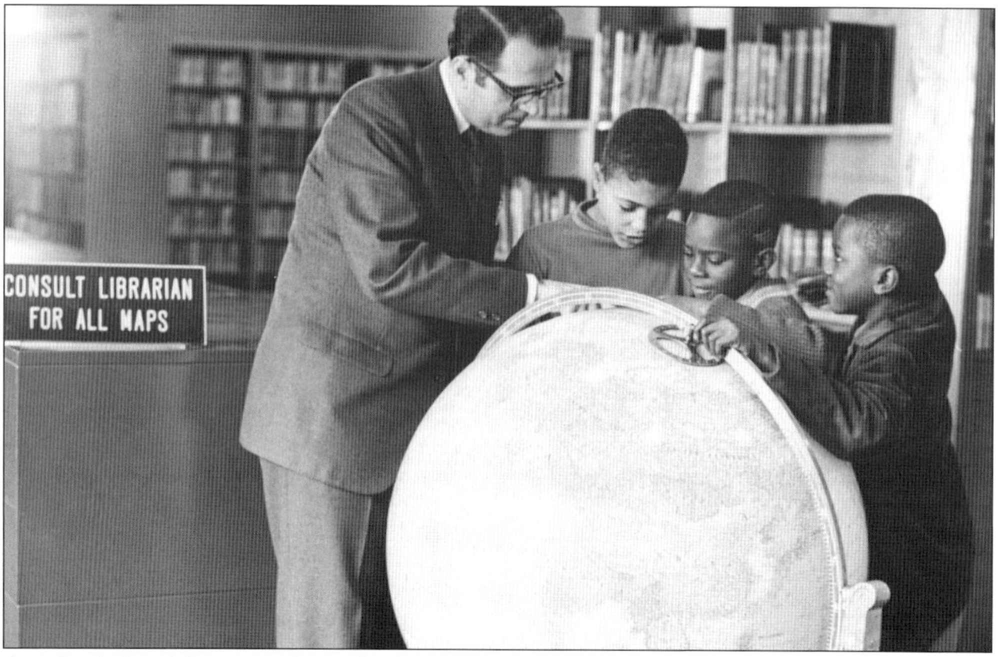

Another beloved feature in Central Library is this large globe, which once greeted visitors in the Grand Lobby. It was donated to the library by a Miss Righter in the 1950s. In the years since, it has seen much use from curious children and adults. The constant poking of thousands of pointing fingers has had its effect over the years; today, the entire New York City area is completely rubbed off the face of the globe.

Many people visit the library without noticing the flagpole in front, which has an unusual history of its own. It is the mast of *Shamrock III*, a racing yacht owned by Scottish entrepreneur Sir Thomas Lipton (of Lipton's tea fame). The yacht famously lost the 1903 America's Cup race to the New York Yacht Club's *Reliance*. The mast was first erected as a flagpole in Queens, then was moved to Red Hook, and eventually found its way to Central Library in 1959. The dedication ceremony is pictured here.

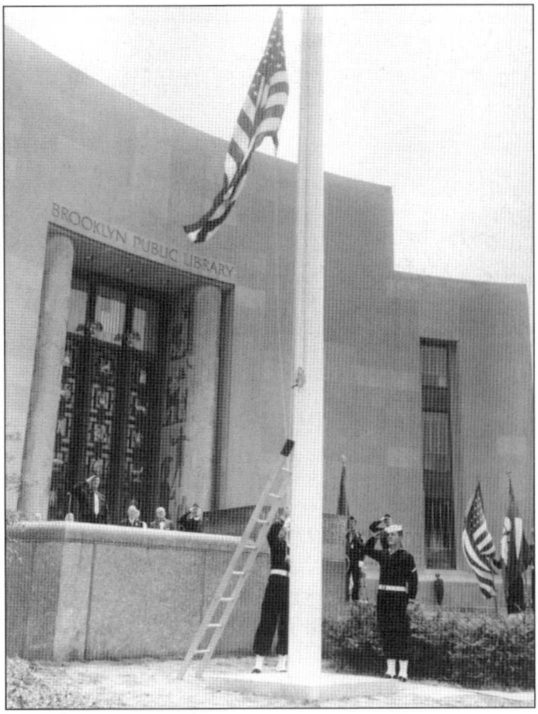

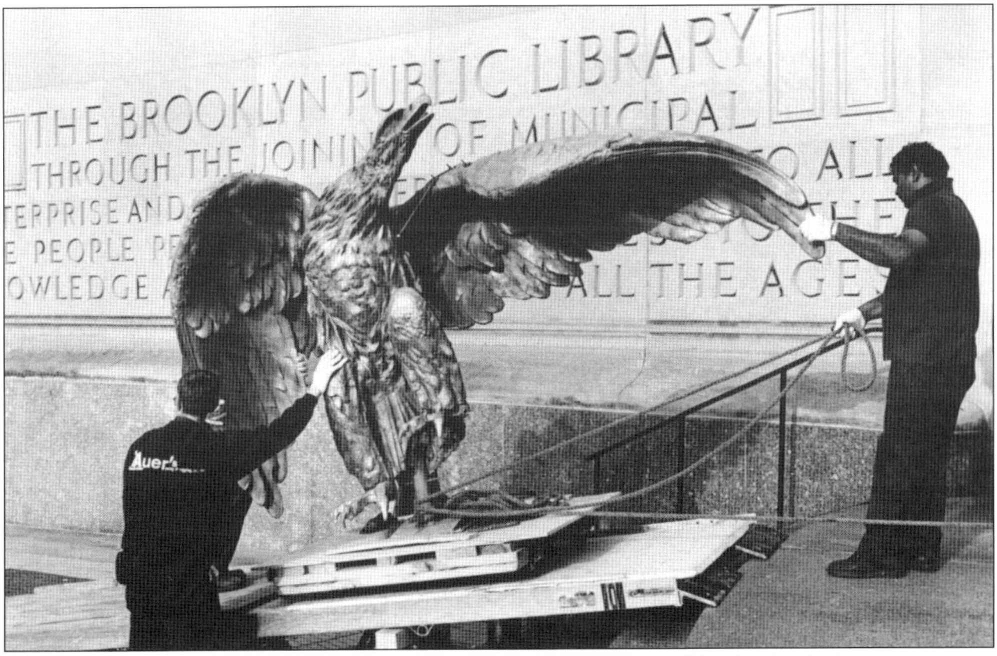

Four eagle sculptures once adorned the headquarters of the *Brooklyn Daily Eagle* newspaper in downtown Brooklyn, including this one. The *Eagle* closed in 1955, and its news clippings and photograph archive were donated to the library. After the *Eagle* building was demolished, this bird found temporary perches at the Brooklyn Museum and the Brooklyn Historical Society. In 1997, the eagle—made of cast zinc and weighing 300 pounds—was moved to Central Library, where it has resided since.

Bibliography

Brooklyn Public Library. *Brooklyn Public Library, Ingersoll Memorial: A description of the new building with verses to science and art by Roscoe C.E. Brown.* Chicago, IL: R.R. Donnelley & Sons Company, 1942.

———. *Annual Reports.* Brooklyn, NY: Brooklyn Public Library, 1890–2016.

Brooklyn Daily Eagle. Brooklyn Newsstand. www.newspapers.com. May 31, 2016.

Ferguson, Ruth B. *The "Hole in the Ground" That Became the Central Building of the Brooklyn Public Library.* Unpublished bound typescript, 1948.

Freeman, Margaret B. *The Brooklyn Public Library: A history.* Vol. 1. Unpublished bound typescript, 1966.

Manbeck, John B. *Chronicles of Historic Brooklyn.* Charleston, SC: The History Press, 2013.

McKee, Marcia. *A Brief History of the Brooklyn Public Library.* Unpublished bound typescript, 1968.

Mumford, Lewis. "The Sky Line: Brooklyn Public Library." *The New Yorker.* October 1940.

Landmarks Preservation Commission. *Brooklyn Public Library: Central building.* New York, NY: the Commission, 1997.

Steen, Signe L. *The Montague Branch of the Brooklyn Public Library: Its History and Development.* Unpublished bound typescript, 1946.

About the Brooklyn Public Library

As an independent system separate from the New York City and Queens libraries, Brooklyn Public Library serves the borough's 2.5 million residents, offering thousands of public programs, millions of books, and use of more than 1,100 free Internet-accessible computers. It is the mission of Brooklyn Public Library to ensure the preservation and transmission of society's knowledge, history, and culture and to provide the people of Brooklyn with free and open access to information for education, recreation, and reference.

The Brooklyn Collection is Brooklyn Public Library's local history and institutional archive housing a rich assortment of research materials including books, maps, newspapers, ephemera, photographs, and films, as well as digital resources. It is also home to the news clippings and photography files of the *Brooklyn Daily Eagle* newspaper (1841–1955). Located in Central Library and open to the public, the Brooklyn Collection aims to promote awareness of the history of Brooklyn and to make as complete a record as possible of all aspects of Brooklyn life available to the public.

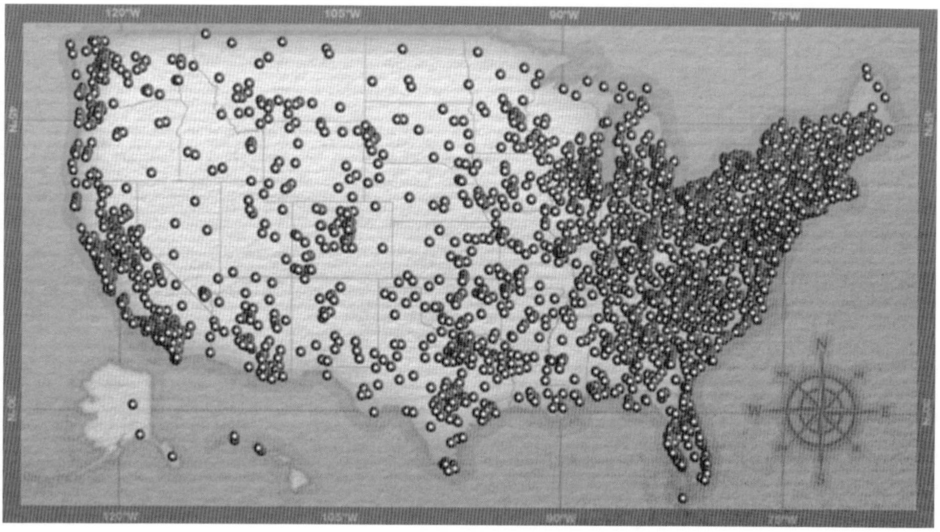

Consistent with our mission to preserve history on a local level, this book was printed in South Carolina on American-made paper and manufactured entirely in the United States. Products carrying the accredited Forest Stewardship Council (FSC) label are printed on 100 percent FSC-certified paper.

MADE IN THE USA